The Qubec
alternative

THe new Bilingualism

The **Center for Study of the American Experience** is a part of The Annenberg School of Communications at the University of Southern California. It provides facilities and support for the identification, analysis, and dissemination of knowledge about the problems and challenges that have helped to shape America's past and present and will be most likely to define America's future. These objectives are pursued through the assembling of conferences, production of edited audio and video tapes and publications from these conferences, and support of visiting distinguished Scholars-in-Residence.

John C. Weaver
Executive Director

Other titles in the Center for Study of the American Experience series:

Rights and Responsibilities
International, Social, and Individual Dimensions

The Arts in Shaping the American Experience

Energy in America: *Fifteen Views*

Political Reform in California: *How Has It Worked?*

THe new BiLingualism

An American Dilemma

Proceedings of a Conference
Sponsored by
Center for Study of the
American Experience
The Annenberg School of Communications
University of Southern California
May 1980

*Edited by **Martin Ridge***

University of Southern California Press
Transaction Books — Rutgers University

Published 1981
University of Southern California Press
Los Angeles, California 90007

Series Editor, Joyce J. Bartell
Designer, Robert W. Giese

Distributed by Transaction Books   Rutgers University
New Brunswick, N.J. 08903 (U.S.A.) and London (U.K.)

Library of Congress Cataloging in Publication Data
Main entry under title:

The New bilingualism.

    Includes bibliographical references.
    1. Bilingualism—United States—Congresses.
2. Biculturalism—United States—Congresses.
I. Ridge, Martin. II. Annenberg School of
Communications (University of Southern California).
Center for Study of the American Experience.
P115.5.U5N4   420'.42'0973   81-15966
                                       AACR2

ISBN 0-88474-104-4

Contents

Contents

III. One Nation, Indivisible?
Panel Discussions on the Implications of Bilingualism

IV. The New Bilingualism: An American Dilemma

Appendix

Preface

When I was invited to become an Annenberg Visiting Scholar at the University of Southern California to study bilingualism/ biculturalism in our society and to arrange a public conference on the subject, several of my closest friends urged me to decline. The topic, they cautioned, could not be approached with scholarly detachment in a public forum; it was too deeply charged an emotional issue for many non-English-speaking minorities in this country, and it had explicit as well as implicit racial, political, and economic implications that were best left to propagandists, politicians, and lobbyists for special interest groups. Moreover, since bilingualism/biculturalism touched so many aspects of American life, faculty members in many departments in the university would feel entitled to participate in the conference and this might well result in a cacophony of academic jargon that would scarcely serve the goals of the Center for Study of the American Experience. Why, my friends argued, bother with so controversial a subject where there were so many risks of offending colleagues and non-English-speaking minorities within the general public.

There were personal as well as professional reasons for becoming an Annenberg Scholar. One year earlier I had participated in a conference sponsored by the National Endowment for the Humanities to assist younger humanists of Spanish-speaking origins in their career development. I discovered, as the only non-Spanish-speaker in the group, how isolated many Hispanic intellectuals felt in the dominant English-speaking culture and how deeply rooted was their sense of frustration. Being bilingual/bicultural had a special meaning for them. I also tended to look at the issue from the vantage of someone who had taught the History of the American West in the Twentieth Century for more than a quarter-century. I have long been aware not only of the virtual invisibility of non-English-speaking minorities in historical treatments of this country but also of the significant demographic patterns that cried out for discussion in a bilingual/bicultural context. My personal experience plus the increasing public consciousness of such issues as bilingual education, the legal puzzles resulting from civil rights legislation, federal regulations and court decisions, and the implications of the newer immigration, all attracted me to a deeper study of the issue. Despite the political drawbacks, the challenge was irresistible.

The immediate reason for agreeing to accept the invitation was the Center for Study of the American Experience itself. Dedicated to serious, honest, scholarly, public examination of important issues in our society, it offered an unusual setting for a civil dialogue on a vital matter. It also provided for a remarkable amount of media attention for the problems that it studied because portions of conferences would be televised and/or taped for radio broadcast on the public radio and public television networks.

The format of the conference had in part been fixed before I joined the Center. Doyce Nunis of the University of Southern California and co-chairman of the conference, Daniel Aaron of Harvard, and John C. Weaver, director of the Center, had already selected Stephen Wagner to prepare his paper on the historical background and Nathan Glazer of Harvard to deliver an address on the issue of bilingualism/biculturalism in a pluralist society. We all agreed that the conference required an international dimension and requested the Canadian and Mexican governments to make available individuals who could explain the policies of their respective nations.

The selection of the participants became a group effort. Since the purpose of the conference was to raise and examine issues, not to formulate public policy, the discussants and participants were selected because they were known advocates or adversaries of a bilingual/bicultural America, they worked in a field where bilingualism/biculturalism was a critical issue, they were thoughtful men and women who might serve to bring the issue of the conference before larger publics, or they were individuals with unusual expertise. Gathering this constituency within a short time proved a difficult task because of the many commitments of such individuals. Not every person invited to the conference was able to attend. Once assembled, however, the participants had no difficulty creating an environment where people would speak, raise questions, and respond freely. There was little formality and the group maintained a self-imposed sense of civility even in the most heated of exchanges.

Transcribing and editing the tapes made during the discussions involved critical editorial decisions. The transcripts were not corrected for errors of fact or interpretation when these were used in argument. Errors were corrected when made inadvertently, and material was deleted to eliminate redundancy or digression. (The participants were permitted to review and correct the edited transcripts.) Because bilingualism/biculturalism is so much a part of the personal experience of the participants, the record contains much autobiographical data that identifies individuals within socioeconomic, ethnocultural, and racial groups. In many of the discussions the words Hispanic, Latino, Chicano, and Mexican-American are used interchangeably but may not refer to the same groups of people. Only the context can make the distinctions clear. Often, too, the word "Anglo" is used as a synonym for English-speaking; it is not intended to refer to people of English-speaking extraction.

The successful preparation of this book rests on the outstanding work of the staff of the Center for Study of the American Experience and its distinguished director, Dr. John C. Weaver, who courageously pursues the goals of his institution, and Mrs. Joyce Bartell, who did far more than most publication directors in seeing this book to completion. Working with them and at the Center, the most dramatic building on the campus of the University of Southern California, was an unforgettable experience. I owe a debt also to Joy Hansen and Gail Peterson of the California Institute of Technology, who helped me see and appreciate the pleasures of using the word processor.

While at work in my office at the Center for Study of the American Experience, and looking out over the playing fields of the University of Southern California, I thought often of my children. This book is for two of them: Judith Lee and Wallace Karsten; John Andrew and Curtis Cordell may write their own books. As always, Marcella VerHoef Ridge made a special contribution.

Martin Ridge, San Marino, California

Conference Participants

Carmen Diaz-Rubin de Armstrong,
Coordinator of Bilingual Education, Thousand Oaks, California

George P. Brockway, *Chairman,*
W. W. Norton and Company, Inc., publishers, New York

Pastora San Juan Cafferty, *professor,*
School of Social Service Administration and
Committee on Public Policy Studies, University of Chicago

Henry Der, *Director, Chinese for Affirmative Action, San Francisco*

Noel Epstein, *Assistant Editor, "Outlook,"* Washington Post

Ricardo R. Fernández, *associate professor of education/*
cultural foundations, University of Wisconsin-Milwaukee;
Director, Midwest National Origin Desegregation Assistance Center;
President-Elect, National Association for Bilingual Education

Aida Ferrarone, *staff journalist,* Imagen, *Culver City, California*

Eugene Fuson, *Editorial Director, KNXT-CBS, Los Angeles*

Jaime B. Fuster, *Deputy Assistant Attorney General,*
Office for Improvements in the Administration of Justice,
United States Department of Justice

The Reverend Max D. Gaebler, *pastor,*
First Unitarian Society, Madison, Wisconsin

Edwin S. Gaustad, *professor of history,*
University of California, Riverside

Nathan Glazer, *professor of education and social structure,*
Graduate School of Education, Harvard University

Josue Gonzalez, *Director, Office of Bilingual Education*
and Minority Languages Affairs, United States Office of Education

The Reverend Andrew M. Greeley, *Director, Center for the Study*
of American Pluralism, National Opinion Research Center,
University of Chicago; professor of sociology, University of Arizona

Conference Participants

Félix Gutiérrez, *associate professor of journalism,*
University of Southern California;
Executive Director, California Chicano News Media Association

Franklyn S. Haiman, *professor of communication studies*
and urban affairs, School of Speech, Northwestern University;
National Secretary, American Civil Liberties Union

The Reverend Wayne C. Hartmire, *Director,*
National Farm Worker Ministry, Los Angeles

Donald T. Hata, Jr., *professor of history,*
California State University, Dominguez Hills

Phil Kerby, *editorial writer and columnist,* Los Angeles Times

Stephen J. Knezevich, *Dean, School of Education,*
University of Southern California

Quentin L. Kopp, *Board of Supervisors,*
City and County of San Francisco

Arnold H. Leibowitz, *Special Counsel,*
Select Commission on Immigration and Refugee Policy,
United States Senate Committee on the Judiciary;
President, Institute of International Law and Economic
Development, Washington, D.C.

David Maciel, *professor of history, University of New Mexico*

Sterling M. McMurrin, *professor of history and philosophy,*
University of Utah;
former United States Commissioner of Education

Salomón Nahmad Sittón, *Director of Indian Languages,*
Office of Education, Republic of Mexico

Doyce B. Nunis, Jr., *professor of history,*
University of Southern California;
Conference Co-Chairman

Conference Participants

Thomas Plate, *Associate Editor,* Los Angeles Herald Examiner

The Reverend Frank Ponce, *Associate Director, Secretariat for Hispanic Affairs, National Conference of Catholic Bishops/ United States Catholic Conference, Washington, D.C.*

The Reverend Carlos H. Puig, *Secretary for Hispanic Ministries- North America, Lutheran Church/Missouri Synod, St. Louis*

Martin Ridge, *Annenberg Distinguished Scholar, Center for Study of the American Experience; Senior Research Associate, Huntington Library, San Marino, California,* Conference Co-Chairman

Moses Rischin, *professor of history, San Francisco State University*

Sharon Robinson, *Director of Instruction and Professional Development, National Education Association, Washington D.C.*

Peter D. Roos, *Director of Education Litigation, Mexican-American Legal Defense and Educational Fund, San Francisco*

Ramón Eduardo Ruiz, *professor of Latin American history, University of California, San Diego; visiting professor, School of Advanced International Studies, Johns Hopkins University*

Abigail M. Thernstrom, *teacher, writer; lecturer, Harvard University*

Stephen T. Wagner, *teacher of social studies, Wayland High School, Maynard, Massachusetts*

James G. Ward, *Director of Research, American Federation of Teachers, Washington, D.C.*

Maxwell F. Yalden, *Commissioner of Official Languages, Canada*

I. Preliminaries

The Conference
in Perspective

Martin Ridge

The decision to hold a conference on bilingualism/biculturalism at the University of Southern California is not a harbinger of a rising tide of nativism in this country, or fear of additional immigration from Asia and Latin America, or concern about potential separatist or nationalist tendencies on the part of non-English-speaking minorities in the United States. It is an effort to treat with sensitivity a question of genuine importance to many people. Despite the presence of some noisy, discredited political and racial extremist elements in the country, this is an era of national calm. It is also a time of widespread interest in our ethnic heritage and in the way that long-persistent and newer non-English-speaking peoples have accommodated to living in a predominantly English-speaking society. This is, therefore, a prudent time to analyze and discuss the issues that may prompt or have prompted thousands of Americans to exercise an option to be bilingual/bicultural.

Racial, religious, linguistic, and cultural minorities are always fearful of conferences devoted to their status vis-à-vis the majority

17

component in society. Since this nation has a long and troubled history of outbreaks of hostility toward minorities and dissenters—it has been said that "nativism is as American as apple pie"—these fears are not without foundation. But muting discourse in a democratic society because of fears that discussion could result in threats to the security of minority elements is unwise policy. In fact, a candid dialogue of the issues surrounding bilingual/bicultural options may go a long way toward dispelling myths, clarifying questions, and setting out facts so that Americans can make rational decisions as individuals when given choices.

The purpose of this conference was to open such a dialogue on many but not all aspects of bilingualism/biculturalism. The idea for the conference originated with John Weaver, director of the Center for Study of the American Experience, after a visit to Canada during that nation's highly controversial, separatist election contest. He saw the social utility of looking at the role of bilingual/bicultural communities within the United States. Too much misunderstanding and too little sensitivity seemed to permeate the subject. He sought a way to bring the issue forward in its most vigorous form. To raise as many issues as possible in as evocative a manner as possible, Weaver recruited Professor Doyce B. Nunis of the University of Southern California Department of History and co-chairman of the conference to prepare a brief conference working paper, which asked, "Should the United States undertake to be officially bilingual/bicultural?" and dramatized the unusual options now open to bilingual people.

What Nunis had in mind when he wrote his paper was the remarkable extent to which both the private and public sector make it possible for millions of Americans to live without using the English language. He saw the range of this activity from foreign-language television transmission to ballots printed in non-English texts. In both official and unofficial ways non-English languages have won sanctioned usage through legislation, government regulations, and court decisions. (As the conference was to show, participants who were part of the District of Columbia's political, legal, and journalistic community refused to recognize that official status could exist unless it was national in scope or granted through federal legislation or Constitutional amendment.)

To place Nunis's evocative statement in an historical context, Stephen Wagner, a teacher who had studied minority groups, prepared a brief, objective, and dispassionate account of the bilingual/bicultural experience of the American people. The Wagner and Nunis papers were distributed to everyone who attended the conference. They provided not only a basis for discussion but also a common ground of understanding for individuals unfamiliar with the bilingual/bicultural aspects of the American past.

The conference was planned to show bilingualism/biculturalism in an international or comparative context. Three formal addresses were presented to highlight the issues involved in bilingualism/biculturalism in the United States, Canada, and Mexico. Nathan Glazer of Harvard, as a keynote speaker, intended to raise larger questions, and he did so by tracing the trend of expanding the bilingual/bicultural options in the United States and questioning whether they would in the long run be healthy for the individuals who selected them or for the nation. Maxwell Yalden, Canada's Commissioner of Official Languages, provided an analysis of the Canadian attitude and policy toward that nation's diverse population. He explained not only the uniqueness of the Canadian experience in multicultural/multilingual life but also that Canada is distinctive. He insisted that it was not a model for the United States. Canada has a geographically concentrated Francophone element that constitutes almost 25 percent of its population and is maintained by a complex and complete infrastructure to nurture its cultural and language needs. Salomón Nahmad Sittón, Mexico's General Director of Indian Eduction, indicated that the Mexican experience is also unique. His country's non-Spanish speakers are indigenous peoples, and the government has been searching for more than a century for a way to bring them into the mainstream of Mexican life. He underscored the complexities of bilingual/bicultural societies where the minority element is also abjectly poor and even, on occasion, physically isolated from the majority culture. Salomón Nahmad Sittón's address was delivered in Spanish and simultaneously translated into English. (The essay presented in this book is an edited translation of his Spanish text.) There can be no doubt on reading the addresses that the conflicting value systems within these nations are evident in the way that each has sought to accommodate to bilingual/bicultural peoples within its borders.

To keep the discussions during the conference from becoming diffuse, the subject of bilingualism/biculturalism was divided into six topics: economics and culture, education, politics, law, religion, and the media. These topics were selected for explicit and implicit reasons. In each of these areas, historically, there have been "nationalizing and Americanizing" institutions that have played a vital role in encouraging the use of English and undermining the efforts of minorities to retain their cultures. These institutions involved in bilingualism/biculturalism were to be reassessed in the context of their current attitudes and policies toward non-English-speaking groups.

The emphasis of the conference was on values, experience, and policy. For example, whether a child will learn a language faster or more effectively by being taught it in his home tongue or by being immersed in the new language for an extended period is an important question, but it is only indirectly related to the focus of the conference. What was of concern were the problems involved in teaching children to communicate when they lived in a society of cyclical migrant workers who travel between nations—Mexico and the United States—or within the United States sphere—Puerto Rico and the mainland. Of importance, too, was the issue of educating children in their home language while they learned English, not only to preserve their culture but also to maintain their self-esteem. In large measure, as the discussions evolved, American policies and practices were subjected to criticism, and the goals of our society as well as its promises and rewards were tested.

The conference was open to panelist-participants and invited guests from the Los Angeles political, academic, business, and professional community. The panelists were selected to present a balanced, not necessarily opposing, view on the subject. Many were experts, distinguished by their work in the field; others were advocates for causes related to bilingualism/biculturalism; still others were academicians who had studied aspects of the issues or problems concerning immigration, minorities, civil rights, and assimilation. Among the invited guests, who were free to participate during the question period at the close of each panel, were many individuals of unusual insight and experience. Their probing comments indicated, as had been anticipated, that there are multiple publics keenly interested in bilingualism/biculturalism. There were few issues related to the subject that were not touched upon. In no case was the discussion circumscribed by the views of the participants.

During the course of the discussion, much of it animated if not heated, the participants often spoke from the heart as well as from intellectual commitment. They rarely had available notes or sources to check or document what they said. At times like these, men and women may misspeak themselves in both fact and interpretation. The proceedings should be read with this caveat. What is remarkable in this conference is not the amount of factual material conveyed, although that is important, but how individuals used what they said to make their cases. This is the critical ingredient that gives this conference significance for the future, because what is given here is a meaningful statement of the complex personal as well as philosophical issues involved.

No-one expected the conference to end on a note of consensus. Such a consensus would scarcely have served a useful purpose. The conference papers were successful because of the issues that they brought out. The prepared papers, addresses, and dialogues demonstrated the deeply held beliefs of minority-language speakers and their advocates. The conference also amply showed how sharply different are current interpretations of recent history, civil rights, and the nature and role of pluralism in the United States.

The content of the conference disclosed genuine misunderstandings, even among experts and intellectuals, about what the issues actually mean to the people involved. A striking fact to emerge from the discussions was the insistence by opponents of a bilingual/bicultural society that it held the potential for economic, political, and social dependency for a non-English-speaking minority. And despite the repeated statements by advocates of a bilingual/bicultural option that the opponents were in fact behaving like the "immigration restrictionist" and "militant Americanizers" at the turn of the century, the opponents ignored the charge. They contended that the real problems were separating private behavior from public policy and, insofar as possible and as rapidly as possible, incorporating people who had in the past taken the bilingual/ bicultural option into the nation's political, economic, and social mainstream.

Should the United States become in fact an official bilingual/ bicultural society is a question not resolved by the conference. The conference papers and the dialogue go a long way toward showing why.

Professor Martin Ridge, *historian of the American West, prize-winning biographer, and for more than a decade managing editor of* Journal of American History, *is Senior Research Associate at the Huntington Library, San Marino, California. He is a former Guggenheim Fellow. During 1979-1980 he was a Distinguished Scholar-in-Residence at the Center for Study of the American Experience, and co-chaired its conference on Bilingualism and Biculturalism.*

Bilingualism
and Biculturalism:
A Time for Assessment
The Conference Paper

Doyce B. Nunis, Jr.

The United States is on the verge of making a set of decisions that will shape its culture, its politics, and its society for generations to come. The issue that subsumes them all is contained in two questions: Should the United States become, in law and practice, a country in which two or more languages share official status and are used widely in public life, business, education, and government? Or should the primacy of English be maintained? *

Surprisingly, many decisions leading to the former outcome have already been taken by Congress, by the federal courts and executive agencies, and by state legislatures, city governments, and judiciaries. In most instances, these decisions have been taken without considering the far-reaching implications of establishing languages other than English as official. *

Spanish, of course, is the principal minority language that competes for equal status with English. The United States has the fourth-largest Spanish-speaking population in the world, and it is the most rapidly growing segment of the nation. Spanish-speaking people have lived on the soil of the present United States since long before the Revolution, but the rapid growth of the Hispanic element—largely owing both to legal and undocumented immigration and to high birthrates—is a recent phenomenon dating from World War II.

For the first time in American experience, some concerned observers have pointed out, a large immigrant group may be electing to bypass the processes of acculturation and assimilation that turned previous immigrant groups into English-speaking Americans. These processes, as we know, worked imperfectly. Racial and cultural differences have persisted among the children and grandchildren of immigrants. But with the exception of legal restrictions imposed on racial grounds, notably segregation and miscegenation laws, these differences have been mainly personal and private. For all their marginality, even segregated Blacks and immigrant Asians have been acculturated if not assimilated and have become Americans in culture and language.

Historically, the period of acculturation and assimilation spread over at least two generations; by the third generation the Americanization of immigrant descendants was generally completed. It cannot be sufficiently emphasized that pride of national origin was not threatened by the "Americanizing" process, as the large number of national-origin organizations and non-English-language newspapers attest. And equally significant is the fact that the members of those organizations and readers of these newspapers define themselves as American. Far from impairing allegiances to America or discouraging acceptance of American citizenship, culture, and language, the consciousness of national or ethnic origin has often enhanced the sense of American identity.

Most immigrants to America *wanted* their children to become Americans, and those who wished at the same time to preserve for their children a knowledge of the language and culture of their national origins did so on a private basis. For example, Japanese children in California went to special Japanese schools on Saturday to learn the Japanese language and culture. The rest of the school year was spent in the public schools. Immigrant Jews followed the same practice in establishing schools that ranged from the orthodox to liberal and radical. For both Japanese and Jew, the maintenance of a distinctive language and culture became a private matter. Today, we see a surprising shift. For the first time, the state itself has become involved in programs that maintain bilingualism and biculturalism. This development demands wider discussion and analysis than it has yet received.

Some cities, states, and the federal government have enacted legislation which *requires* the use of languages other than English. Ballots and ballot measures are printed in English and Spanish throughout the Southwest, in New York and Florida, and now efforts to the same end are under way in Illinois. Executive agencies require instruction in the public schools in Spanish and other languages, and courts have supported executive agencies in this demand. Social service work in some cases must be conducted in Spanish and other languages.

A number of motivations may account for this development: *humanitarian*, to make social services more effective for immigrants speaking a foreign language; *pragmatic*, to make education more effective; *constitutional*, to provide a degree of equal protection, as the federal courts interpret it. But there are *political* motivations as well. These range from the modest objective of providing jobs for members of a group, to the more substantial and controversial one of maintaining the use of a "foreign" language by a considerable population occupying considerable parts of the country. This policy may turn out to be the best for America; cultural pluralism is a philosophy for our diverse country that has a long heritage. But ought the nation take that course without discussion of its implications and possible consequences?

The executive, legislative, and judicial actions that legalize bilingualism apply to all languages, but in fact, "bilingualism" in this country means primarily Spanish bilingualism. Those speaking Spanish are by far the most numerous of the new immigrants—legal and undocumented—and the political pressure for bilingualism comes primarily from Mexican-Americans, Puerto Ricans, Cubans, and from a growing number of other Spanish-speaking peoples. This mounting political pressure raises a truly momentous question: Does the Hispanic population want to become American in the historic sense, that is to say, by encouraging acculturation and assimilation?

The question is not an idle one, because an acceptance of the principle of bilingualism may open the way to a new type of divisiveness in the nation. To the natural strains produced by economic, regional, and scores of other interests, it adds the stresses brought to bear upon the country through interest groups defined by language. The modern world offers examples enough to show how this strain can lead to bitter divisions within nations. Undoubtedly, one of the great achievements of the United States has been the creation of a single nation, a single political system, a single economic market, a single culture, whatever the fruitful variations produced by the diversity of region and ethnic origin. Is this achievement sustainable in the light of the new developments that legalize bilingualism and biculturalism and, indeed, require it in many areas of the national life?

It is the business of this conference to discuss this and a wide variety of related questions and issues. For example:

- What does American history tell us of the relative virtues of acculturation, assimilation, pluralism, bilingualism, and biculturalism?
- What is the present legal status of bilingualism and biculturalism? To what extent are they new developments? Can they be said to have evolved organically from older Constitutional principles?
- Should government actively support bilingualism and biculturalism through legislation and administration?
- What should be the role of education in pressing for acculturation and assimilation or, alternatively, for bilingualism and biculturalism?
- What role do and should various non-governmental sectors play in this development? Business? The labor movement? The media? Religion?
- Is it too early at this point to project some possible consequences of bilingualism and biculturalism on the so-called "American experience?"
- Keeping in mind the ruthless methods employed by some

countries to impose cultural and linguistic uniformity, what can the United States learn from the history of bilingualism and biculturalism in the USSR, India, Canada, Mexico, Spain, and Belgium?

It is to be hoped that the conference will place the issues of bilingualism and biculturalism in a broad enough context for the participants and readers of the proceedings to find a basis for reaching a knowledgeable consensus about public policy.

Doyce B. Nunis, Jr., *conference co-chairman, is professor of history at the University of Southern California, where he teaches the history of the American West. He is a longtime editor of the* Southern California Quarterly, *and has authored numerous books and articles in his specialty, including the history of California. He is a former Guggenheim Fellow and the 1981 Fellow of the California Historical Society.*

The Historical Background of Bilingualism and Biculturalism in the United States

Stephen T. Wagner

In 1862, Justin Morrill of Vermont, later renowned as the father of the land-grant college system, spoke out in Congress against an attempt to require the printing of a German version of the government's Report on Agriculture: "I consider the proposition as unsound in principle, and as utterly subversive of the true doctrine of the country, and I hope we shall continue to hold to the sound and safe practice of printing in the English language."[1]

Despite Morrill's objections, the House of Representatives decided to print 25,000 copies of the report in German. The next day, however, Representative E. P. Walton reopened the matter, emphasizing the Printing Committee's concern with costs, and adding that he "would be willing to incur this expense for these German citizens if I would for anybody, but I submit the question whether we are to have a national language or not."

After another congressman's inquiry as to "whether, in point of fact, we have any legal language or not" was ruled out of order, the House voted to print the report in English only.[2] Though a defeat for those German-Americans who desired official recognition of their language, this decision did not, of course, settle for all time the larger question of the proper status of English and other languages in American law and government.

English was never the only language spoken by the American people. Spanish and French colonists brought their languages to the Southwest and Louisiana, where even today they are the mother tongues of many Americans. One of the first books printed in early Massachusetts was Eliot's translation of the Bible into the Algonkian speech of the local Indians. Most of the English colonies attracted settlers from continental Europe in substantial numbers, and by no means all of these assimilated to an English-speaking culture as quickly as the half-mythical characters celebrated by Crèvecoeur. The Middle Colonies were especially mixed in language as well as national origins.

Before the Revolution Benjamin Franklin expressed alarm at the growth of the German element in Pennsylvania, which amounted to about a third the province's population:

> Few of their children in the country know English. They import many books from Germany; and of the six printing-houses in the province, two are entirely German, two half-German, half-English, and but two entirely English. They have one German newspaper, and one half-German. Advertisements, intended to be general, are now printed in Dutch [sic] and English. The signs in our streets have inscriptions in both languages, and in some places only German. They begin of late to make all their bonds and other legal instruments in their own language, which (though I think it ought not to be) are allowed good in our courts, where the German business so increases, that there is continual need of interpreters; and I suppose in a few years they will also be necessary in the Assembly, to tell one-half of our legislators what the other half say.
>
> In short, unless the stream of their importation could be turned from this to other colonies . . ., they will soon so outnumber us, that all the advantages we have, will, in my opinion, be not able to preserve our language, and even our government will become precarious.[3]

In his *Observations on the Increase of Mankind* (first published in 1755), Franklin indignantly asked

> why should the Palatine [German] boors be suffered to swarm in our settlements and, by herding together, establish their language and

manners to the exclusion of ours? Why should Pennsylvania, founded by the English, become a colony of *aliens,* who will shortly be so numerous as to germanize us instead of our anglifying them?[4]

Yet within a few years Franklin eliminated this anti-German outburst from a reprint of his *Observations.* Indeed, during the War for Independence the Continental Congress sought support from American Germans by publishing for their convenience such important papers as the *Artikel des Bundes und der immerwahrenden Eintracht zwischen den Staaten . . .,* known in the original English as the Articles of Confederation.[5] Franklin's fears of German domination proved groundless, and American statesmen felt comfortable enough about the Germans and other non-English-speaking minorities to refrain from attempting forcibly to Anglicize them.

English, the "Language of Government" Since Independence

Neither the Articles nor the Constitution made English the "official" or "national" language of the United States, nor has any subsequent federal law explicitly done so.[6] Individuals and groups wishing to use languages other than English among themselves have rarely encountered legal restrictions. Nonetheless, from the beginning, English has been used as the language of government, more or less as a matter of course. Requests for the official use of other languages have repeatedly been turned down; Congress in the 1790s, 1840s, and 1860s refused to publish German versions of public documents.[7]

This approach to language issues paralleled the basic national policy which, with few exceptions, governed immigration to the United States for a century after independence: practically no restrictions on entering the country, but no favors to any particular group. As Secretary of State, John Quincy Adams explained to a German nobleman in 1819, "the government of the United States has never adopted any measure to encourage or invite emigrants from any part of Europe."[8] Two years earlier, Congress had approved an extraordinary sale of Alabama lands to a company of French refugees who proposed to cultivate grapes and olives; but the ensuing land speculation prompted criticism of the lawmakers' judgment as well as of the immigrants' bad faith. *Niles' Weekly Register* expressed a representative opinion:

I very much question the policy of any act of government that has a tendency to introduce among us a foreign national language or dialect, manners or character, as every large and compact settlement of emigrants from any particular country must necessarily occasion. . . . [T]he people of the United States are yet wretchedly deficient of a national character, though it is rapidly forming, and in a short time will be as the vanguard of the national strength. Its progress, however, is retarded by the influx of foreigners, with manners and prejudices . . . repugnant to our rules and notions of right.[9]

IMMIGRANTS URGED TO LEARN ENGLISH

Although John Adams's proposal of 1780 for an American Academy along the lines of the *Academie Française* came to nothing, a number of his contemporaries did try to use language as a means of promoting national unity. While Noah Webster sought to standardize spelling and pronunciation, others urged immigrants to learn and use English. Edward Everett, for instance, in 1820 condemned the "inconceivable perversity" of those foreigners who thought it an advantage "to speak a language which your neighbor cannot understand, to be ignorant of the language in which the laws of the land you live in are made and administered, and to shut yourself out, by a Judaic nationality of spirit, from half the social privileges of life." Everett recommended that all immigrants "instead of wishing to cherish and keep their peculiarities of language and manners . . . get over and forget them as soon as possible; remembering, that from the days of the Tower of Babel to the present, confusion of tongues has ever been one of the most active causes of intellectual and political misunderstanding and confusion."[10]

Immigrants themselves frequently urged their compatriots to learn English if they wanted to get ahead in America. A book of "advice and instruction for German emigrants," published in 1856 with German and English texts on facing pages, declared that "as it concerns our means of living, we must, above and beyond all, *rely upon a knowledge of the English language,* and the progress that we make therein has the most important and propitious influence upon our welfare. . . . Whoever does not understand or speak English . . . *continues a stranger here*; his employer entertains a kind of suspicion of him as long as he is unable to speak the language."[11]

The noted political theorist Francis Lieber, an immigrant from

Prussia, complained that Germans, Frenchmen, and other continental Europeans had more difficulty in obtaining government jobs
than Irish and other English-speaking immigrants did.[12] However,
Adam de Gurowski, a Polish revolutionary exile, claimed in 1857
that the cause of the Germans' relative lack of success in American
politics was their loyalty to their mother tongue:

> Only the Germans are the losers by attempting to maintain what in
> itself is not maintainable, what must dwindle in itself; in one word, a
> distinct nationality, a distinct language. In such a manner they may
> form puny confraternities, but never a nation. Thus, willingly seclud-
> ing themselves, instead of coalescing with the native-born popula-
> tion, the Germans have not hitherto acquired the signification and
> influence which their mental culture ought to have secured to them,
> in the yeasty undulations of American intellectual and political life.[13]

Concern about Languages of Non-Immigrant Americans

American political leaders of the nineteenth century generally
saw no need for efforts by the national government to hasten the
assimilation of immigrants. Federal authorities showed a more active concern, however, about the continued use of non-English
languages among three non-immigrant groups: the Indians, the
French-speaking inhabitants of Louisiana, and the Spanish-
speaking residents of New Mexico. Desire to "Americanize" these
people was reinforced by fears that they might pose a political threat
to the unity of the United States if they remained loyal to their own
traditions, including their mother tongues.

INDIANS

From Jefferson's presidency onward, the United States government supported efforts to "civilize" the Indians. Early laws on the
subject rarely mentioned language. In a treaty of 1828 the Cherokees
did secure help in purchasing a press and type for printing in their
own language; and several white missionary societies, evidently
more concerned with spreading Christianity than with promoting
the use of English, established bilingual schools that taught religion
in the languages their pupils understood best.[14] But government
officials increasingly insisted that civilization required education in
English. In 1868 the Indian Peace Commission asserted that "in the

difference of language today lies two-thirds of our trouble. Schools should be established which children should be required to attend; their barbarous dialects would be blotted out and the English language substituted."[15]

Although in 1888 the missionaries won approval for the continued use of Indian Bibles, by that time "there did not exist an Indian pupil whose tuition and maintenance was paid by the U.S. goverment who was permitted to study in any language other than English."[16] Many young Indians were sent far from their reservations for years at a time to boarding schools, where they were forced to give up their traditional hairstyles, dress, customs and languages—surely this was the most coercive cultural assimilation ever sponsored by the United States government. Not until the 1930s did federal authorities begin to encourage tribes to maintain their own languages and cultures.

FRENCH-SPEAKING POPULATION

American policy toward the French-speaking population acquired with the purchase of Louisiana in 1803 was also markedly pro-English, though not so anti-French as to provoke revolt. Jefferson attempted to conciliate the long-time residents of "Orleans Territory," but many of his appointees there, including the governor and several judges, were recently arrived Anglo-Americans. This, as noted by Charles Gayarré in his famous *History of Louisiana*, caused some resentment, which was intensified by the confusion and injustice that attended the sudden introduction of the English language and the common law into the courts.

Some New England Federalists had objected to the annexation of Louisiana, partly because of the French character of its people. Perhaps in an effort to mollify these critics, the 1811 act enabling the Louisianians to draft a constitution and apply for admission as a state specified that "the laws which such State may pass shall be promulgated, and its records of every description shall be preserved, and its judicial and legislative written proceedings conducted, in the language in which the laws and the judicial and legislative written proceedings of the United States are now published."[17] The Louisianians' acceptance of this condition for statehood, Congressman Richard M. Johnson of Kentucky argued, proves their love for liberty, their willingness to sacrifice prejudices at the shrine of independence. They are willing to destroy the only remaining vestige of French nationality, the French language, that we may not only be one in sentiment, one great family in principles, but in language, habit, and external appearance. It is a great sacrifice, one which they ought to make, and one worthy alone of freemen.[18]

The state constitution with which Louisiana entered the Union in 1812 stipulated that the language used for state laws, official documents, and judicial and legislative records had to be that "in which the Constitution of the United States is written."[19] Such formulations, avoiding direct use of the term "English," may have reflected either hostility to the British government in a time of international tension or a desire to emphasize the political rationale for linguistic unity, or both. In any case, they were echoed in later justifications for the preservation of English as the de facto American national language.

SPANISH-SPEAKING PEOPLES

Unlike Texas and California, New Mexico remained predominantly Spanish-speaking for decades after its acquisition from Mexico in 1848. Unlike Louisiana, which had been rather promptly admitted to statehood in spite of its Francophone majority, New Mexico was kept waiting for some sixty years. Not all of the factors contributing to the unusual delay related to the territory's Hispanic culture.[20] But as late as 1902 a special Senate committee, led by Albert J. Beveridge, stressed its disapproval of the continuing widespread use of Spanish in schools and courts, arguing that New Mexico would not be ready for statehood until at least a majority of its people were assimilated to "American" language and customs. The enabling act that allowed New Mexico and Arizona to draft state constitutions passed early in 1910, the same year in which the census showed that, largely because of migration from the other states, "Anglos" had finally become a majority of New Mexico's population.[21] In passing the enabling act, Congress insisted that the "schools shall always be conducted in English" and the "ability to read, write, speak and understand the English language without an interpreter shall be a necessary qualification for all state officers and members of the state legislature." In 1911 Congress withdrew the second requirement but not the first;[22] in 1912 New Mexico became a state.

Language Policies and Practices of the States

Throughout American history the language policies and practices of the individual states have been at least as important as those of the federal government, especially in the nineteenth century when state actions were much more likely than those of officials in Washington to affect the lives of ordinary people. English was, of course, routinely employed as the language of state and local government—and of the public schools—but at times other languages were also used. In general, languages of "old settler" groups, whose occupation of an area preceded or coincided with the arrival of English-speaking Americans, were more likely to be used in government than were those of new immigrants to long-settled places.[23]

Old stories telling how German narrowly missed adoption as a (or even *the*) state language of Pennsylvania belong to myth rather than history.[24] However, Pennsylvania did appoint an official German printer in 1843; and in the "Pennsylvania Dutch" region a great deal of the business of local governments and the lower courts was carried on in German.[25] Likewise, Louisiana before the Civil War published its laws in both English and French and allowed the use of both languages in its legislature and courts; the language of government at lower levels was the language of the local population.[26] Other states—and some territories besides New Mexico—quite commonly printed public documents in various languages. The constitution proposed for Minnesota in 1857, for instance, was issued in German, Swedish, Norwegian, and French versions.[27]

Many early laws establishing public schools contained no language provisions. In 1836 Pennsylvania's Free School Superintendent explained that German-language schools could count as common schools.[28] In 1840 Ohio, responding to considerable political activity among its German residents, explicitly sanctioned German-English schools, which led to the growth of a substantial bilingual school system in Cincinnati.[29] Because of the American tradition of local control over public schools, non-English majorities in particular districts were often able to obtain tax-supported instruction in their own languages even where state laws were silent or hostile. Some Americans were very dubious about public schools in which "the teachers are German, the moral atmosphere is German, the methods part German, and the language of the school, to say the least, as much German as English."[30]

Post-Civil War Suspicion of Newcomers

American suspicion of immigrants intermittently has found expression in politics, notably through the Know-Nothing clubs of the mid-1850s and the immigration restriction movement that flourished from the 1890s to the 1920s. Hostility toward the use of languages other than English has traditionally been regarded as a rather minor element in American nativism. Ray Billington's account in *The Protestant Crusade* focuses mainly on the role played by religious hatred in the pre-Civil War unrest, while John Higham's *Strangers in the Land* identifies anti-Catholicism, anti-radicalism, and Anglo-Saxon racism as the three major elements underlying the later agitation. When labor leaders have supported immigration restriction, their main objective has been to protect American wage rates, not the English language. Moreover, nativists' dislike of the Irish, which was very strong through most of the nineteenth century, shows that in their view the ability to speak English did not in itself entitle an immigrant to be considered truly American.

Nevertheless, many spokesmen for the English-speaking majority, considering full assimilation of the immigrants to be necessary and desirable, regarded the use of English as an almost indispensable means of Americanization. Theodore Roosevelt argued in 1888 that

> the man who becomes completely Americanized . . . and who "talks United States" instead of the dialect of the country which he has of his own free will abandoned is not only doing his plain duty by his adopted land, but is also rendering to himself a service of immeasurable value. . . . A man who speaks only German or Swedish may nevertheless be a most useful American citizen; but it is impossible for him to derive the full benefit he should from American citizenship.[31]

Urging the newcomers to do themselves a favor by learning English, Roosevelt was still confident that the country could and would successfully absorb the immigrants.

FOREIGN LANGUAGES IN THE SCHOOLS

However, even then the "new immigration" from Southern and Eastern Europe was increasing; and as industrialization and urbanization accelerated, cultural conflicts, including disputes over language, were becoming more important in American politics. As in earlier years, the use of languages other than English in the schools gave rise to controversy. Late in the 1880s Missouri's Superintendent of Public Instruction complained:

> In a large number of the districts of the State, the German element of the population greatly preponderates and, as a consequence, the schools are mainly taught in the German language and sometimes entirely so. Hence, if an American family lives in such a district, the children must either be deprived of school privileges or else be taught in the German language. . . . Some of the teachers are scarcely able to speak the English language.

His report for 1889 urged that "the law should specify definitely in what language the instruction of our public schools is to be given. It is a shame and a disgrace to have the English language ruled out of our public schools and German substituted, as is done wholly or in part in many districts in this State. . . ."[32] St. Louis and Louisville, among other cities, dropped the teaching of German from their public schools late in the 1880s.[33]

Parochial schools that used German as the language of instruction found themselves threatened in 1889 when Illinois adopted the Edwards law and Wisconsin, the Bennett law. Both measures, originally passed with little controversy, were compulsory attendance laws, which also required all schools to teach most subjects in English. German Lutherans and Catholics protested strenuously, administered severe defeats to the Republicans in the elections of 1890, and secured the repeal of the two laws in 1893.[34]

Illinois Republicans blamed their defeat in the 1892 elections on continuing disaffection among Germans, Poles, Irish, and other immigrant groups. On January 20, 1893, Theodore Roosevelt assured the Hamilton Club of Chicago that Republican resistance to foreign languages in the schools had been correct:

> America is more than geographical expression, and Americans more than human beings who happen to inhabit a particular section of the world's surface; . . . America is a nation . . . an organic whole, indi-

visible itself, and sharply sundered from all others. . . . American institutions and characteristics include . . . our language—the language in which the Declaration of Independence was drawn up and the Constitution formulated, the language used by Grant in his biography, and by the great statesman whose name and whose priceless worth this club commemorates, Alexander Hamilton, in the Federalist, the language of Lincoln's last inaugural and Gettysburg speech, and of Washington's farewell address. . . . [T]hose of foreign origin who come here must become Americans; they must become like us, and not seek to make us like them. . . .

Americanism is primarily and in its essence a matter of faith, of belief, of spirit and purpose. . . . I want to make as strong a plea as I possibly can against hyphenated Americans of every kind, whether German-Americans, Irish-Americans or native Americans. The word American is broad enough to cover us all. . . . I am an unflinching believer in and supporter of our common school system . . . a system of non-sectarian schools supported by the State, in which the exercises shall be conducted in English and the children are taught to speak United States.[35]

Flood of the "New Immigrants"

Around the turn of the century immigrants were arriving in such numbers, and concentrating so heavily in certain urban areas, that many observers questioned whether they would in fact readily fit themselves into American society. Some openly denied that the United States could properly assimilate the throngs it was receiving. Beginning in the 1890s the Immigration Restriction League, supported chiefly by "old-stock" New Englanders and championed in Congress by Henry Cabot Lodge, sought to lessen the influx. The means proposed for doing so was a literacy test, which, it was assumed, would tend to exclude the "new immigrant" nationalities much more than the English, the Irish, or the Germans.[36] Pseudoscientific racial theories now joined religious prejudice and fear of alien radicals in arousing dislike of the newcomers among well-established Americans, but linguistic differences also helped create negative impressions of the immigrants. The poem "Unguarded Gates" by Thomas Bailey Aldrich was meant as a warning:

> In street and alley what strange tongues are these,
> Accents of menace alien to our air,
> Voices that once the Tower of Babel knew!

> O Liberty, white Goddess! is it well
> To leave the gates unguarded?[37]

On returning to his native land in 1907 after many years of residence abroad, Henry James found himself fascinated by the operation of "the caldron of the 'American' character"—and also quite ill at ease. He objected to changes in the traditional "idea of the country":

> Is not our instinct, in this matter, in general, essentially the safe one—that of keeping the idea simple and strong and continuous, so that it shall be perfectly sound? To touch it overmuch, to pull it about, is to put it in peril of weakening; yet on this free assault upon it, this readjustment of it in *their* monstrous, presumptuous interest, the aliens, in New York, seemed perpetually to insist. The combination there of their quantity and their quality—that loud primary stage of alienism which New York most offers to sight—operates, for the native, as their note of settled possession, something they have nobody to thank for; so that *un*settled possession is what we, on our side, seem reduced to—the implication of which, in its turn, is that, to recover confidence and regain lost ground, we, not they, must make the surrender and accept the orientation. We must go, in other words, *more* than half-way to meet them; which is all the difference, for us, between possession and dispossession.[38]

Boston proved just as unsettling to James. As he watched the Sunday crowd coming up Beacon Hill from the Common,

> no sound of English, in a single instance, escaped their lips; the greater number spoke a rude form of Italian, the others some outland dialect unknown to me—though I waited and waited to catch an echo of antique refrains. No note of any shade of American speech struck my ear, save in so far as the sounds in question represent to-day so much of the substance of that idiom. The types and faces bore them out; the people before me were gross aliens to a man, and they were in serene and confident possession.[39]

James was not always able to distinguish national origins according to appearance; repeatedly he was unaware of the "alienness" of people he met until he heard them speak. He was amazed when he learned that the young fellow he had asked for directions in the New Hampshire woods was an Armenian; the man whom he accosted when looking for the House of Seven Gables in Salem turned out to be another "flagrant foreigner." James did enjoy viewing the graceful old houses of the town—" the only thing was that I had never bargained for looking at them through a polyglot air."[40]

EAGERNESS TO ASSIMILATE

However "alien" they seemed to sensitive natives, most of the immigrants did learn English, often quite willingly. Edward A. Steiner wrote of his shipboard experiences with fellow-immigrants recrossing the Atlantic to visit their old homes:

> It is good to feel that so many of these foreigners learn to love their adopted country. It was interesting also to find that these ten or twelve nationalities which were represented in the steerage of the *Vaterland* were nearly all closely related, but could not understand one another in their native language. . . . [T]o speak to one another they had to use the English tongue. In that conglomerate of races and nationalities, in which language was an iron wall, it was good to hear "American talk," as they call it, and find it a binding link.[41]

Of course, as they used English, the immigrants also changed it. Israel Zangwill, whose popular success *The Melting Pot* Theodore Roosevelt called "a great play" in 1908, emphasized that "as to the ultimate language of the United States, it is unreasonable to suppose that American, though fortunately protected by English literature, will not bear traces of the fifty languages now being spoken next to it."[42] Later research by Mencken and others has confirmed the accuracy of Zangwill's prediction.

ENGLISH MADE A REQUIREMENT OF NATURALIZATION

In 1906 Congress, while attempting to bring order to the casual and often corrupt naturalization procedures that had prevailed in the states for many years, came closer than ever before to identifying American nationality with English speech. Except for those immigrants who had already applied for citizenship, no more aliens were to be naturalized without demonstrating that they could speak English.[43] The enforcement of this requirement doubtless varied considerably from court to court, and it seems unlikely that many judges insisted on near-native fluency in the language. English lessons did become an even more important part of the "Americanization" programs offered by numerous public and private night schools; but even so, for many years substantial numbers of naturalized citizens, let alone resident aliens, used little if any English.[44]

Early in this century the United States government also pursued a pro-English language policy in the possessions it had acquired during the Spanish-American War. In Puerto Rico, for example, from

1905 until 1916 English was supposed to be the sole language of instruction in the schools. In 1916 the rules were altered so that Spanish was to be used through the fifth grade and English from that grade forward.[45]

"America for Americans"

The greatest impetus toward the exclusive use of English in the United States came from the superpatriotism and suspicion of foreigners that swept over the country during the First World War. More than ever Theodore Roosevelt served as a militant spokesman for what became known as "one hundred percent Americanism."[46] No longer confident that immigrants who failed to assimilate were hurting only themselves, he declared in "America for Americans," a speech he delivered in 1916, that "unless the immigrant becomes in good faith American and nothing else, then he is out of place in this country and the sooner he leaves it the better."[47] President Wilson and his supporters also joined in castigating "hyphenates." After the United States entered the war, national unity seemed even more imperative. In the autumn of 1917 Roosevelt drafted and circulated a statement which was signed by prominent Americans of various ancestries:

> We must have but one flag. We must also have but one language. That must be the language of the Declaration of Independence, of Washington's Farewell Address, of Lincoln's Gettysburg Speech and Second Inaugural. We cannot tolerate any attempt to oppose or supplant the language and culture that has come down to us from the builders of this republic with the language and culture of any European country. The greatness of this nation depends on the swift assimilation of the aliens she welcomes to her shores. Any force which attempts to retard that assimilative process is a force hostile to the highest interests of our country. . . .[48]

German-Americans, some of whom had been conspicuous—though hardly successful—apologists for Imperial Germany before American entry into the war, were the prime targets of the anti-hyphenate hysteria; much public pressure and some new state and local laws were aimed specifically at them. Both public and private schools eliminated instruction of and through German; whereas in 1915 about 324,000 students were studying German, by 1922 fewer than 14,000 were doing so. Some states, such as Nebraska, outlawed the use of any foreign language in elementary schools; Ohio singled out German for prohibition. The town of Findlay, Ohio, went so far as to impose a fine of $25 for using German on the street.[49]

Foreign-language newspapers also came under attack. Theodore Roosevelt decried them as "our most dangerous foe."[50] Government agents kept the foreign-language press, especially German and radical papers, under close scrutiny; in several cases they suppressed allegedly subversive periodicals by denying them the use of the mails.

QUOTA ACTS OF THE 1920s

Wartime suspicion of foreigners also contributed to the enactment, over President Woodrow Wilson's veto, of the first law forbidding the immigration of most adult illiterates. (However, literacy *in English* was not required; to pass the test a person merely had to read forty simple words in any language. Even for naturalization English literacy was not required until 1950.) After the end of the war this new restriction proved insufficient greatly to reduce the supposedly less desirable immigration from Southern and Eastern Europe. Accordingly, Congress in 1921 and 1924 enacted stringent quota acts which cut the total number of Old World immigrants to be admitted while favoring the peoples of the British Isles and Northwestern Europe at the expense of other nationalities. No numerical restrictions were placed on immigration from Latin America, and the number of immigrants arriving from Mexico increased significantly in the 1920s. However, while the long-settled Hispanic population of New Mexico continued to educate its children largely in Spanish—often at the cost of isolation from the more dynamic "Anglos" of the state—Mexican newcomers in Texas and California were commonly segregated from Anglo children and not infrequently punished for speaking Spanish at school.[51]

By the middle of the 1920s, with America seemingly once again safe in its isolation—and with immigration greatly reduced—the anti-foreign hysteria largely subsided. In 1923 the Supreme Court, in *Meyer v. Nebraska* and other cases, struck down state laws it felt had unduly restricted the teaching or use of foreign languages. However, it allowed laws mandating the use of English as the sole language of instruction to stand; and by now thirty-four states had such requirements.[52] The "Americanization" efforts which had peaked in 1918-1920 subsided,[53] but their promoters' assumption that immigrants must be encouraged to learn English remained almost unquestioned orthodoxy. With the influx of Eastern Hemisphere immigrants diminished, the number of Americans unable to understand English dropped as well. Official use of any language other than English had come to seem unthinkable.

Development of "Linguistic Rights"

The influence of traditional American language policy is open to debate. Heinz Kloss has maintained that by and large the Anglicization of non-English ethnic groups in the United States has been a matter of voluntary individual choices, not of governmental coercion.[54] Arnold Leibowitz has argued that English literacy tests and English-only requirements in the schools have served chiefly as a means of discriminating against members of minorities disliked by the dominant majority.[55] Interestingly, Leibowitz himself "would question neither the existing official character of English nor the desirability of an open articulation of the language's status. What should be clarified is what follows from such an assumption or articulation. An official language would properly regulate governmental proceedings and establish a customary norm for the country. It should not, however, imply or require statutes aimed at regulating business or social adjustment."[56]

While arguing persuasively that American law and practice have accorded fewer linguistic rights to latecomers in settled areas than to groups who accompanied the English as pioneers, Kloss asserts that the languages which have received greatest protection from the state have been those of groups that were well established before the Anglo-Americans came to dominate them. This generalization hardly accounts for the fate of most American Indian languages; but it does apply to French in Louisiana and to Spanish in New Mexico—and, above all, to Spanish in Puerto Rico.[57]

The Puerto Rican Experience

Puerto Rico has been the great exception to the usual language policy of the United States government. From 1900 on, Spanish has enjoyed legal equality with English in the island's legislature and local courts. (However, to facilitate appeals the federal district court's proceedings have been conducted in English.)[58] Much more controversy has arisen concerning the language—or languages—of instruction to be used in the island's schools. Federal officials long hoped to make the Puerto Rican people genuinely bilingual, but their efforts had only limited success.

In the 1930s native Puerto Ricans in charge of the island's educational system sought to increase the use of Spanish in the elementary schools; they met opposition from Secretary of the Interior Harold Ickes and President Franklin Roosevelt. FDR set forth his views in 1937:

> It is regrettable that today hundreds of thousands of Puerto Ricans have little and often virtually no knowledge of the English language. Moreover, even among those who have had the opportunity to study English in the public schools, mastery of the language is far from satisfactory. It is an indispensable part of American policy that the coming generation of American citizens in Puerto Rico grow up with complete facility in the English tongue. It is the language of our Nation. Only through the acquisition of this language will Puerto Rico-Americans secure a better understanding of American ideals and principles. Moreover, it is only through familiarity with our language that the Puerto Ricans will be able to take full advantage of the economic opportunities which became available to them when they were made American citizens.[59]

However, Puerto Rican Nationalists strongly advocated primacy for Spanish in the island's schools; and, despite a veto by President Truman in 1946, Spanish has been the medium of instruction, even in the secondary schools, since 1949.[60]

Unlike almost every other originally non-English-speaking area ruled by the United States, Puerto Rico never has attracted an Anglo-American "in-migration" large enough to make Anglicization—or even true bilingualism—practical. In Kloss's words: "In Puerto Rico the nominal equality of Spanish, the language of the old-established settlers, and of English led in practice to the predominance of the former; the Anglo-Saxons in Puerto Rico play the role of a minority whose language does not enjoy full equality."[61]

As United States citizens since the Jones Act went into effect in 1917, Puerto Ricans desiring to move to the continental United

States have not been frustrated by the immigration laws. For the most part much more fluent in Spanish than in English, they have presented a special problem to educators and other public officials in places where they have settled in great numbers; as citizens they have, since the mid-1960s, been given government help in their native tongue, as in polling places (where New York's former English literacy test used to exclude many of them from voting) and in the schools.

Cultural Pluralism Replaces "Melting Pot"

Government agencies are now more willing to use languages other than English in dealing even with people who are not native-born citizens but immigrants. The old faith in America as a melting pot has, to a considerable degree, been replaced by a belief—often rather vague—in "cultural pluralism" more or less as promoted in the 1920s by Horace Kallen; certainly the old assumption of Anglo-Saxon superiority is no longer respectable.

Changes in the immigration laws illustrate the shift in sentiment. "Refugee Relief" measures after World World II granted admittance to many thousand Italians, Poles, Jews, and others whom the national origins system would have kept waiting for years. The McCarran-Walter Act of 1952 was both more and less favorable to non-white would-be immigrants than its predecessors: it allowed more Asians but fewer West Indian Blacks to enter the country. Since it retained the quotas favoring Northwestern Europeans, it became law only over the veto of President Truman, who denounced the whole concept of using national origins as a selective principle:

> The idea behind this discriminatory policy was, to put it boldly, that Americans with English or Irish names were better people and better citizens than Americans with Italian or Greek or Polish names. . . . Such a concept is utterly unworthy of our traditions and our ideals.[62]

By 1960 Congressman Walter's defense of the immigration laws seemed outdated:

> Our quota system is based on the image of our own people. It is like a mirror held up before the American people, reflecting the proportions of their various national origins. The main purpose of it is to permit

the speedy assimilation of the newcomer and his absorption into our social, political and economic system more readily than if the immigrants would arrive in numbers disproportionate to the national origins of the people who receive them and make them a part of their own.[63]

Despite Walter's objections, the Democratic party platform in 1960 called for scrapping the quota system. After Walter's death in 1963, President Kennedy pressed for such a change, which was signed into law—significantly, after the Civil Rights Act of 1964 was passed—by President Johnson in 1965. The new law by 1968 eliminated all preferential treatment of immigrants from English-speaking countries.

Bilingualism in the Schools

Early in 1968 Congress passed the first major federal law favoring the use of languages other than English in the schools. Known as the Bilingual Education Act, Title VII of the Elementary and Secondary Education Act offered financial support for projects designed to meet "the special educational needs of the large number of children of limited English-speaking ability in the United States." Many of the act's supporters assumed that chief among those needs was acquisition of proficiency in English; they regarded instruction using other languages mainly as a means to that end. However, others involved in implementing the law rejected this view of bilingual education as a "transitional" device; they sought instead to use the law to promote "linguistic and cultural maintenance efforts," for instance, by improving the Spanish-language skills of Hispanic students already quite capable of learning in English-language classes. The conflict between proponents of these two purposes for bilingual education continues.[64]

Revisions made to the Bilingual Education Act in 1974 strengthened tendencies toward "biculturalism." Only those programs that employed non-English languages remained eligible for funding; moreover, educators were to teach "with appreciation for the cultural heritage" their students brought with them. On the other hand, changes made by Congress in 1978 attempted to re-emphasize improvement in English-language skills.[65]

LAU V. NICHOLS

Since 1974 the federal government has not merely encouraged schools to provide bilingual programs but, in many cases, has required them to do so. In its 1974 *Lau v. Nichols* decision, the United States Supreme Court determined that school districts receiving any federal aid were obliged to provide special help to students unable to benefit from ordinary classes taught in English; failure to do so would constitute national-origin discrimination and thus violate the Civil Rights Act of 1964. This finding upheld the position that the Office of Civil Rights within the Department of Health, Education, and Welfare had taken in 1970. Federal officials have subsequently used guidelines derived from the *Lau* case, along with the incentive provided by greatly increased funding for Title VII projects, to stimulate adoption of bilingual methods and bicultural attitudes.[66] Numerous other recent federal education laws provide money for bilingual programs or require, as a condition of continued eligibility for other federal aid, special efforts to educate persons who lack proficiency in English.

State laws have also become much more favorable to teaching in languages other than English than they had been since before the First World War. By 1976 only eleven states still required that all public school instruction, except for foreign language courses, be in English; and ten states had mandated establishment of bilingual programs in districts with substantial numbers of students whose mother tongues were not English.[67]

Senator Ralph Yarborough had sponsored the original Bilingual Education Act because of his concern about the poor performance of Mexican-American children in the schools of his own state, Texas. Although by the late 1970s Title VII was supporting instruction through the use of some seventy different languages and dialects, Hispanics—including Mexican-Americans, Puerto Ricans, Cuban-Americans, and others—still constituted about 80 percent of the students in bilingual programs.[68]

Bilingual Ballots

The 1975 amendments to the Voting Rights Act of 1965 were also originally inspired by the situation of Mexican-Americans in Texas, where despite the absence of a literacy test only some 38 percent of the potential Chicano electorate voted in 1972. Deciding that English-language ballots and voting instructions placed improper burdens on non-English-speaking citizens, Congress determined that in certain districts election materials must be printed in Spanish or in the languages of various Asian-Americans, American Indians, or Alaskan Natives.[69]

Resentment of seeming favoritism toward these alleged victims of discrimination (as well as toward Blacks) helped prompt Americans of various European origins to seek benefits for their own groups. The resulting Ethnic Heritage Studies Act, first implemented in 1974, has done relatively little to stimulate the use of languages other than English, partly because of lack of desire among the groups concerned, partly because of low levels of funding.[70]

At least one advocate of bilingual/bicultural education has suggested that the United States may soon be compelled by the growth of its Hispanic population seriously to consider adopting Spanish as an "official" language alongside English.[71] Thus far there appears to be little support for such a step. Among other reasons, increasing awareness that several million of the aliens now in the country are here illegally—and that most of these are Spanish-speaking—may reinforce public hostility to further expansion of governmental use of Spanish.

Even so, though Nathan Glazer is probably right in asserting that "it is still . . . part of the general expectation that a general American culture will prevail as the dominant one in our country, and one that does create national identity, loyalty, and commitment,"[72] the role that English, as opposed to other languages, will play in American culture and government now seems less clear-cut than it once did.

NOTES

1. *Congressional Globe*, 37th Congress, 2nd Session, Vol. 32, Part 2, p. 1821.
2. *Ibid.*, p. 1842. For regional and party breakdowns of the vote, see Heinz Kloss, *American Bilingual Tradition* (Rowley, Mass.: Newbury House, 1977), pp. 30-32.
3. Letter to Peter Collinson, May 9, 1753, in Jared Sparks, ed., *The Works of Benjamin Franklin*, Vol. 7 (Boston, 1840), pp. 66-73.

4. *Annals of America* (Chicago: Encyclopaedia Britannica, 1968), Vol. 1, p. 493.

5. Kloss, *American Bilingual Tradition*, pp. 26-27.

6. Absence of an "official" or "state" language, however, does not guarantee equal treatment for all languages. Although German was not officially the "national language" of Hapsburg Austria, it certainly enjoyed privileged status there.

7. Kloss, *American Bilingual Tradition*, pp. 28-33.

8. Letter to Morris von Furstenwarther, June 4, 1819, printed in *Niles' Weekly Register*, Vol. 18, No. 9 (April 29, 1820), p. 157.

9. H. Lallemand, in *Niles' Weekly Register*, Vol. 14, No. 24 (Aug. 8, 1818), p. 393.

10. Edward Everett, "German Emigration to America," *North American Review* (July 1820), pp. 17-18.

11. F. W. Bogen, *The German in America*, 2nd ed. (New York, 1851), p. 11.

12. Francis Lieber, *Letters to a Gentleman in Germany* (Philadelphia: Carey, Lea, and Blanchard, 1834), pp. 201-206.

13. Adam de Gurowski, *America and Europe* (New York, 1857), pp. 109-113.

14. Arnold H. Leibowitz, "The Imposition of English as the Language of Instruction in American Schools," *Revista de Derecho Puertorriqueno*, Vol. 10 (1970), pp. 209-211.

15. *Ibid.*, pp. 210-211.

16. *Ibid.*, p. 212.

17. *Annals of Congress*, 11th Congress, 3rd Session, p. 1327.

18. *Ibid.*, pp. 523-524.

19. Kloss, *American Bilingual Tradition*, p. 112.

20. Warren A. Beck, *New Mexico: A History of Four Centuries* (Norman: University of Oklahoma Press, 1962), pp. 226-241.

21. Kloss, *American Bilingual Tradition*, pp. 127-128.

22. Leibowitz, "The Imposition of English. . . ," pp. 203-204.

23. Kloss makes the distinction between old settlers and immigrants one of the key organizing principles of his study.

24. Kloss, *American Bilingual Tradition*, pp. 28, 142-143; Albert Bernhardt Faust, *The German Element in the United States*, new ed. (New York: Steuben Society of America, 1927), pp. 652-653.

25. Kloss, *American Bilingual Tradition*, pp. 143-147.

26. *Ibid.*, pp. 112-120.

27. *Ibid.*, p. 84.

28. *Ibid.*, p. 149.

29. *Ibid.*, pp. 180-181; Joshua Fishman and others, *Language Loyalty in the United States* (The Hague: Mouton, 1966), p. 223.

30. J. Lalor in *Atlantic Monthly*, Vol. 32 (October 1873), p. 456.

31. Theodore Roosevelt, "Americans Past and Present and the Americanization of Foreigners," *America* (April 14, 1888), p. 2.

32. Fishman, *Language Loyalty in the United States*, pp. 234-235.

33. *Ibid.*, p. 236.

34. Leibowitz, "The Imposition of English. . .," pp. 181-183.

35. Hamilton Club of Chicago, "Third Annual Banquet, January 20, 1893," pp. 18-20 (Theodore Roosevelt Collection, Widener Library, Harvard University). Roosevelt insisted that he wanted to see "men of all the creeds, Catholic and Protestant, Jew and Gentile, taking an equal part in the goverment of these schools." At the same time, the American Protective Association's members were pledging themselves never to vote for Catholics.

36. The bills promoted by Lodge required that adult immigrants demonstrate ability to read in *any* language. For the Immigration Restriction League, see John Higham's *Strangers in the Land* (New York: Atheneum, 1969) and Barbara Miller Solomon's *Ancestors and Immigrants* (Cambridge: Harvard University Press, 1956).

37. *Atlantic Monthly*, Vol. 70 (July 1892), p. 57.

38. Henry James, *The American Scene* (New York: Harper, 1907), pp. 117, 83-84.

39. *Ibid.*, pp. 222-223.

40. *Ibid.*, pp. 117, 255-257.

41. *Outlook*, Vol. 74 (Aug. 29, 1903), p. 1043.

42. Israel Zangwill, *The Melting Pot*, revised ed. (New York: Macmillan, 1919), p. 203. See also, H. L. Mencken, *The American Language*, 4th ed. (New York: Knopf, 1936), pp. 212-222, and his Supplement 1 to that work (New York: Knopf, 1945), pp. 426-439, for examples of immigrant influences on American English.

43. John Higham, *Strangers in the Land*, pp. 118, 356. For the text of the law, see Frederick Van Dyne, *A Treatise on the Law of Naturalization of the United States* (Washington, 1907). The law exempts those applicants physically unable to speak English and those settling government land in compliance with the Homestead Act.

44. E. J. Irwin, "An Americanization Program," U.S. Bureau of Education, *Bulletin*, No. 30 (1923) reported that of the 4,003 residents of Scranton who told school authorities in the summer of 1918 that they could not speak English, 859 were naturalized Americans.

45. Leibowitz, "The Imposition of English. . . ," pp. 219-220.

46. Higham, *Strangers in the Land*, p. 374, casts doubt on Mencken's assertion that Roosevelt coined or at least popularized the term.

47. Theodore Roosevelt, "America for Americans," speech at St. Louis, Missouri, May 31, 1916, pp. 3-4 (Theodore Roosevelt Collection, Widener Library, Harvard University).

48. Wayne Moquin, ed. *Makers of America* (Chicago: Encyclopaedia Britannica, 1971), Vol. 7, p. 131.

49. Leibowitz, "The Imposition of English. . . ," pp. 183-184.

50. Moquin, *Makers of America*, Vol. 7, p. 131.

51. Leibowitz, "The Imposition of English. . . ," pp. 199, 204 (for the treatment of Mexican-Americans).

52. *Ibid.*, pp. 183-186.

53. Higham, *Strangers in the Land*, Chapter 9.

54. Kloss, *American Bilingual Tradition*, p. 283.

55. Leibowitz, "The Imposition of English. . . ," pp. 240-241; Leibowitz, "English Literacy: Legal Sanction for Discrimination," *Notre Dame Lawyer*, Vol. 45 (1969), pp. 7-8.

56. Leibowitz, "English Literacy. . . ," p. 14.

57. Kloss, *American Bilingual Tradition*, pp. 288-289.

58. *Ibid.*, pp. 257-259.

59. Leibowitz, "The Imposition of English. . . ," p. 226.

60. *Ibid.*, pp. 220-231.

61. Kloss, *American Bilingual Tradition*, p. 289.

62. Quoted in John F. Kennedy, *A Nation of Immigrants* (New York: Popular Library, 1964), p. 114.

63. Francis E. Walter to Chester Bowles, Aug. 8, 1960 (Senate Files at the John F. Kennedy Library).

64. Noel Epstein, *Language, Ethnicity, and the Schools* (Washington, D.C., 1977), pp. 9-31; Abigail M. Thernstrom, "Language: Issues and Legislation," in Stephan Thernstrom et al, *Harvard Encyclopedia of American Ethnic Groups* (Cambridge: Harvard University Press, 1980).

65. Thernstrom, "Language: Issues and Legislation."

66. Epstein, *Language, Ethnicity, and the Schools*, pp. 13-16.

67. Nathan Glazer, "Public Education and American Pluralism," in James S. Coleman, ed., *Parents, Teachers, and Children* (San Francisco: Institute for Contemporary Studies, 1977), pp. 102-103.

68. Epstein, *Language, Ethnicity, and the Schools*, pp. 2, 11.

69. Abigail M. Thernstrom, "The Odd Evolution of the Voting Rights Act," *The Public Interest* (Spring 1979), pp. 68-74.

70. Glazer, "Public Education and American Pluralism," pp. 100-101, 105-106.

71. Josue M. Gonzales, testifying before the House Committee on Education and Labor's General Subcommittee on Education, March 1974, quoted in Epstein, *Language, Ethnicity, and the Schools*, pp. 35-36.

72. Glazer, "Public Education and American Pluralism," pp. 107-108.

Stephen T. Wagner *has taught history and social science at Wayland High School in Maynard, Massachusetts since 1969, and has begun teaching German as well. Holding an A.B. from Oberlin College and an M.A.T. from Harvard University, he is a doctoral candidate in Harvard's* History of American Civilization *program, doing dissertation research into changes in U.S. immigration policy from 1952 to 1965.*

II. Three Dimensions

Pluralism
and Ethnicity

Nathan Glazer

For some time I have been recording and commenting on the development of bilingual and bicultural policies in American public education with a certain skepticism. Because I teach about these matters to students who are either enthusiastic about such policies or critical of what they consider the overly timid or limited way in which they are being followed, I have also had to ask myself whether my skepticism is well-based; and I have had at least to question my views.

In this paper I should like to do three things: First, I will describe the extent to which bilingualism and biculturalism are now established in American public education; second, I will mention briefly the arguments that have created my skepticism about these policies; third, I will weigh, in the light of some new considerations I will raise, whether these arguments stand up.

On the first point: We do not know as much as we should about the extent of bilingual or bicultural programs in the United States. Legally, they are now required for any student who has some difficulty in learning English. These requirements stem not from federal legislation—which only provides funds to assist in bilingual or bicultural education—but from two other sources. First, some states now require such education. Second, the Department of Health, Education, and Welfare has interpreted the prohibition, in the Civil Rights Act of 1964, of discrimination by recipients of federal funds on grounds of national origin to apply to children raised speaking a language other than English; this means that school districts must provide some program of bilingual education to be in compliance with the law. The HEW requirement was upheld in rather ambiguous wording by the Supreme Court, thereby enabling the department's Office of Civil Rights to go further and require more definite action by school districts. There are still other legal bases for bilingual education programs, such as consent judgments stemming from court cases under which such programs are mandated.[1] The *Aspira* case in New York City is the chief example.

Interpreting the Legal Bases of Bilingual Education

I have already mentioned the facilitating legislation, providing funds for such education, that has been passed at the federal level. In addition, under other legislation the federal government provides funds for research and development of curriculum materials for education in one's ethnic heritage.

Having described the law, it is, however, much more difficult to describe the reality. Whether provided in response to Office of Civil Rights requirements, or under a consent judgment (such as the one under which bilingual education is offered to the Spanish-speaking children of New York City), or under state law, an initial problem in bilingual education is, to whom must it be provided? The "whom" is generally defined as someone having difficulty in English, but how much difficulty, and how is it to be measured?

Those pressing for bilingual education want it to reach the largest possible numbers; those who provide it, that is, school districts, want to provide it to the smallest possible numbers. After all, it is expensive, it is special education, and all school districts are strapped for money. Thus we find arguments over what tests should be used; what the cutoff point for those defined as requiring bilingual education should be; and whether, if these children do poorly in English, they may not be doing just as poorly in a foreign language. The arguments leave moot the question of which language of instruction should be used.

UNCERTAINTIES IN THE PRESENT SITUATION

Equally difficult to define with any clarity in regulation or court decision is what kind of program must be provided to these children. Indeed, one of my greatest difficulties in coming to any overall decision on these developments is caused by the fact that it is unclear what goes on in such education—what is taught, to how many children, in how many classrooms, by teachers of what background and what training, for how many years—and I do not know whether anyone has such figures and descriptions. But there is no question that any child who has a problem with facility in English owing to foreign-language background has a legal right to something, and that that "something" involves some degree of teaching in the language the child has been raised speaking. There is also a strong bias among those administering these requirements in favor of more than that. Responsive as they are to interest groups pressing for a broader measure of bilingual and bicultural education, they are sympathetic to teaching the ethnic heritage and background in addition to simple instrumental use of the foreign language for a brief period to facilitate educational achievement.

It would be interesting to get some sense of the extent of bilingual/bicultural education now in place. It would be even more interesting—though no simple census or survey can tell us this—to get some sense of what actually goes on in these classrooms. One thing we lack is good ethnographic descriptions of bilingual/ bicultural classrooms. Undoubtedly they range from classes of solid academic content, conducted in a foreign language by well-trained and competent teachers, to—as one anecdotal account puts it—a contemporary history class that was supposed to be conducted in Spanish, in which neither the teacher nor the students knew the Spanish for key terms they were discussing.

Arguments for Bilingual Education

We have, then, institutionalized, through law and practice, bilingual/bicultural education; to what extent and with what effectiveness is unknown. There are several reasons for this institutionalization. One is the desire to improve the educational achievement of children of foreign language background. A second, the hope of maintaining the cultures and languages of immigrant groups, is not formally the objective of either legislation or judicial decrees, but it *is* the objective of those who push for legislation and institute court cases. These two objectives are clearly discernible. A third is somewhat less clear. It is to enhance respect for immigrant cultures among the children who bear them and others, which it is hoped will both contribute to better educational achievement by immigrant children—by way of the greater self-respect induced in the child—and help maintain the culture.

That is the present situation. One hears a good deal of grumbling by congressmen and columnists and writers on occasion, but bilingual/bicultural education seems to be well established, and it is hard to see any development that will reduce its present scale, and more likely it will be expanded.

EDUCATIONAL ACHIEVEMENT ARGUMENT

What reason do we have to be skeptical about these programs? First, bilingual/bicultural education does not do anything for, and is not likely to do anything for, one of the problems it was meant to deal with and the one of greatest concern to Congress, namely, poor educational achievement. Admittedly this argument—does it work?—is always trotted out to show that some innovation, whether it is Headstart, or progressive education, or increased drill, is not the answer to problems of low educational achievement; and bilingual/bicultural education is no exception. It is also true that research findings never seem to affect the fate of such programs much, and in view of how complicated it is to show the positive effect of any one variable on educational achievement, maybe they should not.

But there are more serious reasons for doubting the effects of bilingual/bicultural education on educational achievement. These are historical reasons. It was not necessary to spur the on-the-average higher academic achievement of Jews, Japanese, and other high-achieving immigrant groups, nor was facility in English relevant to explaining the more modest educational achievements of

an English-speaking immigrant group, the Irish. In short, historically, bilingual/bicultural education does not seem to have mattered, one way or another. Its absence did not seem to affect
differential achievement. And that suggests its presence will not
either.

It is not only history that leads us to doubt the significance of
bilingual/bicultural education for educational achievement; it is
contemporary experience (not research). Last year the *New York
Times* reported that Houston faced the loss of two million dollars in
federal funds because it could not find fifteen teachers who spoke
Vietnamese, and whom the Office of Civil Rights insisted it had to
employ to teach the 417 Vietnamese pupils in the Houston
schools.[2] Does anyone who knows anything about these matters
believe for a minute that Vietnamese bilingual/bicultural education
in the public schools will matter for the educational achievement of
Vietnamese children? Other reports indicate that they already sur-
pass native American children in mathematics. There are good
grounds for believing their class background and the excellent
education in some respects—especially in mathematics—of the
schools they attended in Vietnam to be the decisive elements in
affecting their educational progress.

Or consider a newspaper account of a class of children of foreign-
language background in New York City:

> "But soft! What light through yonder window breaks? It is the
> East, and Juliet is the sun!"
>
> With that familiar Shakespearean pronouncement, Wook Nae
> Kim, nine years old, bounded to the center of the fourth-grade
> classroom and spread his arms dramatically.
>
> "O Romeo, Romeo! Wherefore art thou, Romeo?" responded
> Catalina Martin, a native of Ecuador. "Deny thy father and refuse
> thy name!" At the end of the exchange, the class applauded.
>
> When Wook Nae came here from Korea last September, he did not
> speak English. Neither did most of the children in Andrea Gilmore's
> "NES" (non-English-speaking) class in Public School 89.
>
> Standing up in turn, each child introduced himself to a visitor and
> noted his country of origin. There were thirteen children from
> Korea, four from Taiwan, three from the Philippines and Hong
> Kong, and one each from Colombia, Haiti, Vietnam, Ecuador,
> Bangladesh, Honduras, India, Guyana, and the Dominican Repub-
> lic.

And where was Miss Gilmore from? "California!" the children shouted in unison.

"The plane lands every day on the roof," Cleonice LoSecco, principal of the elementary school, said, tongue in cheek. Enrollment increased to 1,600 from 1,353 in 1975, which forced the sending of kindergarten and sixth-grade pupils to other schools. . . .

The elementary pupils are divided into fifty-one classes, including fourteen bilingual Spanish classes and a bilingual Korean class of first- and second-graders, the first such class in the city. In addition, there are two so-called "TESL" classes (teaching English as a second language).

Although she taught Spanish-speaking youngsters in another school last year, Miss Gilmore had no formal training in dealing with a plethora of languages.

"I'm required to teach the usual fourth-grade curriculum," she said, "the Monroe Doctrine, the amendments to the Constitution, even though they don't know English."

As a result, she has relied on inventiveness and imagination to prod her shy students into grappling with English. One day she took them to see the Zeffirelli movie of "Romeo and Juliet." After that, nearly everybody wanted to try the speeches in class.

For Ferdoushi Haguelo of Bangladesh, growing bean sprouts in paper cups broke the language barrier. She had not said a word for weeks until Miss Gilmore put moistened towels and the seeds into a cup. "You're doing it wrong!" said Ferdoushi. Miss Gilmore was thrilled.[3]

How important is a formal program of bilingual/bicultural education, whether mandated by a court or the Office of Civil Rights, to the educational achievement of these children? Of course, not all children will be blessed with a Miss Gilmore. But is the element of bilingual/bicultural education, in itself, crucial for the educational process for these children?

Am I being cavalier in dismissing the significance of bilingual/bicultural education to educational achievement on the basis of these crude references to history and to current experience? Perhaps. Certainly the experience of having to attend school in a foreign language with unsympathetic and prejudiced teachers is bad for children. But I would think it is the lack of sympathy and the prejudice that are the problem, in which case mandating bilingual/bicultural education may not be the answer. In any case, it will take a very long time to find the conditions under which bilingual/bicultural education contributes to educational achievement.

MAINTENANCE OF CULTURE ARGUMENT

Even if the educational achievement argument will not hold, what about the respect argument? Was it not a bad thing that immigrant children were Americanized, forced to give up their parental culture, told to forget ancestral languages in favor of English? Did it not make them less than full persons, did it not make them people with a void, ignorant of their true roots, of who they were? We have heard much of this argument in recent years, from Michael Novak and others.

First, let us recall that there was and is a mechanism for maintaining outside the public schools a consciousness of people and culture. The largest private school system in America was established by the Roman Catholic church, to protect children from the Protestant (or non-religious) influences of the public school but also to transmit ethnic culture. It did this best for the Irish (of course, as in any culture, there are many traditions that can be labelled "Irish," and the parochial schools selected only some of these), but there were also parochial schools for children from French-speaking families, from Polish-speaking families, and for other ethnic groups. There was a problem in that the Irish-dominated church was often unsympathetic to the desires of non-Irish Catholics for an ethnic component in their parochial school education, but the opportunity, nevertheless, existed for parents to maintain knowledge and consciousness of people and culture outside the public school system. In addition to the parochial schools, Roman Catholic and other, there were afternoon schools maintained by many groups, and Sunday Schools.

The Urge to Americanize

A second caution in accepting this argument that public schools imposed the English language and American culture on children whose parents wanted the maintenance of language and culture is that most American parents liked what the public schools were offering. Most had come to this country not to maintain a foreign language and culture but with the intention, in the days when the trip to the United States was long and expensive, to become Americanized as fast as possible, and this meant English language and American culture. They sought the induction to a new language and culture that the public schools provided—as do many present-day immigrants, too—and while they often found, as time went on, that they regretted what they and their children had lost, this was *their* choice, rather than an imposed choice. And every choice involves regret for the path not taken.

Third, the fact was that, whatever immigrant hopes and intentions, the American environment turned out enormously attractive to their children (and often to them). American culture assimilates because it sets its face against the maintenance of foreign language and culture and makes this difficult, and it assimilates because it is itself a new culture, adapted to new immigrants, which makes their transported culture seem less attractive. After all, American culture, or at least certain aspects of it, is very attractive even to youth who do not live in America and do not intend to. How can one fight rock and jeans, or their equivalents in earlier decades?

Pragmatic Advantages of Assimilation

Finally, there were the simple pragmatic advantages to accepting education in English, and in American culture. The public schools had the money and prestige, and they controlled access to whatever-it-is further higher education could give; one did not get very far by being a whiz in Chinese or Hebrew afternoon school, and these schools suffered from being cut off from the larger culture.

But does one fool children about all this by bringing bilingual/bicultural education into the schools? Do children thereby gain an appreciation of their past culture as being equal in importance and significance in affecting their fate to the culture of an English-speaking America? I doubt it. The school is only one thing. Outside, television is still in English, as are movies and major league sports and big-time politics. English is what the President speaks, and the congressman, even if he has a Spanish name. There has been, in other words, an inevitability, once the process of *permanent* migration has taken place, to the relative lesser importance, in reality, of ancestral language and culture, and nothing much can change that. One will never do as well in the United States living in Spanish, or French, or Yiddish, or Chinese, as one will do living, learning, and working in English.

And if bringing the languages and cultures into the public schools will not do much for their relative status and importance, it will not do much to change other people's minds as to their relative status or importance. I think it is therefore a naïve argument to say that putting bilingual/bicultural education into the public school curriculum will make a significant difference in affecting the general respect in which a given culture and language are held.

Neither the educational achievement argument nor the maintenance of culture argument is persuasive to me. It is not clear what, if anything, bilingual/bicultural education will do for educational achievement; and it is hardly likely we will ever find out, in view of how various will be the kinds of bilingual/bicultural education provided, and how complex its interaction with other factors. Nor is it clear that there is either a strong demand for the public schools to help maintain immigrant and non-English languages and cultures (some are not immigrant, of course, as in the case of the American Indians and many of the Spanish-speaking), or that bilingual/bicultural education will help meet this demand in the face of the assimilating power of American culture and the advantages it offers.

CREATING JOBS FOR ETHNIC TEACHERS

There are other arguments for bilingual/bicultural education, of course. For example, bilingual/bicultural education is one way to bring into the teaching force persons of a given culture and background who are poorly represented within it and who are important to relate to children of that language and culture. This seems a better argument than the two I have given, but even this is not completely convincing. After all, we have seen huge transitions in the ethnic composition of the teaching force without bilingual/bicultural education. In New York City, Protestant teachers were replaced by Catholics, and Catholics by Jews, and Jews are now being replaced by Blacks and Puerto Ricans. The relative rates of change raise some questions. Also it is true that transitions in the past have generally occurred *after* the composition of the students

had changed, and there was no necessary close statistical corre-
spondence between the ethnic composition of the student body
and the teachers. But need there be? Nevertheless, it is worth
pointing out that whatever the general soundness of this argument, the push for jobs for persons from given groups is probably
the strongest force leading to more bilingual/bicultural education;
and the resistance to giving these jobs to members of these groups
is probably one of the strongest forces in opposition to bilingual/
bicultural education.

Why Not Bilingual Education?

But it is not the weakness of the educational achievement argument or of the respect argument that has been most significant in
opposition to bilingual/bicultural education. It is revealing that the
most forceful arguments have been made not by persons who
themselves come from the white Anglo-Saxon Protestant group,
the old majority. The most forceful critics, I would hazard, have
been Jews. Stephen Rosenfeld of the *Washington Post* was perhaps
the first to raise the question in a major national forum of why
public funds should support bilingual/bicultural education. Noel
Epstein has written an effective monograph that is rather skeptical
about bilingual/bicultural education as it has developed.[4] And I
have been a critic.

UNITY-DIVISIVENESS ARGUMENT

The argument that appeals to these and other critics and carries
the most weight in raising skepticism about bilingual/bicultural
education is not the educational achievement argument or the
cultural respect argument. The critics, after all, want to see higher
educational achievement, and they are people who argue for respect. The argument they advance is that of unity-divisiveness,
which says that bilingual/bicultural education prevents the development of a common culture, a common loyalty, a common allegiance. The critics seem to be saying that it was a good thing that
people of many stocks were molded here into one nation speaking
one language, that it would have been a worse country had this not
happened, and therefore it could be a worse country because it
now is happening less.

I have asked myself why I believe this, and I can give some pragmatic reasons, starting with the assumption that, had our people been less assimilated and Americanized we might have been more badly divided than we were in two world wars. In answer, one can say that the maintenance of language facility and cultural loyalties does not necessarily undermine an overarching loyalty to the federal republic. Patriotism in Switzerland does not seem to be lessened by its four official languages. Furthermore, it is hardly likely that we will want, for a long time to come and, it is hoped, ever, to test the loyalty of our new immigrant groups in hostilities with their countries of origin.

CONFLICTING VALUES AND ALTERNATE LOYALTIES

It would seem the pragmatic arguments for a common language and culture and an educational system that imposes them do not stand up very well. One cannot avoid issues of value, which are hard to justify pragmatically. Those of us from the immigration that was Americanized in language and culture think it was a good thing, and we simply prefer that kind of country. And with our skepticism we are telling the newer elements, principally Spanish in language, that we think our path—the path of the immigration that ended in the 1920s—is better than that of the current immigration, even as we recognize that the newer immigrants (their leaders, at least) are pressing for bilingualism clearly not for pragmatic reasons, either, but for reasons of the values they hold.

How does one solve such a conflict? The degree to which it is a conflict is revealed in a recent 5-4 Supreme Court decision on whether public school teachers have to be citizens.[5] Any 5-4 decision reveals a deep value conflict; it could have been 5-4 the other way. Here are pragmatism and emotional, irrational value commitments lined up on one side, represented by the teachers who will not give up foreign citizenship but who are clearly good teachers; and here is another set of values (also emotional, irrational, if you will) on the other side, claiming that teachers induct into citizenship, and that students have to be educated to values as well as to skills.

I realize this is a different situation from one in which bilingual/bicultural education is required, where the issue is language in the public schools, not citizenship. And yet at bottom the issue is the same. The demand for bilingual/bicultural education is not purely linguistic or pragmatic. It is not only for educational achievement and jobs. It is also a demand made out of an alternate loyalty, loyalty to a culture and language that must inevitably be linked to foreign countries.

I have suggested that my views, having been so sharply challenged by my students, are somewhat more uncertain than they were, and I will suggest some reasons now why my own opposition to this development has been moderated.

NEW IMMIGRANTS AND NON-IMMIGRANTS

The groups for whom bilingual/bicultural education is being instituted, and who are most active in demanding it, are different from the old immigrants from Europe in a number of important respects. First, many among these groups are not immigrants— they are American Indians, Puerto Ricans, and Mexican-Americans resident for many generations in this country. Without untangling all aspects of their complex political status, we know them to have full rights as American citizens; the presumption, still part of American naturalization law, that naturalized citizens should know English, does not apply to them. Indeed, we have decreed by law that for all those of Spanish origin, for American Indians, and for Chinese and Japanese, inability in English should be no bar to full participation in the American political system. The Voting Rights Act now requires that those who speak these languages and are unable to exercise their voting rights in English must be given assistance, written and oral, in their native languages. Thus their status is already rather different from that of the European immigrant, who could not become a citizen if he did not know English, and who had no right to assistance in his language in exercising his political rights, even though this might have been given as a matter of convenience rather than of law.

"Undocumented Aliens"

A second respect in which these groups who are the main claimants for bilingual/bicultural education differ from the older immigrants is that many have only an uncertain and fleeting attachment to this country. These are the "undocumented aliens," who may or may not have decided they want to stay here permanently. It may be understandable that for them the Americanizing experience of the public school is something they might find repugnant or to which they would be indifferent. A useful comparison here is with the foreign guestworkers of Germany, whose children must be educated; it is a fair question, in view of their legal status as only temporary German residents, whether it would not be wiser to educate them in Turkish or Serbo-Croatian or Greek than in German, since most of them are expected to return to their home countries. (Fewer and fewer informed Germans, it should be noted, now expect this.)

Decline in Patriotism

Further, in the country at large, we see a substantial difference from the United States of the old immigration: It is less unambiguously patriotic or chauvinistic. There is, first, an embarrassment (at least among intellectuals) over how American power has been exercised in the world, and a strong sense that we are not better than most other countries. Why then should we impose some view of the virtues of American loyalty on new immigrants, when old settlers only partially accept it and are themselves doubtful of whether this loyalty is a good thing?

We seem in our culture today to be in a situation in which no single course receives unambiguous and universal acceptance, and thus it is hardly likely that we will roll back bilingual/bicultural education so as to reinstate a single-minded loyalty to American culture, society, and polity, with universal emphasis on learning English. And I would be the last, despite my criticism of the arguments for bilingual/bicultural education, to urge such a rollback, because I see the reasons why we have changed, and I see that it is unrealistic to expect new immigrants to be like old (though many are), or persons of non-English language and non-American culture who are not immigrants to behave like immigrants. I see, too, that the country is different now and Americans no longer want to place a single-minded energy into the creation of a common people and common culture.

Alternatives for Change

But given this situation, it is still possible to urge a looser and more tentative approach to development of bilingual/bicultural education policies. Unfortunately, this is not easy, because we have developed these policies not pragmatically, not even in the give-and-take of political debate, but through court order and agency regulation, and they are thus given a rigidity and a presumed sacrosanct base in Constitutional right that does not favor tentative and experimental steps. This does make for problems, because it treats all alike although they are not. To require the same for all is properly bureaucratic. But I wonder who raised the question of the need for Vietnamese-speaking teachers in order to fulfill Office of Civil Rights regulations in Houston. I doubt that it was the Vietnamese themselves, because, it is my impression, they are very much like the old immigrants, want to learn English fast, and prefer to maintain their religion and culture and language outside school, through the family, their churches, or their voluntary organizations. I would guess many other substantial streams of immigrants are of the same mind, over all. Do Koreans want a public school commitment to bilingual/bicultural education? Do Indians and Pakistanis? Do many of the immigrants from Latin America, leaving aside Mexican-Americans? We do suffer from the fact that these policies are being developed and imposed by national bureaucracies, applying their own rules, and by federal courts, and that important distinctions between groups and what they think is best for them will be ignored.

VOLUNTARY PARTICIPATION

A second point: One way of taking into account the differences between groups and within groups is to make these programs, in greater measure than they are, voluntary. In the case of the New York City consent judgment, there was an unsettling dispute in which the plaintiff lawyers for Aspira wanted to *require* students deemed after testing to need bilingual education to take it, even in the face of the opposition of their parents. Fortunately Judge Marvin Frankel rejected this demand. A true voluntarism will permit each child or its parents to select what they think is best.

OUT-OF-SCHOOL PROGRAMS

Finally we should consider to what extent we want these programs in the public schools, as against providing assistance to parents and ethnic groups to develop programs outside the public schools. The reason I suggest that we explore this is that *within* each group we will find considerable differences as to what they want to teach in the way of culture, and this undoubtedly affects what they want to teach in the way of language. Most of these programs are, or are supposed to be, transitional, but the tendency is for children to stay in them for a number of years and to take subject matter courses in those languages. Thus there is an issue as to what kind of emphases the public schools will present in their bilingual/bicultural education. Will they teach that we robbed Mexico of its territories—in which case there will be conflict with patriotic school boards? Will they teach that Puerto Rico should be independent—in which case there will be conflict with those Puerto Ricans who want Puerto Rico to become a state or maintain its commonwealth status? Some groups are strongly divided over their history, over the role of the church, over the role of the socialist or communist movements.

Consider, as an example, if the public schools had had to teach Jewish immigrants something of their language and culture. There would have been disputes over whether they should teach Hebrew or Yiddish (or Ladino), Zionism or anti-Zionism, Orthodoxy or Reform, as the "true" language, culture, and religion of the Jewish people. In any event, of course, hardly anything was done in the public schools. When Jewish children formed one-third of the children in the New York City public schools there was no reference to Jewish history in the textbooks, no reference to Jewish religion, hardly any reference to any Jew. It was only in the 1930s that some modest opportunity to study Hebrew as a language in the high schools was offered, and that, I am sure, was in part because Hebrew is one of the classical languages that, in early colonial days, had been required or taught in our rudimentary colleges.

I do not argue that what happened in the past was for the best. I only draw from it the example that groups of non-English language and culture may be so divided that the public schools would have to provide a bland pap acceptable to all and satisfying to none. Under these circumstances, might we not experiment with providing vouchers so that parents can find the kind of bilingual/ bicultural education they prefer?

Whatever course we develop, I would urge the virtues of tentativeness and experimentation, and what they lead to is voluntarism in the choice of programs, the provision of a variety of programs, and consideration of whether we should not encourage efforts to provide the programs outside the rather rigid frame of the public schools.

NOTES

1. Nathan Glazer, "Public Education and American Pluralism," James S. Coleman, ed., *Parents, Teachers, and Children: Prospects for Choice in American Education* (San Francisco, 1977), 85-109; *Bilingual-Bicultural Education: A Handbook for Attorneys and Community Workers* (Cambridge, Mass., 1977).

2. "Sweet Houston Sound: Vietnamese Language," *New York Times*, March 4, 1979.

3. "Elmhurst Flourishes as Melting Pot," *New York Times*, April 4, 1979.

4. Noel Epstein, *Language, Ethnicity, and the Schools: Policy Alternatives for Bilingual-Bicultural Education* (Washington, D.C., 1977).

5. "High Court Upholds Denial of Teaching Posts to Aliens," *New York Times*, April 18, 1979.

Nathan Glazer is *professor of education and social structure in the Graduate School of Education at Harvard University. Co-editor of* The Public Interest *since 1973, he is known for his studies and publications in the fields of urban policy and social concerns, including in particular, ethnicity. He is a former Guggenheim Fellow, a member of the American Academy of Arts and Sciences and the National Academy of Education, and a recent visiting scholar with the Russell Sage Foundation.*

The Bilingual Experience in Canada

Maxwell F. Yalden

Because it is always a good idea to begin by getting one's facts straight, I would like to set out, as concisely as I can, a picture of language relations in Canada, past and present, both from the perspective of the demography involved, and of the approaches of various governments to what they have perceived to be a suitable linguistic balance. Having done that, I will try to present my own views of what are the permissible inferences from Canadian strategies to the American situation as I understand it.

In considering the Canadian situation, I would also ask that one basic observation be kept in mind. Because language is, in some ways, the most deep-rooted and all-pervasive element in our individual and collective identities, any policy of change should make sure of its purpose and direction to the greatest extent possible, as the basis for a sound action program, some of whose results are bound in any case to be less than predictable. In other words, one should have the clearest possible idea what one is about and prepare one's ground accordingly. If nothing else, even if we have not always been able to follow this maxim, Canada has the advantage over its neighbor of long years of trial and error in trying to reach this clarity of mind and purpose.

History of Canada's Linguistic Situation

European languages have coexisted in North America, of course, for several centuries. French was the first to establish itself across the vast territory that stretches from the Atlantic to the prairies, rather as Spanish took possession of large areas to the south. In what was to become Canada, the advances accomplished by French *voyageurs* were in time duplicated by those of English traders. The beginnings of language contact in Canada, and the linguistic disputes which they inevitably engendered, go back to the days of Louis XIV and beyond.

After the French territories were ceded to the English under terms of the Treaty of Paris (1763), the English-speaking majority gradually spread out over much of the country while, with exceptions, the most significant French-speaking enclave came to be concentrated along the banks of the St. Lawrence, forming the nucleus of an eventual province of Quebec.

From its earliest beginnings, Canada's rulers had given equal recognition to English and French. The Royal Proclamation of 1763 granted French official status, and when the Constitutional Act of 1791 divided the then Canadian territories into Upper Canada and Lower Canada, both languages were granted equal status in the legislative assembly of Lower Canada.

At this point one may ask, what possessed the British conqueror that he did not, in Lord Durham's phrase, "subordinate the French"? By 1838 the result of not doing so was, in the same gentleman's eyes, the spectacle of "two nations warring in the bosom of a single state." However, if the original motivation of the British was a mixture of idealism and expediency, by 1838, when Lord Durham proposed the systematic assimilation of French-Canadians to the English language and British ideology, it is more than doubtful that such a policy could have succeeded even if it had been accepted and vigorously pursued.

Since that time, the cousin languages, English and French, have continued to swing between mutual animosity and mutual tolerance for 150 years. And notwithstanding Lord Durham, our governments have usually made a virtue of necessity by confirming what to many non-Canadians appears to be an incongruous arrangement.

CONSTITUTIONAL ROOTS

The Act of Union of 1840, which reunited the two territories in the Province of Canada, officially sanctioned the use of French in the legislative assembly. This policy was maintained by the British North America Act of 1867 creating the Canadian federation. That act, together with subsequent amendments, has of course come down to us to this day as the Canadian constitution. It is, therefore, particularly worth noting that it recognized:

- both English and French as legislative and judicial languages in federal and Quebec institutions;
- the right to denominational schooling (which was closely associated with the French-English distinction); and
- the official character of both languages in the various Canadian territories, some of them shortly to be brought into confederation.

At this crucial point in Canadian history, the demographic distribution of French-speaking and English-speaking Canadians was considerably different from what it is now. Although exact census data do not exist, it is clear that the use of French in that large area of western Canada known as Rupert's Land had remained widespread and enjoyed various degrees of official recognition.

When Manitoba was created by the Manitoba Act of 1870, both the French-speaking populations and the tradition of official bilingualism were strong enough to warrant exactly the same form of recognition of English and French as had been granted in Quebec by the British North America Act. Meanwhile, in Ontario and Acadia, both of which also had substantial French-speaking populations, French had no official status.

We sometimes forget, in this connection, that our forefathers— particularly in view of the immensity of the lands they occupied—were quite capable of tolerating and even promoting forms of individual liberty which our own overcrowded age has tended to iron out. As Heinz Kloss reminds us in *The American Bilingual Tradition*, the United States too has always entertained mixed feelings about the need for linguistic uniformity: in some respects the melting pot is a relatively recent utensil.

At any rate, it is true that the Canadian federation was founded with a strong presumption that not only was linguistic coexistence possible but that it offered a juxtaposition of cultures that was of mutual benefit. Our governments believed, and for the most part continue to believe, that where there is an overriding commonality of purpose and considerable decentralization of authority, official bilingualism is both manageable and affordable. It is a presumption that has seldom gone unchallenged, but which certainly reflects the higher pragmatism in being at once realistic and just. It stands firmly in the North American tradition of respecting local liberties as much as possible.

It is, however, a tradition often honored rather more in word than in deed. For instance, in the years leading up to and immediately following the founding of the Canadian federation, respect for religious and linguistic dissent took some particularly hard knocks in the eastern part of the country. The French-speaking Acadians of Nova Scotia lost their right to have separate Catholic schools even before confederation, in 1864. In 1871 the Catholic schools of New Brunswick were shut down and teaching of and in French was forbidden. The same fate befell the Catholic, French schools of Prince Edward Island six years later, in 1877. Here again are signs of the institutional Jekyll-and-Hydeism that has dogged Canadian linguistic history: measures of enlightenment and tolerance coexisting in the same frame with acts of deliberate repression.

NEW IMMIGRATION, NEW ATTITUDES

Starting in the last decade of the nineteenth century, Canada entered a new phase of development. Its huge underpopulated areas were progressively settled both from the East by descendants of the original settlers and by immigrants from many other countries. In the process, as the federal state grew, the original rationale for language rights became obscured.

Already in the 1890s, the legal existence of French in Manitoba and the Northwest Territories had been put in question by the repeal of section 23 of the Manitoba Act (an action which only a few months ago, after ninety years on the statute books, was judged unconstitutional), and by amendment of the Northwest Territories Act to the same general effect, an action which was to undercut the status of French in the Yukon and the eventual provinces of Saskatchewan and Alberta.

By the First World War, the status and use of French outside Quebec had suffered other severe setbacks. Perhaps more important, many recently arrived Canadians had small sense of the spread and standing that language had once enjoyed. After 1914 the cry of "one language, one school, one flag" was to be further exacerbated by resistance in Quebec to military conscription. At least two more acts of linguistic repression characterize this general period: Ontario's Regulation 17 (1913), which effectively put a stop to publicly supported French-language instruction in that province (which has the largest population of Francophones outside Quebec) until the 1960s; and Manitoba's decision of 1915 to ban further "bilingual" teaching in that province, an example that was to be followed in practice by the other western provinces.

But if the first half of the twentieth century in Canada was marked by an aggressive and uncomprehending reaction outside Quebec to the dogged persistence of the French fact, the second half has begun to reverse that trend, to the point where Canada is now within hailing distance of a new linguistic deal.

Since the Second World War, more and more measures have been adopted to protect and enhance the French heritage in Canada. Once again, it would be misleading to suggest that this trend has flowed from a universal change of heart. On the contrary, there is a running dispute between those who regard French in Canada as alien, unsettling, and unnecessary, and those who not only believe that French should not be banished from the scene but also know full well why it cannot be.

Contemporary Canada: Individual and Institutional Bilingualism

Perhaps the social and institutional realities of Canadian bilingualism today can best be described by dealing with them in the following order: 1) the contemporary rationale for a bilingual and multi-cultural society in Canada; 2) the current demographic trends and reactions to them; and 3) government actions to clarify and consolidate institutional guarantees and services to our official-languages communities.

THE CONTEMPORARY RATIONALE

The problem before us is, in some sense, a universal one. In the words of our Royal Commission on Bilingualism and Biculturalism, "The universality of bilingualism stems from three factors: there are more languages than nations; some languages are more widespread than others; and populations are increasingly mobile." Specifically, we have to determine to what extent it is possible, fruitful, or expedient to make legal and practical accommodations whereby linguistically distinct groups can nevertheless pursue common goals.

Both our countries have been committed from their creation to recognizing the normal diversities of human nature and maximizing individual liberties. In spite of differences of structure, we share the ideology of pluralism. One might suggest, then, that the question before us today is, philosophically speaking, whether linguistic diversities are somehow different from other diversities which we find not merely tolerable but stimulating.

In the Canadian case, there is a long tradition of sometimes rational, all too often demagogic, debate on this theme. One strand of this debate climaxed in the early and mid-sixties with the work of the Royal Commission. At the risk of oversimplifying the findings of an inquiry which extended over several years, let me summarize some central conclusions:

- both history and demography having already consecrated the use of English and French as national languages, the state should ratify and support that use;
- the equal status of English and French should, as far as possible, be based on individual choice rather than strict territoriality; and
- there is room within an officially bilingual state for other forms of linguistic and cultural pluralism so that bilingualism

and multiculturalism can only complement and reinforce each other.

However successful this rationale for institutional bilingualism may turn out to be, it has one important corollary which immediately distinguishes it from the language philosophy of the United States. Where Canada tends to cultivate, if not exactly cherish, linguistic diversity, the American trend has generally favored linguistic assimilation to the English-speaking mainstream. Our problem is to give our official-language minorities the space they need to be themselves; yours is—or at least appears to have been in the past—to enable the minorities to integrate more effectively.

DEMOGRAPHIC TRENDS AND POPULAR REACTIONS

While the linguistic demography of contemporary Canada is complex, it is dominated by the phenomenon of polarization. This "growing tendency," as a recent Task Force on Canadian Unity describes it, "toward the geographical concentration of Canada's French- and English-speaking populations," clearly raises questions about the effectiveness of institutional bilingualism.

Both the vitality and mobility of different language groups, of course, are closely bound up with the phenomena of modernization, urbanization, and secularization. Social and economic conditions have as much to do with the status and viability of languages as do the laws of the land. Thus there is an obvious relationship between the growth of Quebec nationalism, which has led up to proposals for "sovereignty-association," and the perceived rapport between the French and English languages in Canada as a whole.

The belief that the respective status and use of the two major languages in Quebec were potentially dangerous to the majority French culture led in the 1970s to a series of language laws culminating in 1977 in the Charter of the French Language or what is often called simply Bill 101. Aimed at reinforcing the French character of the province, this legislation has had inevitable repercussions for the English-speaking community in Quebec. While it would be misleading to represent that community as a downtrodden minority barely staving off assimilation, they have experienced in one short decade a number of the setbacks to their linguistic freedoms which befell the French communities outside Quebec over a period of a century and a half.

In these circumstances, while one could not hope to explain all the interactions now at work to determine Canada's linguistic future, I must try to propound a particular view of what is possible, given the present language balance in Canada. As I see it, it is feasible to retain our bilingual character, provided certain conditions can be met, namely that 1) reciprocal guarantees for English-speaking and French-speaking Canadians can be written into our Constitution and at the same time given increased practical expression; 2) individuals and families can move from province to province in Canada without entirely foregoing their most fundamental language rights or being unduly pressured to conform; and 3) we can convince enough people that the chauvinism that rejects any language but its own is a drag upon our aspirations and potential as a people.

For the time being, Canadians are living through a period when both the believers and the non-believers in bilingualism are leaning toward radical solutions. But a number of positive signs indicate that governments are waking up to the value and significance of their minorities and taking more seriously their obligations toward them. We are still some considerable way from stemming the flow toward extreme and institutionalized territoriality, but there is no reason to think that it cannot be done—or that Canadians lack the means or will to do it.

GOVERNMENT ACTIONS

The work of the Royal Commission on Bilingualism and Biculturalism culminated in the federal Official Languages Act. Passed unanimously by Parliament, it launched the first decade of a lengthy process of language reform. Still anything but complete, this reform seems to comprise at least three major dimensions: the formulation of *language rights;* the development of *institutional resources* to make them work; and the *explanation* of what is going on and why it is important.

Language rights can be said to include the right to communicate with and enjoy the services of federal institutions in either English or French; the right to be heard in either language in criminal proceedings; the right to educate one's children in French or English; and more sporadically, the opportunity to obtain social services from provincial or municipal governments in either language. Those rights represent a degree of choice for Canadians as regards the way they orient and conduct their personal lives. They also offer the linguistic minorities the right *not* to assimilate, the right to maintain a certain difference.

The clear expression of language rights has two great advantages: it lets people know where they stand and it sets administrative goals toward which we can work. For the last ten years of language reform in Canada, the most clearly expressed right, and the forerunner of the rest, has been the right to federal services in English and French. From an American perspective that may sound like a tall order—and in some ways it is. But among all the administrative difficulties and attitudinal hang-ups involved, one is conscious also of an incalculable and underexploited resource at our disposal, namely that we already have two great languages and two large language groups to work with.

But minorities cannot live by bilingual income-tax forms and postal services alone. Education is the keystone to self-fulfillment as a member of a linguistic minority—and, in Canada, education is a provincial prerogative. The effectiveness of language education in Canada and its implications for the United States will be discussed later, but one should note here that both English-speaking and French-speaking Canadians are just beginning to understand how crucial this right is, not just for the continuity of one's culture, but as a token of mutual respect between language groups.

In Canada, the role of the national government has been to set an example by putting its own house in order, and also, no less vitally, to induce other governments and institutions to act upon aims and premises that they do not necessarily share. Which brings me once again to the importance of education, in the broadest possible sense of that word.

Nothing is less abstract or theoretical than language relations between people; to describe them is one thing but to alter them is something else again. One lesson that Canada has been learning in the last ten years or so is that, if you lay out enough money, you can eventually bring about significant institutional changes. But, if you can also affect for the better the attitudes of those responsible for the changes, and the opinions of those who have to live with them, you can achieve a great deal more at less expense.

Inferences from the Canadian Experience to the Situation in the United States

Enough has probably already been said about differences in our respective philosophies, histories, and human geographies to indicate my wariness about pushing the Canadian experience or conclusions about it too far onto the American stage. It would be better to get down to cases. The most obviously practical and relevant question is that of language education.

And indeed the schools involved precisely that sector of bilingualism in which, in my experience, Americans are most inclined to look to Canada for enlightenment. This is yet another reason to get clear in our minds the very different backgrounds, goals, and methodological assumptions that apply in each country. The rationale for bilingual education in the United States is clearly rooted in the civil rights principle that citizens should not be socially or politically handicapped by the degree of their ability to acquire the dominant national language. In Canada, let me remind you, there is a commitment to provide minority-language citizens with the choice and opportunity *not* to assimilate completely and irrevocably to the majority mainstream.

To understand how language education actually works in Canada, you must also understand how the relations between English and French vary according to their particular social context. French, for instance, is the majority language (80 percent) in Quebec, but it is the language of only 26 percent of all Canadians, and is dwarfed into near insignificance at 2 percent of a North American population whose wide-ranging English media are almost inescapable. Outside Quebec, French-speakers constitute a majority of the local population only in relatively small pockets, almost all of them in Ontario and New Brunswick.

Language Education in Canada

Against that background, you may better understand why, in Canada, we can recognize at least four basic patterns of language education:

- English schools for Anglophone children in which French may be offered as a second language course in a non-intensive way;
- French schools for Francophones, particularly though not exclusively in Quebec, where courses in English as a second language are similarly available for a few hours a week;
- so-called mixed schools where children of the official-language minority (usually French-speaking) receive some but not all course offerings in their own language, either separately or together with majority-language children; and
- an increasing number of "immersion" classes and schools in which Anglophone children across the country, especially in the early years of schooling, receive more than 50 percent of their education in French.

Our underlying goal is more and more seen to be the fullest possible parity of educational opportunity for both major linguistic groups. Already, from the standpoint of the Francophone minorities outside Quebec, this is a major theoretical and practical advance, as compared with an era when they were barely allowed to cling to their language and, even then, at considerable social and psychological cost. Most interesting in this regard is the variety of reaction that this renewal of minority French education gives rise to in the English-speaking population. Some see it as singling out one language minority to the detriment of others; some choose to endorse and use the additional language as an enriching extension of their own identity.

These variations in English-speaking reactions, like the variations in schooling patterns which to some extent reflect them, are, I believe, of particular interest and concern to Americans today. What people want to know is, in Canadian experience, how does full-fledged "Big B" bilingualism actually affect the society and the people most directly involved.

I have already said that a Canada that wishes to remain true to itself and united for the future has never really had any choice about formally recognizing its linguistic duality. All that one can reasonably speculate about, in my opinion, is the probable consequences of different forms of recognition. In effect, this same question is built into the bilingualism issue in America: what are the repercussions of granting to one or more minority languages some degree of recognition—and to what extent do you really have a choice about granting such recognition?

QUEBEC AND SEPARATISM

Let me try to make my point by beginning with the second part of that question. I am frequently asked in the United States whether the present political polarization of Quebec and the rest of Canada is not a consequence of our policy of bilingualism; has not increased recognition of French fueled the fires of separatism? In all honesty I must say that, on the contrary, had Canada's efforts to modernize its official languages policy been more timely and more convincing, I do not think the question of Quebec's autonomy would have taken the form it has.

There is not much doubt, at least, that Quebec's present claims to sovereignty are in large part attributed to the need to ensure a more dependable future for the French language and culture in that province. The argument is that this cannot be accomplished in a Canada in which French-speakers are inevitably outnumbered and, moreover, that the original constitutional balance has proved too lopsided by imposing almost exclusively on Quebec the social burden of individual bilingualism.

For the record, one should note that the constitutional line of argument, unlike the more pessimistic social one, is not peculiar to the advocates of separation. It is shared by a great many Canadians who perceive the logic and necessity for arriving at a new linguistic deal within confederation.

Canadians are not in the business of *introducing* recognition of minority language rights; we are looking for ways *to update* a principle of equality to make it more consonant with contemporary life and institutions. Therefore, so far as English-French relations on the Canadian landmass are concerned, the necessary reciprocities will still have to be arrived at whether Quebec separates or not.

BILINGUALISM AND THE LEARNING PROCESS

Where, then, do the various types of language education fit within the new model of Canadian federation that is struggling to be born? Although educational structures in Canada are not notably avant-garde, the country's new patterns of language education do seem to offer an optimistic glimpse of things to come—a foretaste of how it might be, if enough people were convinced that it should be so.

In the first place, there is an explicit recognition that the official language minorities are entitled to an education in their own language and that linguistic cohabitation in mixed schools is not the answer. What we are witnessing, in fact, is a more and more determined effort on the part of French-speaking minorities outside Quebec to rid themselves of the imputation that they are just one more linguistic minority like any other, with no choice in law and nature except to assimilate; and therefore to build up an adequate network of autonomous French-language institutions from schools and school boards to hospitals and credit unions, comparable eventually to the Anglophone infrastructure that exists in Quebec, thus shielding them from further erosion of their language.

At the same time as the minority is trying to throw off the dismal aura of a people condemned to disappear—and, it would seem, succeeding—the majority is also beginning to attune itself to a new reality in which the citizen who has something to say in Canadian matters will seek to say it in French as well as in English. The recognition that the old hit-or-miss method of, perhaps, twenty or thirty minutes of second-language instruction a week rarely produced anything like fluency has thrown the spotlight on the "immersion" programs in which children study non-language subjects in their second language. It is this phenomenon which has been seized upon by some American commentators either to prove or disprove different hypotheses about the potential effects of bilingual education in the United States. We should therefore consider some of the questions that may arise.

Is Bilingualism Harmful?

First, the question of *whether bilingualism itself is good for the individual or somehow impedes cognitive development and self-expression.*

Insofar as there can be a simple answer to what is obviously a very complex question, all the evidence that I am aware of suggests that individual bilingualism is at the very worst neutral with respect to the normal interaction of the human brain and its environment. Bilingualism will, of course, vary both in form and in degree, but in itself it has, if anything, more advantages than disadvantages from the standpoint of cognitive development. In short, the idea that coping with more languages than one is unnatural and muddling is not borne out by the observable facts.

Language Status

A more significant series of questions relates to *the circumstances in which the individual becomes bilingual: how and why this occurs and how it relates to personal motivation and the values attached to the languages involved.*

There certainly appears to be a relationship, although not yet thoroughly researched and understood, between the scholastic achievement of a child who is being educated in his second language and the extent of his security and competence in his first language. It would also seem to me to follow that if the first language is itself perceived as a lower status language, the child's incentive toward adequate mastery of his mother tongue is diminished and a chain reaction of linguistic, academic, and social difficulties may result.

For this reason, one should be extremely cautious about applying the educational experience of majority-language children to children whose mother tongue is a minority language. The fact, for instance, that English-speaking Canadian children are able to make good learning progress in French immersion programs without in the least impairing their mastery of English is no reason to suppose that children of the French-speaking minority can be submerged in English schools with comparable academic and linguistic results. The difference lies in the relative status of the two languages as determined by the total environment in which their education is taking place.

Applications in Education

This leads us to a third question: *How are the status and socio-economic circumstances of first and second languages to be reflected in the educational process?*

That there are a number of important choices to be made in this respect is amply demonstrated by the decisions which many French-speaking Canadian parents and administrators outside Quebec are called upon to make. Should they foster the use of the mother tongue at home and support it through cultural aids such as radio and TV? Should they send their children to English school at the earliest opportunity—knowing that they will eventually have to function in a predominantly English society? Should they hold out for, and do political battle for, physically and administratively separate institutions, or work through mixed schools and mixed school commissions?

Notice, however, where our Francophones outside Quebec and Northern New Brunswick are concerned there is seldom any question as to whether the minority individual should or will acquire the majority language. The acquisition of English, in those conditions, is assumed to be almost as much a part of the natural process as puberty and pimples. The English community may sometimes resent the perpetuation of the Francophone distinctiveness, but it has no reason to regard it as a threat to the dominant majority culture. On the contrary, it is the minority language and culture that are endangered, and for children of that minority to achieve solid development in *both* languages, it is essential that they be given every institutional encouragement to study and live in their mother tongue as much as possible.

MERITS OF MAINTAINING MINORITY LANGUAGES AND CULTURES

It is not for me to comment on American practices in this regard. But I believe you do expect to hear my opinions about the merits and consequences of maintaining minority languages and their distinctive cultures in face of deep-rooted feelings that this can only mean laying up social and political headaches for the future.

By way of answer, I have to say that, if our experience is in any way relevant, it is ultimately more divisive to begrudge the minority legitimate means of self-expression than to accept that goal. Whether they are encouraged in their difference or driven toward conformity, it is in the nature of minorities *not to assimilate*. The fact of a common language has not eradicated cultural and even linguistic differences which make the English, Scottish, Welsh, and Irish consider themselves as separate peoples. What one has to decide is how to make the best, the most democratic, use of such differences to build the overarching national structures we need. This, I suggest, is the positive view of cultural diversity.

I see no point in denying that, in your country no more than in my own, "the positive view of cultural diversity" faces numerous attitudinal and practical difficulties, among others a fundamental distrust of what is perceptibly different, and, speaking practically, finding the right balance of bilingual services and educational conditions to maintain the self-respect of the minority, as a minority, while giving it the chance to contribute to the larger good. In these circumstances, for those who believe that the advantages of diversity—a diversity that is appreciated, cultivated, and has an acknowledged place in the scheme of things—outweigh the advantages of uniformity, attention can be focussed on how to make it work. To my mind, that means enabling the minority to help itself in these ways:

- by acknowledging its right to be what it is and enabling it to define as clearly as possible how it expects to live in and contribute to the larger community;
- by using the minority language as a social tool to enable the young to learn and the not-so-young to belong and to participate; and
- by demonstrating our convictions in the concrete form of aid, institutions, and human resources.

I hope I have been able to bring to you a clearer notion of the concepts, definitions, and social conditions that make Canadian bilingualism what it is. I think it was Barbara Tuchman who observed that it is what people believe about themselves that determines their history. When we are considering the relations of language and power, it is obvious that people's beliefs are not always easy to reconcile. The best we can do is to keep our concepts and definitions as clear as possible and to seek to win people to them by careful argument and well-documented example. In an area that is rife with myths, we need to do everything we can to keep the debate within reasonable bounds.

You will no doubt take or leave my arguments for recognizing linguistic and cultural diversities within the state. But, where the example of Canada is concerned, I would like to stress again that both the balance of our history and any reasonable projection for the future confirm the view that the struggle to define ourselves linguistically is an on-going one and, if sometimes bitter, a healthy one; and there is less social danger in the long run in tolerance and understanding of linguistic differences than in specious uniformity.

Maxwell F. Yalden *is Commissioner of Official Languages for Canada, a position he assumed in 1977 after four years as Deputy Minister of Communications. Educated at the Universities of Toronto and Michigan, he joined the Canadian Department of External Affairs in 1956. After overseas posts in Moscow, Geneva, and Paris, he returned to the Department in Ottawa, becoming Assistant Undersecretary of State in 1969.*

The Bilingual Experience in Mexico

Salomón Nahmad Sittón

Social sciences, particularly anthropology, have contributed the basic elements in research for constructing a thesis that with time has been modified into a well-forged instrument which will permit complete and free development of ethnic groups within society. In view of all the efforts made to the present time, it is not irrelevant to foresee, about the end of the twentieth century, a new policy relating to the Indians that is designed to induce not only superficial but also very deep changes from a society which has exhibited a particularly unjust attitude toward the native population of our country.

One main objective of this talk is to introduce briefly the successive stages in the development of education in Indian areas of Mexico, and to advance some viable expectations, since education is one of the most important factors for the Indians' progress and their participation in national development.

After having tested, in both word and deed for more than five decades, the viability of a considerable number of theories and projects in Indian education, Mexico now must critically review the policy that has been applied to the fifty-six so-called ethnic groups (subsumed under the general category of "Indians" on the ground that they have languages of their own) who inhabit our country and who, if we credit the accuracy of 1970 national census figures, add up to 3,111,415 persons, or 7.7 percent of the total population.[1]

The areas inhabited by Indian groups have been labelled "marginal" because the natives are isolated, both physically and culturally. This characteristically marginal living condition in which Indians are enmeshed is indicated by their almost utter lack of any social services, medical care, or—the most neglected area—education.

This utterly hopeless situation has been constantly highlighted by members of academic and political circles who insist in pointing out that, in allowing this deprivation to perpetuate (which, in addition, involves exploitation and spoliation of Indian communities), Mexico, regardless of being a free nation, will maintain a form of domestic colonialism.

Early Development of Public Education

Clearly, it would not do to talk about any policy concerning Indians that failed to take into account the Mexican Revolution and agrarian reform, for the revolution caused the breakdown and finally the dissolution of former economic, social, and political structures that had prevailed before 1910, thus allowing the cooperative participation of all social segments of our nation.

Eventually, however, the bloody phase of the revolution came to an end and gave way to its institutional stage. It was then that the State undertook the immense task of formulating a program designed for the peasants, who constituted the majority of the population of our country, and who were active participants in the armed fight against the unjust forms of domination, spoliation, and exploitation to which they had been subjected.

In order to achieve its objectives, the State proceeded to distribute lands to improve living conditions of the peasants, and organized the education of the people to further their economic, social, and political self-liberation. Since 1915, social scientists have worked within the new policy; their contribution being a theoretical scheme which, along with the empiricism applied to daily work, provides an account of social phenomena that constitutes the reality of Mexico.

CONFLICT OF CULTURES

In the twenties, Mexico was divided into two conflicting cultures—on the one hand, the urban population, consisting mainly of descendants of European colonizers, and on the other hand, the peasant population referred to as native. At the end of a century of independent life marked by economic and political instability caused by constant imperialist intervention, the government of the country looked forward to the cultural homogeneity of Mexico so that it might be considered a Westernized society. To this end, it was necessary to incorporate the Indian people into national life, hoping to unite, in the shortest time possible, the diverse cultures coexisting in our country.

In 1921, the Ministry of Education was reestablished, and Indian policy permitted creation of the Department of Indian Education and Culture. Traveling teachers began to work in Indian communities under a carefully designed program in which the teachers first studied the natural conditions of the villages, then provided elementary schooling, did social community work, and introduced new agriculture and cattle technology.

In 1923, the so-called Houses for the People (Casas del Pueblo) were founded. The purpose was the over-all improvement of the Indian communities. Efforts of the schoolteachers were aimed at motivating members of the community to feel that whatever they achieved was their own doing, and then providing them with suitable training so they could earn an honest livelihood and join the wider society.

Integral to the working of the Rural Mexican School is the thesis that every member of the community has the right to attend school, regardless of age or sex. The lesson we learned from experience gained through field work and the results of the Rural School during those initial years of its activities was that there was no tradition to serve as a guide; the teachers had to create a special program for each village, covering all the specific needs of that community.

Later on, Cultural Missions were founded, and they became an effective supplement for the activities of the rural schoolteacher, providing him with the support he needed so that the community would be able to generate its own self-development by the use of its own resources. Due to the growth of the Cultural Missions' responsibilities, it became impossible to satisfy their needs, and therefore the Cooperative Centers were formed, which eventually brought about creation of the Institute for the Training of Teachers.

In 1922 the first Normal Rural Schools were founded. Later renamed Regional Peasants Schools, they were intended principally for the full-blooded Indian communities, but in those communities they failed, although in the peasant—half-breed—communities this was not the case. Unfortunately, the approach employed a Western cultural point of view, completely forgetting the traditional Indian culture.

BOARDING SCHOOLS

In 1926 the House of Indian Students was inaugurated in Mexico City by President Calles. Indian youths were brought there to be educated within the national cultural context and, when returning to their villages, could transmit what they had learned to their fellow villagers in order to stimulate their progress and enhance the community as a whole.

With the purpose of educating the Indian population in their own environment, eleven boarding schools had been established by 1932 based on experience gained through the House of Indian Students. In 1936 the Autonomous Department of Indian Affairs was created, and it set up thirty-three boarding schools with almost 3,000 pupils. Furthermore, some Brigades for the Betterment of Indians were assigned to the department, along with village commissions whose function it was to defend the interests of Indians within the inter-ethnic areas.

President General Lázaro Cárdenas, who had an accurate insight of the problem, not only gave economic and political support to the Department of Indian Affairs but also, thinking about future projects, founded the National School of Anthropology and History with a view to the training of social and linguistic investigators who would attend the needs of Indian communities. At the same time he founded the National Polytechnic Institute and the School of Rural Medicine for the training of physicians who would be able to practice in rural and Indian areas. The celebration of the First Inter-American Indian Convention was his final and culminating success in the field of education. The convention was to discuss problems that all ethnic groups on the Latin American continent have in common.

Within his revolutionary approach, General Cárdenas established the basis for Indian education. This included the appropriate rules, one of which, approved by UNESCO, reaffirmed the principle that the personality, dignity, sensibility, and moral interests of Indian students had to be respected, along with their positive ability for organization and the typical expressions of their culture. This implied that when formulating programs, two fundamental aspects had to be taken into consideration: complete mastery of educational theory, and a profound knowledge of Indian cultures.

EDUCATION LINKED TO ECONOMIC AND TECHNICAL DEVELOPMENT

In 1946 the law which had promulgated creation of the Department of Indian Affairs was repealed, and about the same time the boarding schools changed their name to Economic and Technical Training Centers, with the objective of linking formal education with economic and technical development. There were 2,173 students in the twenty-one centers that were functioning in 1945, and in the same year, 329 completed their studies. The youths came from twenty-two ethnic groups.

The previous Department of Indian Affairs, in its *Work Résumé,* said of its eleven Missions for the Betterment of Indians:

> Given the magnitude of the Indian problem, with a population dispersed over vast extensions of our territory, who are enmeshed in complete poverty, century-old subdevelopment in their agricultural and industrial methods for the exploitation of natural resources, what the Missions have accomplished in five years of hard work could be mistaken as negligible, but this is not the case.

The average annual budget received by the Department of Indian Affairs during General Avila Camacho's administration was 3,638,000 pesos [almost $300,000], and during this presidential term, 21,832,173 pesos [roughly $1.75 million] were used exclusively for Indian education.

As mentioned previously, in 1946—ten years after its creation—the Department of Indian Affairs went out of existence, and all personnel, effects, and equipment were transferred to the Ministry of Public Education to become the General Department of Indian Affairs. Here it was relegated to a secondary position without having developed its methods either theoretically or practically. At the same time, it lost the ideological content from which it had arisen and became completely bureaucratic. In 1968 it was abolished and its activities divided among various departments within the ministry.

Indian Education, 1950-1970

From the beginning of its history, Mexico has been, and continues to be, a country characterized by a plurality of coexisting cultures and languages. Social scientists, educators, and teachers have been faced with the problem of uniting the nation through common language. They have been seeking appropriate methods to enable almost four million Indians who speak more than fifty languages[2] to use the official language, and thereby achieve the goals so anxiously awaited by our nation—unification through a common language.

The coexistence of ethnic and half-breed groups, the latter forming the majority and the former dispersed all over the country, has resulted in the marginality and exploitation of those who do not participate in the national cultural pattern. This condition is imposed upon the Indian population as opposed to non-Indians. One of the determining factors of this subordination is ignorance of the official national language.

ALTERNATIVE PHILOSOPHIES

In the educational policy relating to Indian groups, two basic tendencies can be clearly discerned. The first derives from developmental positivism and, consequently, considers all forms of non-Western culture as primitive and lacking any intrinsic value. It defends the argument that in order for our society to achieve its desirable uniformity and homogeneity, Indian groups must be absorbed by and incorporated into the wider society with the help of coercive means which, if they were strictly enforced, would cause linguistic and cultural barriers to tumble down. This position advocates a thesis whereby the Indian population has to be educated through the exclusive use of Spanish, and rejects any suggestion of the viability of making use of vernacular languages.

The second position follows a completely different course, based on the belief that the right way to educate ethnic groups is through use of their own languages, applying a bilingual method whereby the Indians would become familiar with using Spanish. Likewise, this second line of educational thought hints at the suitability of an education with a bicultural content, combining elements of the student's culture with cultural elements both national and universal.

In spite of the fact that for a long period of time the former thesis managed to prevail in educational policy for Indian groups, it failed to realize the intended goals. In fact, the latter thesis, which was followed only at an experimental level in some intercultural areas of Mexico, proved far more effective because it succeeded in penetrating Indian zones and partially introducing some elementary knowledge of the Spanish language among the Indians.

After 1952 the National Indian Institute (Instituto Nacional Indigenista, INI) could show the Ministry of Public Education the benefits of a bilingual system for training of members of ethnic groups who eventually would carry out the bilingual and bicultural educational task themselves. As early as 1963, on the occasion of the Sixth National Assembly of Education, the use of bilingual methods by teachers and *promotores bilingües* [bilingual agents] was approved as the basis of national educational policy for intercultural regions.

BENEFITS OF BILINGUAL APPROACH

Bilingual education involves use of both languages—the mother tongue and the national one—as methods of teaching. When the mother tongue is the teaching instrument in the first years of primary school, it proves an effective means for mastery of the national language, which is learned as a second tongue. Furthermore, bilingual education produces far better results because it encourages a greater degree of communication through a warmer and closer relationship between teacher and pupil. Finally, it helps to enhance the psychologically balanced development of the student, helping him to acquire a sense of confidence and certainty about his capacity to learn more. If, in addition to being bilingual the education is bicultural, the mother culture of the pupils will be taken into account for both content and teaching methods of educational programs.

Another quality of bicultural education should be mentioned: because the native who teaches in an ethnic group is a member of that group, he has better opportunities than any outsider to participate in the life of the community. In addition, he can freely choose from his cultural environment those elements he knows will be excellent auxiliaries of his teaching work. At the same time, other members of the ethnic group learn to appreciate the richness of their own culture, and as soon as they are instructed about their having rights and duties as members of a wider society, surely they will find it necessary to participate in fitting the inherent values of their culture into those of the nation.

LEGAL FRAMEWORK

Between 1950 and 1970, no essential modifications were made in the law creating the National Indian Institute (INI) nor the one concerning the ministries and departments of the State within which, in Article 13, Fractions XV and XVI, the functions of the late Department of Indian Affairs were transferred to the Ministry of Public Education.

The law founding the National Indian Institute in 1948 to meet the drafts passed by the First Inter-American Indian Convention assigned the institute the following functions:

> It is to be the legal organ of the State for investigation of all problems relating to the Indian groups of the country.
>
> It is the only organ empowered to put forth and to advance before the federal government the measures to be taken for the betterment of these groups.
>
> It will act in the capacity of an advisory body for public and private institutions on affairs pertaining to Indian communities.
>
> Through its authorized agencies called Coordinating Centers, the National Indian Institute is empowered to control and coordinate

any action the qualified governmental agencies for Indian groups undertake.

During this period, through presidential decrees, eleven Coordinating Centers and one Sub-Center were established, along with creation of the Indian Patrimony for the Mezquital Valley (designed to attend to the needs of the Otomí Indians inhabiting the State of Hidalgo) and activation of the Inter-Ministerial Commission of the Yaqui Indians.

EDUCATION AND ECONOMIC DEVELOPMENT

The Rural Education Project failed to fulfill the great initial expectation of furthering economic development, at least so far as the Indian areas were concerned. As already mentioned, the number of native students who succeeded in completing their studies at the boarding schools could be considered as negligible when compared with the magnitude of the educational needs of Indian areas. On the other hand, the Rural School attracted more attention and yielded good results in those communities not exclusively made up of Indians, because peasants were more receptive to instruction by the teachers.

Since a lack of educational measures suitable to the cultures of the Indian areas persisted, the peasants refused to let their children attend rural schools. In order to implement public education for the Indians, structural changes within the intercultural regions were necessary and, especially, the securing of land ownership as demanded by the Indians. Notwithstanding the fact that the Indians worked the land and cared for their cattle using technology of ancient origins in some cases and coming from the colonial period in others, the result did bring the people a frugal living. The hope that loans, modern agriculture and cattle-raising technology, health services, roads, and supplementary food resources would accompany the educational systems failed. It was self-evident that planning and methods needed thorough review so that education and a complete program of economic, health, agricultural, fishing, and forestry development might be realized.

On the basis of previous experience, the National Indian Institute proceeded to reexamine and formulate anew the pilot project of the Chiapas area, and for the first time to use bilingual natives as intermediaries between the official institutions and the communities; they were expected to have some influence in their communities and to use their mother tongues for both formal education and to persuade the community to participate in its own development.

This program, which started in 1952, was not in harmony with the idea of sending teachers who spoke only Spanish to Indian areas to enforce the compulsory use of that language by children. These teachers usually arrived at the Indian communities with all the prejudices typical of representatives of half-breed groups and without any knowledge of the native languages. For these reasons they were rejected both by the Indian groups who considered them foreigners and by members of the oppressing class, and could not participate in community affairs.

EXTENT OF EDUCATION, 1950-1970

Between 1950 and 1963, in the six Indian regions where bilingual education was in use, the National Indian Institute maintained 350 *promotores,* and 237 schools with an enrollment of 19,009 students. The percentage of student population by grade was: pre-school, 44; first grade, 31; second grade, 19; third grade, 3.5; fourth grade, 2.0; fifth and sixth grades, 0.5.

In 1964 the number of *promotores* and bilingual teachers was increased, based on the Sixth National Education Assembly's approval of the national educational policy for intercultural regions and the use of bilingual methods by *promotores* and teachers who had a complete mastery of both Spanish and the Indian language of their native villages.

By 1968, 2,150 *promotores* were operating in twenty-five Indian regions; in 1970 there were 3,815 *promotores* and bilingual teachers in charge of 1,601 schools with a total population of 125,895 Indian children. In the same year, twenty-six boarding schools for Indians were functioning side-by-side with the boarding schools for elementary education; together they had 5,835 pupils. Twenty-four Brigades for the Betterment of the Indians were operating along with thirty village commissions. The Ministry of Public Education and the General Department of Indian Affairs, in their last budget for 1968, allotted 45,191,707 pesos [$3,618,000] to this end. Pupils of two boarding schools sponsored by the National Indian Institute were given 100 scholarships, in addition to which the Institute spent 1,400,000 pesos [$112,000] for the furtherment of education in Indian areas. Of the yearly scholarship vacancies, 33 percent were granted to the Agriculture and Livestock High Schools with boarding facilities, to enable them to admit Indian children who had completed their elementary studies.

FINANCIAL AND HUMAN RESOURCES PRIOR TO 1970

Education in Indian areas was financed, essentially, by the federal government, and only in very few places was economic assistance received from the governments of the twenty-nine states into which Mexico is divided. We have already seen that the budget allotted to Indian areas in 1970 was insufficient to satisfy the enormous educational needs of those communities. Private initiative was represented only in the labor force supplied by the Indians and the regional raw materials used for school construction.

The investment in education made from 1964 to 1970, however, allowed a great number of youths who were graduated from the Indian boarding schools and other schools with a complete training course to be admitted as *promotores bilingües* for further education in the Federal Institute of Teaching.

The recruiting of bilingual teachers and *promotores* increased the demand from Indian communities for more schools, and raised school attendance significantly. In communities where teachers were not bilingual, an attitude of rejection by both teachers and community was reflected. More noticeable was the teacher's rejection of his community because he could not adapt himself to the Indian cultural patterns and, usually, he insisted on eradicating the local language, tradition, and cultural ways.

Among the bilingual teachers, however, only twenty were skilled and qualified enough to head the Culture Division of the Coordinating Supervising Centers. In bilingual mastery and linguistic training, the result had been very poor. The schools of anthropology and pedagogy had not trained more than a dozen skilled and qualified bilingual teachers, and most of them, unfortunately, were not engaged in any bilingual education activity.

PROBLEMS IN EDUCATION OF THE INDIANS

Although the educational situation in rural areas had indeed improved between 1950 and 1970, it was proportionately at a much lower level in comparison with urban educational status. The problem was even more serious in Indian regions because of the scarcity of conventional services and the faulty performance of those few that were functional. Among deficiencies, we can mention the alarming percentage of students who dropped out and the low level of performance in most classes. Because of teacher absenteeism and budgetary limitations that hindered supervision, the Indian zones still showed a high rate of monolingualism, as well as bilingualism characterized by very poor Spanish. Also, population growth exceeded the rate of expansion of educational services, which, in turn, reinforced their marginality and underdevelopment.

The lack of formal education in the Indian areas leaves this population only few opportunities and alternatives for ascending the social scale with the help of education, and contributes to the strong oppression exerted upon them. Because they keep their cultural patterns, they adhere to traditional ways of production and commercial relations, using asymmetrical methods based on barter of their products. In order for an educational system to be effective within Indian areas, it must elicit changes in the habits of communal life and, eventually, transform the people's natural resources so they can increase their standard of living.

The 1970s: Reorganization of Services for Indian Areas

In 1971 the General Department of Pre-School Education for Indian Areas was created, assuming the functions previously held by the General Department of Indian Affairs, which lately had been divided among various departments of the Ministry of Public Education. To this end and responding to urgent demands coming from the Indian communities, the working system was reformed, and all cultural *promotores* and bilingual teachers who were rendering a national service were officially appointed to government positions. This decision came from experience gained between 1964 and 1970, when their services began in a rather disjointed way to fulfill the technical resolutions issued by the various Inter-American Indian Conventions and by the Council of Indian Languages. Particular attention was paid to the UNESCO recommendation which reads: "The use of the vernacular language provides a way through which national unification can be achieved in a shorter time than when the national language is directly taught to an illiterate community."

Thanks to experience gathered by bilingual *promotores* working within ten Indian areas, a majority of the authorities in charge of educational affairs reached the conviction that there was a need to provide institutional status to bilingual education in our country. Therefore, the decision was made to employ as many bilingual teachers as possible who had been welcomed in a highly rewarding manner by their native communities, thereby permitting the teacher to be accepted within his community as a friend and educator.

This system of formal education was also intended to promote community interests, both socio-economically and culturally. Here again, the bilingual teacher was a link between the federal and state governments and the community.

EMPHASIS ON BICULTURALISM IN TEACHING

Recently some Mexican linguists specializing in pedagogy related to the Indian field said of bicultural education:

> No educational project may be considered complete if its social context is not taken into account, as interpreted from two points of view: first, that relating to an understanding and evaluation of its own culture; and second, that referring to a knowledge of how the non-Indian society functions and acts, and consequently, the role that native groups, with their strong human resources, play in the development of Mexico.

The Indians should understand the social and cultural causes that contributed to their being ignored; only then will they be able to face this problem, show their capability, and thereby gain a sense of dignity based on reality. Educational methods and programs must take into account the cultural features of each of the different groups and socio-economic areas. This kind of education awakens the interest of the adult population and promotes active participation not only in the technical development of school centers but also in supplying ideas about what they consider most useful to be taught to their children.

The frame of mind of the Indians has been influenced since colonial times by complete social and economic submission. But when the will of the community is recognized by inviting its members to participate in the contents of educational programs, the frustration of dissociation and insecurity reflected by their depreciation of their own values is avoided. Only in this way can functional education be achieved.

The revaluation of each culture and its relationship to the contents of the educational programs permits the intermingling of education with the daily life of the community. The knowledge of the structure of the national society and how it functions, linked to an understanding of the facts and values which have permitted Indian groups to survive—often through a strong internal cohesion—will encourage a rapid and successful development of our country. In this way the creative expressions and elements of ethnic groups, which unfortunately have been wasted until now, can be brought into action.

INTERCULTURAL AREAS

From their very first contact with Western culture, the Indian populations of Mexico were steadily expelled from their original lands to inaccessible and inhospitable areas. Notwithstanding this isolation, the colonizers penetrated even those regions to establish cities from which they could exercise economic, political, religious, and social domination over the Indian communities and villages. This is how present inter-ethnic areas were structured, and the means through which the Indian and half-breed populations established permanent contact.

Even though many changes have taken place in Mexico since independence and the revolution, many social structures and features originating during colonial times have been perpetuated. Therefore, educational policy in these areas should cover not only formal aspects of instruction but also should aim at breaking down the obsolete relationships related to colonial times. To this end, bilingual *promotores* and teachers have the task not only of instructing children but also of exercising influence over the community to give the existing asymmetrical social structure a more symmetrical form.

INI AND THE MINISTRY OF PUBLIC EDUCATION

With the objective of carrying out its programs in each inter-cultural region, the federal government counts on the help of two institutions dedicated to attend to the problems of ethnic groups: the National Indian Institute which, through eighty-five Coordinating Centers, establishes the links to achieve a well-functioning relationship with all government organizations; and the Ministry of Public Education which, through the General Department of Indian Education, has the main educational task based on the theory of bilingualism, the most appropriate method of working with Indian communities. Each institution operates with a Director of Regional Indian Education, various area supervisors, and a fluctuating number of bilingual teachers in each region who act as school directors or who lead groups from the community. The institute and the ministry work together in the educational field toward regional development, and in this way achieve the in-tended goals of well-guided social change.

At the end of school year 1979, 11,165 cultural *promotores* and bilingual teachers in these two organizations handled 4,221 schools with grades from elementary to higher education. Some 918 board-ing schools were managed by 419 bilingual teachers, distributing 46,900 annual scholarships to students, most of whom lived a considerable distance from their schools.[3] These teachers and *promotores* came from Indian groups and serviced a total of 326,398 children at various levels of elementary education.

In addition, there were 3,286 *promotores* in the program for teach-ing basic Spanish to 65,720 pre-school children. The total number of students educated under these two programs in 1979 was 392,118. The programs were overseen by 249 supervisors, who were in turn supervised by 82 regional directors.

As noted before, financing of the educational system for the socio-economic development of the Indians is essentially from federal government revenues. For 1978, from a budget of 1.3 billion pesos for elementary education, most was allocated to pay the salaries of bilingual teachers and *promotores*, to maintain twenty-eight Social Integration Centers, and to run thirty Brigades for the Betterment of the Indians and the village commissions. In addition, from the budget of the National Indian Institute 61,000,000 pesos were set aside for scholarships, boarding schools, scholar furniture, educational materials, and the like.

According to the Federal Education Law, which came into force after 1973, bilingual instruction is considered part of the educational system. Because bilingual methods are different from those usually employed in formal systems of elementary education, it follows that special textbooks and teaching materials must be made available both in Spanish and in the native language of each area.

Through the Social Integration Centers or Coordinating Centers, both INI and the General Department of Education are now adding to their programs for Indians special training in collectivization of agriculture, stressing the benefits it provides their farming tasks based on traditional systems of communal work. These programs are aimed at awakening in the Indians a growing sense of social status, and the need for organization into pressure groups to defend their economic, cultural, and political interests at local, state, and national levels.

It is the large number of *promotores* and bilingual teachers who provide the motor to run the field-working phase and implement the national policy for education and socio-economic development of inter-ethnic areas. The National Indian Institute and the General Department of Indian Education have joined efforts in a well-articulated coordination to achieve the established goals. But because of the lack of legal advice for settlement of the aforementioned basis of coordination, there are in both the Institute and the General Department of Indian Education strong currents that tend to disrupt that cooperative action.

Present Progress and Future Needs

From what has been reported thus far we may infer that the revolutionary process of developing the Indian areas and providing Indian education has failed to follow an ascending line. This account clearly shows its cyclical outline: a period of active promotion of Indian education is followed by another period during which educational institutes are left without any political or economic support and consequently lose their original focus and become only bureaucratic institutions.

During the present presidential term, particular attention is being given to the process interrupted at the end of General Cardenas's presidency, and therefore the majority of the population has been mobilized in a search for new opportunities.

During 1979 the educational systems servicing 85 Indian areas gave formal elementary education to 366,000 children of school age. The population of school children in these areas is approximately 525,000. Between 1979 and 1982 a great effort has to be made, so that at least 95 percent of these children take advantage of the facilities. This means that, in order to handle 600,000 children at thirty per class, by 1982 the number of bilingual teachers must be increased to 21,000, or approximately 3,500 yearly.

Formal education must also be extended to the children who live in scattered villages. The scholarships now given to 46,900 students distributed among 918 boarding schools have to be increased to fund the 2,000 or so boarding schools that will be required, with fifty students per school, to accommodate the 150,000 children who, according to the latest census, live in scattered villages without educational possibilities. This objective would provide 100,000 scholarships for children who can be found mainly in those communities with the densest Indian population. If they are not given this opportunity, they will continue to be marginal, and, therefore, eventually the illiterate and monolingual population will increase and be subjected to more exploitation and discrimination.

At the same time a higher school attendance is achieved at the elementary level, more youths will have completed elementary instruction and should be channeled into the technical and agricultural schools. To this end, we must increase the number of scholarships between 1979 and 1982 to 12,000, that is, 3,000 yearly until a figure of 24,000 is reached. For a population of 600,000 children, this represents a minimum of 4 percent.

When these youths finish their high school education, they should be recruited as agricultural and livestock *promotores,* so there are at least two or three skilled youths in each of the 7,500 Indian communities within the 135 intercultural areas. These youths would lead and promote technical, administrative, and cultural changes for the development of the Indian economic structure. This overall program will require the assistance of university-trained technicians who will support this army of agricultural *promotores* and bilingual teachers. The technicians will face and attack, through the Indian Coordinating Centers, the problems of each and every community, using a central program developed at regional and national levels. This plan should generate radical and substantial changes so that the population of six million Indians expected by the end of the century can be absorbed into the national population, a harmonious and symmetric articulation of the Indians with the rest of society.

There should exist a permanent bilingual educational system, which would shape teachers skilled in bilingual education and those linguistic technicians needed at high school and higher educational levels, according to the recommendations of UNESCO and international Indian agencies.

EDUCATION AS A STEP TO SOCIAL JUSTICE

At present the Indian population is still dissatisfied as a result of the previous decline of attention to their many needs. Should this decline be repeated, even more frustration would be generated and, along with the growing cultural separation between urban and Indian populations that would result, might cause a significant social crisis.

The agrarian reform should continue, and those forces which have stopped its progress for many years must be destroyed. The Indian communities should receive, in the same measure and at the same time, both their lands and systems of education, in order that the process of self-liberation might be completed. The bilingual educational system should be supported by the agrarian reform, and at the same time both teachers and bilingual *promotores* should stimulate social changes for the development of agriculture and livestock activities.

The Mexican people have only two alternatives: The first is to give Indians a status of equality and dignity in their cultural patterns, as we are trying to do by means of our educational plans; the second is the inheritance from colonial times—domination, exploitation, and submission.

The peasant and Indian populations of Mexico are allied because in many aspects their living conditions are similar. It is not possible to carry out a program for the rural half-breed peasant population without a parallel program which takes into consideration the social and cultural conditions of the fifty-six ethnic groups who live in our country. The need is acute for more economic resources. According to current prices and salaries, it is estimated that by the end of 1982, fifty new Coordinating Centers will need to be created, and 5 billion pesos will have to be invested by the General Department of Indian Education. The political and economic support given to an integrated Indian policy covering the entire population is basic, aside from the need to have coordination among all the institutions established in the Indian areas. This would allow us to receive a program of social justice which the revolution promised these marginal groups in Mexico.

Plans for the Future

The program of public education has still wider aims and objectives. When the General Department of Indian Education was established within the jurisdiction of the Undersecretariat for Elementary Education, the federal government for the first time gave its tacit recognition to basic bilingual education. According to the *Regulations of the Ministry of Education*, printed in the official government publication dated September 11, 1978, three fundamental objectives were set forth:

- to propose educational contents and methods, as well as norms of teaching techniques to be applied to non-Spanish-speaking Indians;
- to organize, develop, carry out, supervise, and evaluate the programs for the teaching of Spanish in Indian communities;
- to carry out these programs and services of elementary education, particularly within those communities that are almost exclusively monolingual.

The actual school-age Indian population living in areas where our services are available is approximately 525,000. Of this total, only 326,000 children receive bilingual education, and only 15,000 ever reach the sixth grade. The rest of the school-age population, living in other areas, receive monolingual education. The Spanish language should reach 150,000 pre-school-age children, so that the bilingual educational system will completely cover at least 750,000 children, providing a functional elementary education in Spanish. The objective is to make Spanish not only a means of communication within the wider society but also a living tongue within Indian areas.

Current methods for teaching Spanish are rudimentary and insufficient. Adapted to local needs, they must be diversified and made extensive enough to cover all areas of education from preschool through elementary. To this end, a team of technicians—specialists in bilingual and bicultural education—will be chosen from our present employees. To reach our objectives we must:

- develop educational methods and techniques relating to conditions and problems we face within the Indian areas;
- conduct research and training in the field of linguistics on a practical level;
- in collaboration with the National Indian Institute, adapt materials and textbooks of the first to sixth grades in the four basic elementary educational components;
- prepare, publish, and distribute bilingual reading material, in coordination with the General Department of Communal Cultures, the National Indian Institute, and the General Department of Publications and Libraries;
- in cooperation with the institutes of higher education and the universities, develop Indian linguists, and rescue, develop, and spread the cultural linguistic legacy of as many Indian groups as possible;
- create new administrative zones to provide services to all Indian areas;
- give training in the latest educational innovations to elementary schoolteachers who are already bilingual;
- increase the training of supervisors and bilingual teachers at the superior level, so as to provide enough personnel to cover all phases of education in all inter-ethnic areas;

- recruit and train *promotores* and teachers of the Spanish language and thereby reinforce the complementary programs related to social development, health, and production.

Boarding school services will be increased as will support for elementary bilingual/bicultural education for scattered villages until all areas have been covered. Through a close collaboration of INI and CAPFCE [the federal committee for school construction], efforts will be made to build and equip school facilities.

Taking advantage of the available time of the communications media, we shall try to rescue, develop, and disseminate the cultural and linguistic heritage of our Indian groups. Existing programs and the main centers in Mexico that nurture Indian cultures will be strengthened.

In order that the objectives and aims of the Mexican government may be achieved, the following programs which constitute the spinal cord of all Indian educational systems must be applied:

- the program of pre-school Spanish language training (to introduce and strengthen the use of Spanish within Indian areas);
- the program of elementary bilingual education for all Indian children of school age; (both of the preceding programs will be reinforced by our network of boarding schools that services the scattered populations);
- the program of educational and academic training to raise the quality of our present and future staff;
- educational programs through public radio and television;
- programs to reinforce the educational plan designed by the General Department of Communal Cultures for the rescue and development of Indian culture;
- programs of formal and informal education that reinforce existing plans of economic development designed by INI and COPLAMAR [the federal planning commission for isolated areas];
- programs which will make available human resources at all levels of skill.

NOTES

1. This census does not take into consideration children under five years of age, estimated to be 700,000 in number, giving an Indian population figure in 1970 of 3.8 million. Because of the difficulties faced when gathering the data, the actual total may have been still higher. Considering an annual increase in population of 3.5 percent, it is estimated that in 1979 the Indian population stood at 5 to 5.5 million persons.

2. The 1970 census reported that, of the 3,111,415 Indians then over the age of five, 1,544,904 (or 3.5 percent of the total Mexican population) were monolingual, speaking only their Indian languages. The balance had a rudimentary mastery of Spanish.

3. During school year 1978-79, 12,000 scholarships of $370 per month were distributed to provide gifted Indian youths the opportunity of continuing their education. Eight thousand of the scholarships were for secondary education and 4,000 for high school students. During the previous school year of 1977-78, the Bank of Mexico granted 120 scholarships of $500 per month for higher studies in universities or technological schools.

Salomón Nahmad Sittón *is General Director of Indian Languages for the Secretariat for Public Education of Mexico. A social anthropologist with higher degrees from the National School of Anthropology and History, he has been a university professor, a researcher, and since 1967 an administrator. He is a prolific scholar, with fifty-one publications to his credit and membership in numerous prestigious academic institutions in his country.*

III. One Nation, Indivisible?
Panel Discussions on the
Implications of Bilingualism

Implications of Bilingualism:
Culture and Economics

"For individuals from homes where English is not the first language, the role of a second language is significant in their view of their culture and their economic opportunity."

Speaking from personal experience was Ramón Eduardo Ruiz, professor of history at the University of California, La Jolla, who moderated the opening panel discussion of bilingualism/biculturalism in the American experience. Panel participants were Noel Epstein, journalist and author; Donald Hata, professor of history, California State University, Dominguez Hills; David Maciel, professor of history, University of New Mexico; and George P. Brockway, social critic and chairman of the board of W. W. Norton and Company, publishers.

Ruiz told an old story from Mexico about the son of a wealthy Mexican family who was sent to the United States to study at an American university.

Ramón Ruiz: Shortly thereafter a letter arrived in Mexico City from the son explaining, "I find English difficult to learn; meanwhile I am forgetting my Spanish." The parents, much concerned, replied: "Come home at once, before you revert to your childhood and forget how to speak."

When I entered school in the United States, I did not know a single word of English, and those wonderful American teachers put me back one year until I learned English. My mother used to say that was unfortunate because I learned so much English I was unable or unwilling to carry on a conversation in proper Spanish. I had to go back and learn my native tongue all over again.

Noel Epstein, an editor and writer for the *Washington Post* and author of the 1977 book, *Language, Ethnicity, and the Schools*, expressed grave doubts about the purpose of the conference and a fear that it might damage bilingual programs. He theorized that hostility to bilingual programs was rooted in incipient nativism and misunderstanding, and discussed how ethnicity diminishes among non-English speakers as they enter the American mainstream.

Noel Epstein: I have a promotional button, the only button I have ever saved, and it says, "Technology is the answer, but what was the question?" For more than a decade, in Washington and elsewhere, some people have been suggesting that being bilingual and bicultural is the answer, and a good many other people have been scratching their heads in recent years and asking, "But what on earth was the question?" Much to my astonishment I note that one of the background papers prepared for this conference states that the question everybody is waiting for is whether the United States should become officially bilingual (or multilingual) or whether the dominance of English should be continued. The United States, as far as I am aware, is not facing this question. Nobody I know of, especially in Washington, has thought that this is the question they have been addressing. I would suggest that the more widely that kind of question is asked, the more damage will be done to some very important efforts on behalf of bilingual education programs in the nation's capital as well as elsewhere, including in California.

Now to the specific topic assigned to this panel. Economics and ethnicity or economics and culture, particularly minority cultures, do not get along very well. In fact, they are outright enemies in many respects. The evidence suggests that the more linguistic and cultural minorities succeed economically in the majority culture in this nation, the more erosion there will be of most members' ties to their initial language and culture. That, of course, does not include a small group of what might be called "ethnic professionals" who are often paid and devoted by profession and inclination to maintaining the minority culture and language, including leaders of ethnic groups as well as anthropologists, linguists, sociolinguists, and others. But for the majority of people, the more they are accepted into the mainstream economy, the weaker the ties to ethnic language and culture. It is important always to keep in mind that one of the powerful ways to maintain minority languages and cultures is to discriminate against their users. That is certainly one reason why many Hispanics in the Southwest have continued to live chiefly in Spanish into the second, third, and sometimes fourth generation, especially in the geographically separated areas such as rural New Mexico. Any kind of separation from the majority—from contact with the majority culture—tends to help maintain the minority language and culture. On the other hand, a very large threat to ethnic cohesion is tolerance in the majority society toward the minority group.

There is nothing new about this in American history. It goes back, for example, to the Pilgrims. We teach in school, in our homes, and on television that the Pilgrims came here to escape religious intolerance. The reality is the opposite. The Pilgrims came to these shores to escape tolerance. The Pilgrims fled to Holland to escape religious intolerance in England, and in Holland they found a very tolerant society, certainly in the context of those days, and their children were being tempted into the mainstream of that society. As William Bradford explained in the 1600s: "And of all the sorrows most heavy to be born was that many of their children by these occasions and the great licentiousness of youth in that country [that is, Holland] and the manifold temptations of the place were drawn away by evil examples into extravagant and dangerous courses, getting the reins off their necks and departing from their parents." Lawrence Cremin of Columbia Teachers College has remarked: "In effect the Pilgrims came to America as a community seeking to preserve its religious and cultural integrity."

I think it is worth emphasizing that the Pilgrims came here to escape tolerance, not intolerance. Today there are many Hispanic-Americans, as there have been leaders of many other groups, who fear that too much tolerance, too much success, particularly economic success in the majority economy, will help erode ethnic ties, linguistic as well as cultural. That is one reason why they have been pushing for government to provide what are—casually and carelessly—called language and cultural "maintenance" programs. This is a very human hope, but their desires for government-sponsored and government-financed language and cultural maintenance efforts generally have failed from the outset, certainly so far as bilingual education is concerned. Their plea has been rejected in Washington repeatedly. I think that the whole cultural and language "maintenance" argument, at any rate, is widely misunderstood. But it is clear that economics and ethnicity are not very good friends.

> David Maciel, a Spanish-speaking professor in the University of New Mexico who teaches Mexican and Chicano history, expressed his feeling that bilingualism cannot be assessed because it has never been adequately tested to see what it could produce if proper training programs were in place. He spoke from experience and conviction.

David Maciel: I have lived closely with the bilingual/bicultural problem, as have many people in my community, that is, the Chicano community. The first time I went to Washington to deliver a paper at an academic conference, the chairman, who was not a Chicano, said: "I am amazed that you do not speak with a Spanish accent. Most Chicanos that I know who are from the Southwest speak with a noticeable Spanish accent." That did not really strike me as odd at the time, but about a year later I went to study in Mexico at a very prestigious, elite, and exclusive institution of higher learning and research. It was a program started in 1971 to expose Americans to the Mexican background of Chicano studies. After two weeks in Mexico I was invited to a faculty dinner party where I was the only Chicano. Well into the conversation my host said, "Let me get this straight: you *are* a Chicano?" And I said, "Yes, I certainly am. My specialty is Chicano and Mexican history." He said, "That is really amazing. You do not look like a Chicano." I said to myself, "Can this be happening to me here in Mexico?" Then he went on to say, "You do not speak Spanish with an American accent—you speak Spanish well; and Chicanos, if they speak Spanish at all, it is horrible Spanish, and they cannot make themselves understood."

Obviously, for the Chicano community the question of bilingualism/biculturalism is of profound influence and importance. It involves their politics, involves their heritage, their legal questions, their own identity and their place in society—in a real sense, their culture.

There are three basic questions that we should ask in dealing with bilingual/bicultural education in the Chicano community. First, why was bilingual/bicultural education advocated by Chicano academics, students, and the greater community? Why did they see it as a particular solution for the deplorable educational statistics that the census very clearly indicated? Second, how were the bilingual/bicultural programs begun in the 1960s and early 1970s structured? What was their content? What texts were used? How were the teachers trained? And finally, what has the balance sheet displayed in regard to bicultural education?

It is my experience that bilingual/bicultural classes rarely incorporated much on culture. What then has been the emphasis of instruction in bilingual/bicultural programs in the Chicano community?

This is my first year as a member of the faculty in the University of New Mexico. Last semester I taught a course that has been in existence for three years—a history of New Mexico supposedly taught in Spanish. This brings me to an interesting contradiction, because by law today New Mexico is a bilingual state. Of the twenty-five teachers who took my course, twenty-one were Chicanos already teaching in bilingual/bicultural settings; they were bicultural instruction specialists. But I could not conduct the class in Spanish nor could I require all my readings in Spanish. They simply did not know enough Spanish. This is not the fault of this particular group of teachers. It demonstrates how the courses have been set up, what the aims of the people running the program were, and what the problems with bilingual/bicultural education are.

Many of the ideas about ethnic hostility and group assimilation raised by Noel Epstein were shared by Donald Hata, like Maciel a university professor of history, but Hata felt that his personal background demonstrates the unusual problems of the Japanese community to which he belongs. In a special sense Hata pleaded that English is not enough.

Donald Hata: I would like to reinforce Noel Epstein's initial reservations about raising this issue now. I am a fourth-generation American of Japanese ancestry, born in East Los Angeles. When I began college, I puzzled my freshman English professor at the University of Southern California because my ordinary speech was part street-Chicano and part street-Black. The folk culture I knew did not include little poems out of the Transcendentalist Movement, but was essentially alien to the mainstream of American life.

It was not until I became an historian and began to try to find some meaning, perhaps some historic roots, that I began to realize how differently ethnic and racial groups have seen each other, far apart from the conventional, predictable white-versus-Black confrontation.

Japanese-Americans are very often regarded as a model minority. They have gone far beyond Theodore Roosevelt's exhortation to be 100 percent American, and in fact are seen to be 200 percent American. And, in the process, they have adopted perhaps some of the worst as well as the best of whatever American culture is. To what extent is that model minority stereotype rooted in facts? First, surveys done since 1960 reveal that of all males in California, Japanese-American males can be counted on to have perhaps 11 percent more baccalaureates, a higher-than-average standard of academic achievement. But if you look at economic statistics for those Japanese-American males, you find that regardless of their level of academic achievement, professional degrees included, the average white male in California has perhaps 57 percent more chance to make at least one-third more annual income than a Japanese-American male.

When we probe further we come up with some speculations. As Japanese-Americans advance through the ranks of whatever their jobs may be, private or public, they reach a plateau—they reach the lower management level and then stop, because it is at that point that interviews become very important. I think that we have to discuss this in terms of mastery of English, all the dimensions of what we consider fully mastering and utilizing, exploiting the language—verbal manipulation. The ability to think on one's feet, the ability to project an assertive posture, is something that is apparently not a part of the conventional stereotype of Japanese-Americans. They are good middle-Americans and, indeed, economically there they stay with few exceptions. They rarely get to the highest ranks in the economy, or positions of leadership or policy-making.

Like many native English-speaking Americans, publisher George Brockway had no visceral response to the language issue, but he was concerned with the fact that the presence of prejudice in the world has perpetuated myths about culture that have been detrimental to the maintenance of a singular American culture.

George Brockway: I am not sure what is meant when "culture" is used as in a "bicultural situation" or a "bicultural problem." For example, I do not think that one has to be Greek to read Homer or Plato or Aristotle, and, at the same time, I do not see why any citizen of the world should not read them and be as familiar with them as with Shakespeare or Mark Twain or Cervantes.

As I read what is written on the subject of biculturalism, it seems to me that the whole celebration of ethnicity disguises a strong belief that culture is genetically transmitted. Well, it is not genetically transmitted. A newspaper reported an incident in Colorado where all the kids who had Spanish surnames were assigned to one school, whether they spoke Spanish at home or not. The idea is that language is somehow genetic. This idea is quite pervasive. It is part, I am sure, of the explanation for the enormous and fantastic success and interest of the book *Roots.*

This interest is identical, in my opinion, with the older and generally frowned-on interest of the Daughters of the American Revolution, or of the First Families of Virginia. No white man alive today came over on the Mayflower. No white man alive today signed the Declaration of Independence. No white man alive today fought in the Civil War. And no Black man alive today came across on the middle passage, suffered on the middle passage; nor did any Black man alive today suffer under an overseer's whip. We have, or we should have, one culture—a culture that is available to all.

Another aspect of current thinking that indicates an underlying feeling that culture is genetic is rooted in a proposal now often advanced. It is the idea of compensatory treatment, which is even advanced by the courts. Blacks are entitled to compensatory treatment in education not only because of their difficulties in the primary and elementary grades but also, it is said, because of generations of ill-treatment. I do not know what the generations part has to do with it. My grandfather enlisted as a drummer boy in the Civil War and, as a result (which sometimes happens in the army), he took to liquor. Consequently he never was educated, and he was not able to see that my father was educated. But I was educated, and I do not suffer from those generations of deprivation.

There is no doubt that there are prejudices loose in the world—prejudices loose in the United States—and people do suffer, but they suffer in their present persons and not in their generations. It would be very helpful if that issue were clarified by making this distinction, that it is a present deprivation that is the issue and not some alleged genetic inheritance.

> Moderator Ruiz responded to the comments of the panelists by pointing to the roots of the hostility toward bilingualism and the nature of the bilingual community. He also argued for a national allegiance that is based on equality of opportunity and results in cultural diversity.

Ramón Ruiz: One implication of what we have been discussing is that we have a language crisis that we have just discovered. Given what we know about that crisis, it is the Spanish language that is the danger. We have been overwhelmed by people who are of Mexican descent and speak Spanish. I share Noel Epstein's observation that the United States is not facing the demise of the dominance of the English language, but it is not an accident that this discussion is taking place in Los Angeles where Mexicans have settled and where we now have at least one million Mexicans.

George Brockway, I think, raised the point that language is often equated with culture, that people who speak a foreign language are presumed also to keep a foreign culture. I am not sure that is true. The assumption is that people of Mexican descent, many of whom speak Spanish and have a foreign culture, do not bear allegiance to the United States. A careful reading of major American newspapers—the *Washington Post, New York Times,* and *Los Angeles*

Times—indicates that this view seems to come at a time of great fear and insecurity in the United States. I suggest that perhaps the old book by Oswald Spengler, *The Decline of the West,* might be profitable reading at the present time. In other words, as we have become very conservative, more so than we have been in the past, these views come out.

Another implication of the major questions raised by the conference paper concerns anti-foreign-language hysteria, which is endemic to United States history. When I entered the army I used to hear such things as "Talk American, boy" coming from Missourians. I also recall reading that use of the German language in this country was banned in the First World War. And I am old enough to remember the attack on Japanese-language schools here in California during the Second World War.

The reality is that most Americans, not all but most, have traditionally distrusted neighbors who spoke more than just English. Richard Hofstadter of Columbia University, in his book *Anti-Intellectualism in American Life,* insisted this was an offshoot of that long and traditional practice of anti-intellectualism in American life. We are not in danger of losing our unity or our identity because of a language threat. Language is not the issue.

The basic question is both economic and social. Languages, "foreign languages" if you wish to call them that, survive in the United States and have always survived in the United States until the immigrant groups using them get ahead. Past history of American life shows that assimilation follows jobs and upward mobility. Therefore, why do some people of Mexican descent in the United States continue to speak Spanish? Actually most Americans of Mexican descent do not, especially those who are the most successful in terms of upward mobility. The Chicano movement is not an expression of the Spanish-speaking group. It is an expression of those who have moved beyond language and are concerned about other issues.

There are two groups that continue to speak Spanish, and they are very unlike each other. One, of course, is the large group of poor people of Mexican descent in the United States who have been denied the fruits of the American Dream. This group speaks Spanish because it has not been given the opportunity to move into the mainstream of life in the United States. Then there is a tiny group, an almost miniscule group, of educated intellectuals, cultured, sophisticated people who do speak Spanish and who are almost binational by cultural definition. And they have established a bridge between Mexico and the United States. They often live in border cities, places like El Paso, Laredo (but not San Diego, which is a curious border town). They are a minority of privileged intellectuals, whether they are in business or in education.

But those who speak only the Spanish language and maintain it for a long period of time are those who have been denied opportunity to change and advance. These are the victims of discrimination and prejudice, and if we are concerned about unity and disunity, if that is a major worry for all of us, and if we define that in terms of language, there is an obvious solution to the problem. It is to stop discrimination and prejudice, to open the gates of opportunity to all, to make equal opportunity a fact, not simply in theory but also in practice.

The issue we are discussing here raises a number of questions about goals. Where are we going? What do we want to do with ourselves in the United States? What kind of country do we want to build? We all agree that we want a strong country. Most of us would agree that we want a rich country—a country rich in culture and educational possibilities. We can define that in two ways. One, of course, is to offer equality of opportunity and equal results to all in the socio-economic area. This includes Hispanics, obviously at the bottom of the ladder, the twenty million who will appear in the next census. But the second thing that leads to richness in a plural society is a variety in cultures and languages where cultures meet on an equal plane, where Americans of all backgrounds profit and enrich the society because they are different, because they speak different languages. Thus we acquire something of a taste for foreign cultures. This is not a disadvantage. This is not a danger. It is not divisive.

Those who fear these things should remember that allegiance to the United States, our country, cannot be legislated. It has to come through opportunity. Allegiance is won by making the United States the kind of country that makes people proud to be Americans, and that, of course, comes down to equality: equality of opportunity, equality of jobs, equality of respect, and obviously, in the long run, equality of results.

Reiterating that the Japanese accepted American culture—even its worst dimensions—Donald Hata pointed out that domestic nativism closed off continued cultural ties between Japanese in the United States and those in Japan, and that Mexican-Americans are now similarly threatened.

Donald Hata: That fact that Japanese-Americans today are so well accepted in relevant because about the turn of the century people were meeting in groups, probably much like this one, talking about all those Japanese immigrants. They were going to inundate California. They were not Christian. They worked on the Sabbath. They did not do anything at night. You never saw them at the opera, or at any community functions. They simply reproduced. Western civilization was threatened.

And what has happened? The nativists were all wrong. The nativists were the ones who should have had more faith in the appeal of whatever-it-is we call American culture, insipid as it is. (Cello-wrapped carrots are more expensive but somehow inherently better than those in the vegetable bin uncello-wrapped. McDonald's hamburgers. Colonel Sanders. We are even exporting this to the land of my ancestors, and they thrive on it.) There is something compelling about being an American in spite of the insipid, mundane, mindless qualities of those elements of our culture that do not have any links to the Old World roots. We should be very careful of arguments that are being used today: the numbers game—there are so many of them and they continue to come in; they are going to take away jobs. This could be a straw issue.

It happened with the Japanese, and what was the result? One reason why my immediate predecessors had to acculturate was because they were cut off from their own culture by the nativist theme that I see dangerously behind these kinds of discussions—not intentionally, perhaps, but there nonetheless. There was a drastic change in immigration policies in 1924, and Japanese immigration was simply cut off. I do not rule out such an action as a possibility with respect to American foreign policy in the future, because some tricky things are now being done to policy regarding Mexican nationals who are laborers in this country.

> For David Maciel, social status as well as the close ties between nativism and hostile attitudes toward educating minorities remain the critical themes.

David Maciel: Perhaps if we looked at the Mexican-American community and the Cuban community, we would get a very good idea of the policies toward bilingual education. It comes down to the social hierarchy of this country, particularly in the Southwest where the Mexican-American community has always served as a cheap labor force. If we look at every southwestern state from California to Texas, we see that the great agricultural, mining, and other empires were made with the toil of Mexicans. As a Texas grower said around the turn of the century, "I'm all for educating people, but once you start to educate Mexicans they stop working."

In Miami the question has not been as heated. The letters to the editor have not been as passionate as here. In Arizona when bilingual ballots were printed, for three weeks there were repeated letters to the editor about squandering all those millions on such an unimportant thing as assisting Spanish-speaking people to vote.

As late as 1974-1975 the media in this country were very anti-Mexican immigration—perhaps not the *Washington Post* but certainly *Newsweek* and *Time.* Even ex-CIA director William Colby was quoted in various interviews as saying that the greatest threat to the United States in the upcoming decades was not the Soviet Union or China; it was this silent invasion of people coming from Mexico into the United States.

Shortly thereafter, Gallup took a poll on this question; and the poll showed very clearly, although for some reason it was not well publicized, that 89 percent of the people in this country who were polled did not at that time want any further immigration to this country, particularly Mexican immigration. Why? Colby, in various of his interviews, stated that it was because the Mexican-American population was going to grow. They were going to change and shift the balance in voting power, in education. They would create social problems in the Southwest.

For the Mexican-American community, bilingualism and biculturalism were clearly tied to the question of dominance. Historically, that has been well outlined.

> Heated debate has not always accompanied efforts to utilize for-
> eign languages but it would be an error, argued Noel Epstein, to
> believe that the Cubans in Miami escaped it. Furthermore, he ob-
> served, no policy about equality of opportunity can assure equality
> of results.

Noel Epstein: It was stated that Americans have always distrusted those who speak a language other than English. Historically, the distrust has been most notable during difficult times,
either war periods—1917-1918 and 1941-1945—or bad economic
times, when jobs were threatened. That is another link between
economics and culture. It certainly goes back to Benjamin
Franklin's concerns about the Germans in Pennsylvania.

But it is not always there; in better times people do not feel as
threatened. When we are in more pressed and troubled times, as
we have been for fifteen years, this type of issue does arise. There
must be more equal opportunity, but there is not anything that one
can actually create, at least through government, that will provide
absolutely equal opportunity. There are many arguments about
equal results; there is at least an arguable question whether one can
expect or require equal results.

In response to David Maciel's point that there was not as heated
a debate in Miami as elsewhere: in fact, there has been a very
heated debate over the bilingual issue in Miami. I have even been
told—although I did not have a chance to confirm this—that some
Cuban-American leaders wanted to stop some of the bilingual
programs because too many English-speaking children were learning Spanish and becoming too competitive for the jobs that require
Spanish.

Contrary to what is popularly believed, it is still very much an
open question about how large the American community of Mexican descent is in this country. Some very prominent members of
that community believe that it is not anywhere near twenty or
twenty-two million people. David Broder of the *Washington Post*
quoted Joseph Aragon, the former Carter-White House aide, as
saying the estimate everybody is talking about is setting up some

very high expectations that will in no way be fulfilled. The census figure is going to be more like fifteen million. The Black population is far larger than that, speaking in the context of Black-Hispanic tensions that are out there. It is a mistake to assume that the Mexican-American population will prove to be so large, and certainly a mistake to assume that most of the people will necessarily be Spanish-speakers.

There are new studies—including one in California that has caused quite a fuss—that have to do with speaking, not with reading and writing. One study, commissioned by the federal government, by people who were generally sympathetic to the bilingual-education movement, states there is absolutely no threat, certainly not anything like the Quebec experience. They talk about erosion in native language use among language-minority groups, including (although not as extensively) the Hispanic population. There is very serious erosion in use of Spanish at all levels—reading, writing, speaking, understanding.

Ramón Ruiz: A large number of people of Mexican descent do not speak Spanish or certainly do not speak it well. But I have never believed that the issue was merely language.

Noel Epstein: We do not disagree. Even fewer read and write it well, according to the evidence. The same thing is true of Yiddish and a lot of other languages.

Ramón Ruiz: This is not simply an American experience. Many years ago I published a book on Mexican education, and a part dealt with the Mexican experience with so-called Indian groups. All the attitudes that we have here in the United States can be found in Mexico, and not simply in the recent past, but beginning with the Spanish conquest. Anthropologist Shirley Brice Heath in her book *Telling Tongues* details this clash between those who would deny people the right to speak a native language and those who would preserve it as a cultural asset.

In Mexico people have learned that you cannot stamp out an Indian language. There are as many people speaking an Indian language today, as many people classified as Indians, as in 1920 or 1930. The Mexican experience is one of a terrible inequality in society, where the poor today are poorer than they were in 1940, and the gap between the rich and the poor is wider today than it was in 1940. What we have learned from the Mexican experience is that language is a defense mechanism. People use their native language not simply because they cannot learn other languages, not simply because they do not have equality of opportunity, but because it is a wonderful way of defending oneself against the exploiter, which in this case was the majority of the Mexican population.

We are not going through anything uniquely American. My guess is that what we are going through is what is experienced by most countries that have various language groups in their midst with a clash of values and cultures because of social and economic issues.

The moderator invited comments and questions from the floor. The first speaker was Professor Nathan Glazer of the Graduate School of Education, Harvard University, who challenged the panel to reassess the issue in terms of past national policy.

Nathan Glazer: There is more of an issue than the members of the panel suggest, and even some legitimacy to the evocative questions raised in the background paper for the conference. Does the fact that this is now an English-speaking society relate to policy decisions of the past—policy decisions which members of the panel might disagree with or find objectionable, but taken in order to achieve that result? Or is this an English-speaking society because American culture, insipid as some might insist that it is, is so attractive that regardless of any policies we had, the result we have today would have followed? In other words, if one could have become an American citizen without knowing English, let us say, would it have mattered? Had there been constitutional requirements and defenses and Supreme Court decisions that required some actions in the mother tongues of students, would we have the same dominance of English today? Were the policies we adopted in the past related to what we are today? Will the policies we are adopting now relate to what we will be in the future? I am not saying that what we will be is not much better than what we are. I think that panel members implied that these policies are terrible and in some sense are not related to what we became.

Noel Epstein: It is self-evident that many actions were taken to promote the use of English among immigrant groups, refugee groups, and indigenous groups as well. In the earlier part of this century there was widespread fear of South and East European refugees. We had policies toward the American Indians involving boarding schools and the removal of children from their parents and from their culture.

Would things have worked out differently without official policies? I am very reluctant to try to rewrite history, particularly in such a complicated area as this. It is true and implicit in one part of Professor Glazer's questions that there was a large voluntary element to adoption of the English language and American culture, however you may define what being an American is. (I do not know how to define an American.) There is no question that, regardless of government action, many of the parents voluntarily urged their children to learn English, and the children became the translators in the home in typical situations and taught the parents English. Frequently, of course, the problem was much greater for the parents than it was for the children. Children, particularly in younger ages, have much greater flexibility at adapting to new cultures and learning new languages, although this too has been questioned.

What would have happened otherwise, I just will not speculate. Admittedly there were laws on the subject in most states, if not all. I do not know how many said that classes could be taught only in English. I do not know whether that requirement forced something that otherwise would not have happened. My speculation, in which journalists sometimes are allowed to engage, is that, for the most part and with some large exceptions, we would have ended up where we are today.

Donald Hata: One of the entrapment qualities of these questions is that we are being asked to name some convenient generic enemy. Who did this? Who established the policy? The State of California prohibited any—as they called them—"Orientals" from attending the public schools and, therefore, cut them off before they even had any systematic chance of acculturating through language, and yet there was a great desire among the immigrants to learn English, not for any great love of country, but for the very reason they came here—to make a buck. If you wanted to get off that coolie team or stoop labor team and become an entrepreneur who was going to sell produce to the white man in the market, then you had to know a few words of English. That applies to a number of other immigrants as well.

David Maciel: It has been not so much directed policy that has influenced acculturation of Mexican-Americans, although people were categorized and were reprimanded for speaking Spanish. This was true in schools even in such predominantly Spanish-speaking cities as San Antonio, El Paso, and Albuquerque until the 1950s. But there is an even broader question: How were Latins portrayed in the society as a whole? *That* is the image Mexican-American children growing up were seeing around them in the media, in textbooks, and in movies. This is the reference of the question being raised. We should not consider only policies in law but also societal views. Those views were very important in a child's formulation of his own identity.

A second question and comment from the floor came from a representative of the Northrop Corporation, a major employer in the Los Angeles metropolitan area.

Donald Page: We are trying to get more Hispanics into our company, and we are having great difficulty. I have spent hours recruiting in East Los Angeles. We open store-front hiring halls, and no-one comes in to speak to us.

But the thing that really bothers me in talking about bilingualism is what do we mean by "bi"? Do you realize that in this city we may have the largest Korean community outside of Seoul, and we brag that we have the largest Hispanic community outside of Mexico City. We also have a very large Japanese population, second outside Japan only to Hawaii, I think. So when we talk about "bi," what language are we talking about?

George Brockway: I would agree that there is a question of definition. And I would go a step further. It seems to me that a real issue that has not been discussed gets over into politics—the printing of ballots in Spanish and in some other languages. This performs an act of self-segregation that puts those who are unable to read English enough to vote an English ballot at the mercy of their leaders. This is rather like the situation that Karl Marx describes. The small peasants of France have parallel interests but no national interest, and their parallel interests lead them to support Louis Napoleon, and it ends with Louis Napoleon running them. He becomes their boss. This is historically what has happened to every ethnic group. The political leader turns out to be not just a leader but a boss. This is because the society being so led cannot be perpetuated because of the language barrier. Why *do* people want bilingual ballots?

Noel Epstein: The foreign language ballot is much more an effort to give access to the right to vote than an effort to promote use of that language and officially recognize it. As for it being "self-segregating," my impression is that there is choice in ballots. A voter is not automatically given a ballot that segregates him. As for "bi" in "bilingual," the "bi" happens to be aimed at the individual, not at the society. We are talking about a multilingual, multicultural society which, incidentally, is very different in degree from the Canadian or Belgian experience. There are certainly language minority groups in Quebec, for example, that are not French and that are getting "zapped" along with others in the whole Francophone movement. The word "bi" refers to individuals.

One problem has been that bilingual programs have been very poorly implemented. That does not mean that bilingual education will "solve" the learning problems of the children involved; there has been a very misleading suggestion for years that there was a cause-and-effect relationship between language and doing poorly in school. There is as large a relationship, if not a larger one, between being poor and doing poorly in school. Spanish-speaking children who are poor and disadvantaged are probably going to suffer the same problems as do English-speaking children who are poor and disadvantaged.

One must understand that bilingual programs, as supported by Washington and in most states that have separate state programs, are assimilationist programs. This is what is troubling ethnic leaders who worry that there might be too much success. Then they will weaken their ties to the "rabbis" and the "priests" of the movement. I would rather see the students and youth and adults get bread, and later I will worry about the caviar, about reading *Don Quixote* in Spanish. If the kid is poor and reading poetry in Spanish in the East Los Angeles barrio, it does not impress me at all.

The Canadian Commissioner of Official Languages, Maxwell F. Yalden, returned to the line of questions taken by Professor Nathan Glazer.

Maxwell Yalden: I am puzzled by this panel, particularly by Noel Epstein, who, if I recall correctly, began by telling us that the questions put in the background paper for this conference were not real questions. Indeed, he told us it could be dangerous for the present programs of bilingualism in the United States to pose such questions. Yet, if I understood him just a few seconds ago, he was saying that there is a real issue, a very serious issue. Perhaps he could tell us a little more clearly what the real issue is in the United States, because as I look from north of the border it does not seem very clear.

I would also add that there does seem to be a tendency to be rather dismissive of this question, which is a policy question for the conference. The panel has not shown in any way that it is not an important question, and I do hope that they will do so now or tell us what *is* the important question.

One final observation. I am not a demographer or statistician, but I do know enough not to make predictions about how many Hispanics will be counted in the 1980 census. Noel Epstein knows that many people will not turn out to answer that census, and the total, whether fifteen or twenty million, will not be a great deal more accurate than it is now. Again, looked at from Canada, it is a large number and the concentration is very interesting.

Noel Epstein: I am not a scholar but a journalist; I try very hard to be careful in what I say. The United States is not facing the question embraced in the conference statement which reads: "The United States is on the verge of making a set of decisions that will shape its culture, its politics, and its society for generations to come. The issue that subsumes them all is contained in two questions: Should the United States become, in law and practice, a country in which two or more languages share official status and are used widely in public life, in business and education and government"—which suggests the Canadian-type model—"or should the primacy of English be maintained?" There is nobody facing that decision that I am aware of; that is not a question facing any policy maker in Washington or in most states that I know of.

There *are* questions facing those policy makers, particularly as they apply to bilingual education, which is the area that I have concentrated on. It has been settled policy in Washington that the bilingual education program, Title VII of the Elementary and Secondary Education Act, as passed again in 1978, is a transitional program—is assimilationist. Therefore, in San Francisco the federally funded part of the program involving Chinese-speaking students will have a transitional requirement. It will have a five-year limit. Maintenance programs will not be required, though they have always been available to the population of any state that wanted to set them up voluntarily. Neither in the courts nor in the national legislature is anybody facing the question of whether to make Spanish an official language.

There are certainly issues, particularly in the bilingual education area, that I have tried to cope with for many years, and the main issue grows out of a lot of misunderstanding. The issues have to do with the role of the federal government generally in bilingual/bicultural education.

First, how do you best help students learn in English? How do you get them into English-language classrooms, which has been the primary objective of Washington from the outset of the program. Should there be any uniform, national requirement coming out of the Office of Civil Rights based on equal opportunity, or should the local school districts be given flexibility in trying more than one approach, since all the evidence suggests that there is no one best way to help these students?

Second is the maintenance issue, which again and again has been rejected in Washington. There have been suggestions from people like Joshua Fishman of Yeshiva University, who made a plea for maintenance. Even Josue Gonzalez, who is now head of the Title VII program, will tell you that it is overwhelmingly a program designed to teach English. The problem with the maintenance issue is that it gets confused with "language equality," which is not what most people in the bilingual-education movement want. They would be more than satisfied, I think, if students were offered the choice of continuing to learn just one class during the school day in their native language after they have become proficient in English. In other words, this "maintenance" would be just a variation on a traditional foreign-language program.

There is no feeling of jitters among the general population about teaching second languages in this country. In the school setting, where you have what might be called among the education jargonists "limited maintenance," we are not advocating teaching physics or any other subject in the native language.

The greatest problem in the bilingual-education movement today is that bilingual education and bilingualism as practiced are diametrically opposed. No doubt it will confuse many people, but bilingualism is not promoted by bilingual education in this country. Almost all bilingual education here is intended to move children into English-speaking classrooms. And language- and cultural-maintenance programs do not, for the majority of bilingual education advocates, mean "language equality." "Maintenance" and "language equality" unfortunately have been equated in people's minds; it is that kind of thing that prompts the appalling reaction expressed by Tom Bethell in his piece in the February 1979 issue of *Harpers*, suggesting that those who want bilingual education are those who never liked America to begin with and want the country to fall apart. I suggest that raising the question as it was raised in the conference paper is going to generate that same kind of reaction, needlessly threatening those very programs that are designed to help the kids move on into English.

I would hope that children could maintain their native languages to the extent that they have at least a voluntary opportunity to continue them in one class—not 50-50, half the class in one language, and half the class in the other, but a single class. For the rest, so far as maintaining the native language is concerned, I would leave it where it has always been: in the family and in the home, in the ethnic group, in the church and in the synagogue. But those are volatile issues in this country because they prompt very emotional and irrational reactions, and what is really needed is some calm discussion.

According to moderator Ramón Ruiz, the issue has ramifications that Noel Epstein did not explore; in fact, reinforcing and enhancing cultural integrity should be one key aspect of bilingual education.

Ramón Ruiz: Noel Epstein has talked about the technical side of bilingual education, but there is another side that is even more important. The goal is not to make people bilingual (although that may result in some cases), but essentially to teach English. It is not unique to the United States, it was developed in Mexico long before it was employed here. It was developed as a response to the failure to teach a dominant language directly. The direct approach has not worked, for obvious reasons. The economic question is basic to all of that.

But there is another element for those who have a Spanish background and that has to do with the fact that they are an easily distinguishable minority. There is the question of color, a question of physical characteristics. Both are crucial here, as is the sense of inferiority, of insecurity that comes from being placed in this position in the United States, sentiments brought by poor families from Mexico. All of this is, of course, exacerbated here in the United States.

Hispanic culture (the culture of Spain and Portugal) until recently was unrecognized as important for the teaching of European culture, history, and languages. Children who go through public schools sense this directly; they do not have to be told, they know it immediately. There is an absence of Hispanic role models in public or private education. Therefore, the teaching of a foreign language, Spanish in this case, is much more than simply a language exercise. It is a way of communicating to the students that there *is* a language that is equal to English. There is a grammar to it, a sense of importance to it. That is a part of what we are talking about. Although it may not be noticeable to those who are not of Hispanic descent, to those who *are* of Hispanic descent it is especially important, crucially important.

The question of language here is not simply a linguistic problem, a technical problem of how to teach English through another language, be it Spanish or something else. It is also a cultural question. To ignore this is to misunderstand what is involved.

The fact is that no-one is here at this conference because of language, because of wanting to maintain Spanish as a wonderful part of the United States. I have never heard anyone say that— even the most bitter Chicanos have never said that, or if they said it, it was out of anger and frustration and despair. But what is missing here is the recognition that the problem exists not because these people have created it, but because of the absence of opportunity.

To go back to American history and ask whether this was legislated in the beginning begs the question, because no matter if or how you legislate, the problem is not going to go away. It is there. It is a reality, because something does not work within our society, and until we grapple with that we are not going to answer the question. We are not even going to be asking the right question.

The rejoinders did not satisfy Commissioner Yalden. An exchange followed.

Maxwell Yalden: I am not at all convinced by Noel Epstein. There are a lot of people in this country who think that the question in the conference paper is a serious one, including those who put it in the program. We are all well aware what Washington policy is on transitional versus maintenance, but the fact remains that there is a rather large number of people who believe in the maintenance point of view.

Noel Epstein: I was not suggesting that there are not many people, essentially in the Hispanic community, who want to see maintenance, but many if not all of them, so far as I am aware, have already resigned themselves to the fact that maintenance probably will have to come out of private efforts, not out of government-sponsored efforts in the public schools. And that is why we in the United States will not have to decide about making bilingualism "official," which was the question posed in the conference paper. Whatever happens on the private level, nobody questions the right or the needs of individual families or individual persons to maintain their languages and cultures.

Maxwell Yalden: Do members of the panel of Hispanic back-ground and their associates agree that maintenance should not be a publicly-financed program in this country?

> There was no direct response to Commissioner Yalden's question. Donald Hata felt this was a matter for the later panel on education. David Maciel was more interested in the economic and political dimensions of bilingualism and the reasons why there have been responses outside the Hispanic community to demands for bilingual/bicultural programs. He was also concerned about the structure of bilingual programs.

David Maciel: The question raised earlier about the equality of programs gets back to economics. Every bilingual program that I have seen has had serious limitations. The programs were de-signed with those limitations and were designed to fail. That the implementation, the training, the input were inadequate is based on economic concerns.

Bilingual/bicultural education has to be looked at in the broad spectrum of the Chicano struggle; it was one proposal for bringing about social change. That is, Chicano academics, communities, people, students, teachers saw the unresponsiveness of the educa-tional system among many other injustices in this country and they turned, as one possible solution, to bilingual/bicultural education. And look what happened. It was as a direct response to that pressure that bilingual/bicultural programs were started through-out the Southwest. Chicano studies, too, were not started because people really believed in the positive values of the cultural pluralistic model or in some of the issues that we have been talking about today; they were started by pressure, by pressure from community leaders, activists, legislators.

We have to take into account how people responded to that pressure. What were their attitudes? If we did that kind of analysis, we would see some of the problems that bilingual/bicultural edu-cation has had. Even today the advanced reports of the census, which were in March 1978, show that the dropout rate has not significantly bettered for Chicanos than before bilingual/bicultural programs were started. Nor is the number of Chicano students entering the university particularly better as a whole. Educational statistics today, in spite of bilingual/bicultural programs, in spite of

Chicano studies and other things, show results not particularly as successful as people in the late 1960s and early 1970s perhaps thought they would be. Bilingual/bicultural education has to be looked at in the complexity of the Chicano struggle. Our people saw it as an alternative to something that obviously was not working.

The Secretary for the North American Ministries, Hispanic Board for Missions, Lutheran Church-Missouri Synod, wanted definitions.

Carlos Puig: It would be helpful for all of us if we get our terminology correct, and I would like to hear the panel define bilingual, bilingualism, bicultural, and biculturalism. I think this is extremely important because we are actually using the word "bilingual" when what we mean is language as a second language.

Noel Epstein: Many people have debated this very question in scholarly journals for a long time. Most agree there is no such thing as being completely bilingual. We tend to use different vocabularies for different situations: certain vocabularies for personal relations at home and in neighborhoods, another vocabulary in schools and jobs. We also are never, so far as I am aware, equally proficient in two languages. There is no such thing as that kind of balance. What is meant by being bilingual is having some significant degree of proficiency in both languages.

Unfortunately, what is happening under many of the programs, as David Maciel suggested, is that many people are coming out bi-illiterate, which is a very serious problem. It sounds funny but it is not funny at all; the kids out there do not have much of a chance in life as a result of it. It is very sad.

"Bicultural education" essentially means teaching in the native language the history associated with the language.

Ramón Ruiz: I have met bilingual people. It is difficult but possible to be so. But bilingualism is not biculturalism. I have rarely met a bicultural person. Many Americans have learned to speak Spanish fluently, even perfectly. Yet I have never met a North American who was bicultural because that is a question of values. It is being able to feel values in two different cultures—to feel them in the same way, to sympathize with the aspirations of people with a different culture and overcome patriotic and nationalistic barriers. That is extremely difficult to do. You come down on one side, because language does not give you the cultural dualism that some people assume comes with language. Language is a technical proficiency just as learning to play the piano is. That is a very different thing.

Noel Epstein: I disagree very strongly. Language is absolutely central to culture, not some kind of technicality. It is the central part of culture, and to suggest that it is a technical thing, some technical proficiency, is beyond my comprehension. I really do not agree with that at all.

> The nature of American culture, aside from language, and the origin of American culture, were questions raised by Ricardo Fernández, professor of education, University of Wisconsin-Milwaukee.

Ricardo Fernández: As a student of the American experience, especially ethnicity, I have often wondered if there is something that has evolved as this country has developed over the last two hundred years that uniquely relates to the issue of culture. In particular I am a bit puzzled by the reluctance of the panel to address the issue of culture and biculturalism.

If we look at, for example, France, before we can talk about it we must understand that France is a combination. In other words, the consciousness, the nationalism that creates something called "France" has evolved over many, many centuries. It is a defined geographical area, a fairly homogeneous set of people sharing the same language, the same culture, much the same religion; and ultimately in the sixteenth century somebody said, this is France. It is really the result of a long process.

In the case of the United States, the process is the other way around. It starts with a number of people somewhat homogeneous who declared some two centuries ago that this is the United States, and subsequent to that, millions of people came into this country from different racial backgrounds, different religious backgrounds, different linguistic backgrounds, different political ideologies—probably the most diverse migration that has ever taken place in world history. When we talk about "an American," it seems to me it is a very different kind of thing from a resident of France saying, "I am a Frenchman."

So I wonder, when we talk about what constitutes an American in this debate on bilingualism/biculturalism, what exactly do we mean? Are we talking about a common set of values, as Ramón Ruiz has pointed out? What are those common core values that everybody agrees on? I was thinking as I listened to Donald Hata (relative to the Los Angeles desegregation case) that there are some sociologists who say that, for the sake of school desegregation, the traditional definition of minorities should not include Asian-Americans because by all standards they are so successful that they are not subject to discrimination of any kind. And I know that there are some Asian-American scholars who clearly disagree very strongly with eminent sociologists who are going before courts as experts. My question is, what exactly is American culture? How does that fit into this whole debate on bilingualism/biculturalism? Why is it that Americans a generation or more removed from immigration have been so reluctant to learn other languages?

Donald Hata: I find it impossible to go beyond what I have already said in describing American culture. That which is not tied or linked to Old World roots across either the Atlantic or Pacific is insipid or mundane. Perhaps it need not be so insipid and mundane and mindless, if we realize that multiculturalism is a very real part of our lives.

George Brockway: I would like to take exception. While there are some linguists who hold that language and culture are essentially identical, it is by no means a majority of linguists. It is only one very small school of linguists extending from Herder and it is not the majority school of linguists today.

On the question of culture and of values, I agree with Donald Hata. This is not a sociological question but a historical question. American culture is American history. This has been obscured for generations of Americans. It has been obscured by the widespread practice in American schools of teaching not history but something called "problems of democracy." We find in American history our common heritage. Lincoln is our common heritage, regardless of where we came from. So are Washington, Jefferson, and all the rest. The broad culture is also a common heritage. Cervantes is as much mine as Ramón Ruiz's, although I have to read him in Putnam's translation rather than in Spanish. This is a historical question, and this is what culture is. Culture is not a public opinion survey or a sociological balance of whatever sociologists balance.

A Canadian conferee from the Department of the Secretary of State, Ottawa, asked if the American habit of monolingualism denied this country a valuable resource.

Gilbert H. Scott: I would just like to mention that in the Canadian experience we believe that we have a number of people who are fluently bilingual. About a year ago at another conference, a comment was made that the United States, by having followed a policy of unilingualism, either by intent or by default, has deprived itself of a very valuable natural resource, and that is the facility to function in many languages, and by extension has not done as well as it might have in international affairs. Would the panel like to comment on that?

The moderator considered this a very significant point and ended the discussion by commenting on it.

Ramón Ruiz: I have just finished a review of a book done by two *Miami Herald* reporters—*The Winds of December*—a study of the fall of the Batista regime. It contains two hundred interviews with Cubans of all walks of life, both in the United States and in Cuba. Earl Smith, the United States ambassador in those troubled times, did not know a word of Spanish and could communicate with the Cubans only through a translator. This is a comment on the point you are raising. There have been many people who have been abroad representing the United States who would have done a much better job had they known a foreign language.

Implications of Bilingualism:
Education

Perhaps the most critical area of discussion of bilingualism/ biculturalism in contemporary society is education. Dean Stephen Knezevich of the University of Southern California's School of Education moderated the panel on that subject, and the participants were Pastora San Juan Cafferty, associate professor at the School of Social Service Administration, University of Chicago; Ricardo Fernández, associate professor of education, University of Wisconsin-Milwaukee, and director of the Midwest National Origin Desegregation Assistance Center; Josue Gonzalez, director of bilingual education and minority languages affairs for the U.S. Department of Education; Sharon Robinson, director of instruction and professional development, National Education Association; Abigail Thernstrom, lecturer at Harvard University and author; and James Gordon Ward, director of research, American Federation of Teachers.

Dean Knezevich referred to the classic objective of a system of education as transmission of the cultural heritage of a nation. Part of our heritage, he said, "we recognize as being uniquely American, but what of other cultures? Things that make us great perhaps can also help generate controversy."

Josue Gonzalez spoke first. Although his duties include directing the Title VII program of the Elementary and Secondary Education Act, largest funding source for bilingual education in the country, he would not at the outset defend the narrow basis for bilingual teaching under current legislation. He preferred to speak within the less restrictive generic concept of the subject, and his remarks demonstrated a philosophical and intellectual commitment to learning, more than one language and to retaining languages learned at home.

Josue Gonzalez: I am very pro-bilingualism, perhaps because my professional life has been dedicated to the study and teaching of languages. It is healthy to be bilingual/bicultural, however that term may be defined. Bilingualism and bilingual education are as American as apple pie. We have always as a society and as an educational community favored the teaching and learning of languages. We have in the past even required people to be knowledgeable in more than one language in order to award them higher degrees, which I regret has not always been true in the recent past.

Education has a much broader mandate than simply to teach math and science and reading and writing in one language. We also have a responsibility to prepare young people for the world, and in doing so we need to teach those communication skills that are important in other countries as well as this one. Ours has been an ethnocentric educational system. We have been inadequate in teaching and learning languages. We ought to do something about that, and, if we value the teaching and learning of languages for all students, then it is an error to say that people who are already bilingual should stop being bilingual and that we should teach languages only to those who do not already speak them. That seems very undemocratic.

The recent report of the President's Commission on Foreign Languages and International Studies made some very strong recommendations. Languages are a national asset. They are individual and group assets. They are not liabilities. They increase our capability to communicate and understand each other and, therefore, they should be promoted. It is much better, in my opinion, to have a level of language proficiency in more than one language (which might be called bilingualism) than to have a tokenistic, passing acquaintance with language, as happens in so many cases, particularly as a result of public education where having studied

French or Spanish or German for a year or two, one is still unable to communicate in that language with native speakers.

Pastora Cafferty, who has completed a number of projects and studies on Hispanics in the United States, was concerned about the special need for bilingual education experienced by Puerto Rican and Mexican-American laborers who live in a pattern of cyclical migration. Her discussion of the issues was unique, and she raised questions that were new to many attending the conference.

Pastora Cafferty: There are a number of arguments for and against bilingualism in this country, particularly regarding Hispanics. They are political, pedagogical, cultural, and philosophical. I am using the term "bilingual education" to mean education in two languages to the degree that an individual is functional and literate in both.

First, bilingual education is necessary, indeed essential, for Hispanics, and I will try to show why. Second, transitional bilingual education is necessary culturally and important for other migrants to retain their own culture, but it may be transitional education that is sufficient. And third, acquiring a second language is a cultural enrichment, a good thing for monolingual speakers in this country, as good as acquiring a knowledge of art or literature. The three must be separated or they become confused.

The history of bilingual education in this country really is very complex. The parochial schools maintained bilingual education until the Second World War, but publicly funded bilingual-education programs date back to 1843 in the city of Cincinnati for the Germans and continued until the First World War. The Germans have an excellent history of it in the Midwest. There were some publicly funded bilingual-education programs in Louisiana and in the Southwest. It is interesting to note that even after New Mexico adopted a law banning the teaching of two languages in its schools, it was allowed because of the unrest that would have been brought about had the law been enforced. However, most bilingual education has been transitional. Immigrants for the first and second generations have gone to their language schools, and as they became more fully integrated into American society, economically perhaps, or moved away from their original community, they tended to go to monolingual English-language schools.

Hispanics are different, because of a very serious fact—that of cyclical migration. Wherever a country has contiguous borders, the labor market dictates a cyclical migration. This is true in Central and South America, and to some extent in Europe and the African countries. We are no different. And cyclical migration for the Hispanics is no different than it is for the Canadians, although Canadians, being English-speaking, are cyclical migrants that we barely notice. Mexicans, Central Americans, Cubans (who are not cyclical migrants) are another problem. Individuals who travel between two monolingual societies need to be bilingual in order to survive. ✓

While we tend to lump Hispanics together, the Puerto Rican experience is different. Puerto Ricans are American citizens traveling within national boundaries between two monolingual societies. They tend to travel between the island and the mainland in five- to seven-year cycles, and studies show that it is not a matter of going back to the island to retire. It is a matter of young families coming here and enrolling a child in school, pulling him out in the third or fourth grade and taking him to the island systems, which essentially are as monolingual as our own. Puerto Rico, in fact, does not have a history of bilingual education; it has a history of mixed monolingual systems imposed by the American federal government. Not until 1973 did the United States put money into Puerto Rico for bilingual programs. Therefore the Puerto Rican child, who is likely to move between San Juan and New York as any other American citizen is likely to move between Albuquerque and Chicago, is forced to deal with two monolingual societies without adequate provision to make him bilingual.

The extent of cyclical migration for Mexicans is harder to determine. However, recent studies show that as many as 90 percent of Mexican families in northern Mexican towns have had at least one member of the family live in the United States and work and return more than once. Very often these are families with young children.

We are not talking about creating a bilingual society; there is good reason for American monolingualism: we go from sea to shining sea with a dominant English-speaking society. We have a history of at least two centuries of English dominance both politically and economically, and we have some xenophobia and perhaps some legitimate fears of a nation of immigrants who, if they were not forced to learn English, would not be able to communicate with each other. A bilingual individual can participate both in his own society (whether it is in the barrio here or, more important, if he goes back to his own monolingual country) and in the English-speaking society. The pedagogical objectives are to create an individual who can function in both societies.

There is a good deal of controversy about how effectively this can be done. I agree with Noel Epstein's thesis that it has not been done well, but the argument to discontinue bilingual education or diminish it because it has not been done well, if applicable, would also end the teaching of math, reading, and writing in our public schools. We need an improvement in bilingual education and also a redefinition of the policy. Transitional programs will never do well now. I read a doctoral dissertation in which the author, writing about Spanish-speaking children in bilingual and monolingual programs, draws the conclusion that children in bilingual programs learn better in both languages. Some studies with French-Canadian children in Maine show that those in bilingual programs assimilate better—that is, they are comfortable living in the United States, they are comfortable with their French-speaking parents. The children in monolingual English programs reject their parents and have difficulty adjusting in school; and the children who are monolingual in French reject American society.

The bilingual individual should be able to function in both societies. This is a practical solution that will make the millions of Hispanics in this country able to assimilate—and the goal is assimilation—equally well here and also equally well at home.

The significance of civil rights legislation in the development of bilingual education was the primary concern of Ricardo Fernández, president-elect of the National Association for Bilingual Education. He felt that without strong efforts the cycle of inadequate education would only reinforce the inability of non-English-speaking children to function adequately in mainstream America.

Ricardo Fernández: In the United States, the recent use of languages other than English as a vehicle of instruction dates from the late 1950s. Instruction was then posed in terms of national defense. The country was threatened by Sputnik—the Russians were getting ahead in technology—it was in the interest of the United States to promote the learning of languages along with the study of hard sciences. That push has lasted through the present day, although it has diminished somewhat.

In the early 1960s, in part as a result of the civil rights movement and the efforts of Blacks to achieve equality of opportunity, there was some grumbling from the Southwest. For the first time the Civil Rights Commission made a study that included five states in the Southwest. It came up with some appalling statistics, showing that Chicanos and Mexican-Americans were falling miserably behind in school, dropping out, and in fact being deprived of any meaningful opportunity to get an adequate education and, therefore, to get ahead in society. As a result of the report, Congress began to discuss the issue, and Senator Ralph Yarborough from Texas initiated the idea that something be done for Mexican-Americans. He proposed the first version of the Bilingual Education Act, which focused exclusively on Spanish. But then somebody told Senator Yarborough that there were people in other language groups in the same situation. He said, "Then we have to define it not in terms of Spanish-speakers but of limited-English-speaking ability." The original legislation, passed and approved by Congress in the late 1960s, used that terminology.

Although it was a very modest effort initially, it grew significantly because the states picked up on the federal effort. A number of legal developments followed. The most important was the *Lau* decision, which provided added impetus. Since that time, many arguments have been offered for and against bilingual education. Some question it on the issue of achievement. Does it help achievement? Does it actually work? Fundamentally it could also be looked at in another dimension—discrimination as defined by civil rights legislation and by government agencies in charge of interpreting the *Lau* decision. As I understand that, we could look at bilingual education as a measure of equal opportunity to participate in educational programs that are offered by school districts. If, in fact, some individuals are unable to participate because they do not speak the language that is used to deliver that instruction, they are being deprived of their civil rights.

There are, in addition to the educational dimensions, some other areas in which this type of discrimination could be addressed. We could look at the delivery of social services. People who do not speak English in the city of New York have been found to receive significantly fewer services than English-speaking persons, yet they have the same needs and are all entitled to the same type of services. In the area of health care in California, the state code requires informed consent, but a number of women underwent sterilization, apparently consenting, who would never have done so had they known English. Thus, discrimination on the basis of language goes well beyond education.

It seems to me that fundamentally the issue is whether a child has a right to an intelligible education. The interpretation given so far by government agencies and by courts is that there is a duty on the part of the school system to take affirmative steps to "rectify the English-language deficiency." The question is how that is to be done. The Supreme Court in the *Lau* case stated: "It seems obvious that the Chinese-speaking minority receives less benefits than the English-speaking majority from respondent school system, which denies them a meaningful opportunity to participate in the educational program." The argument is simple: If the child does not understand the language of instruction, he is not going to be able to participate as fully as children who do. The question then becomes, what is the obligation of the school system to remedy that?

There are two approaches. One is to spend all the time teaching English, which means that children are not going to learn other subjects. The rationale for instruction using the home language is that while the child is learning English one can proceed to teach him content. An argument against this type of approach is that using the home language of the child for instructional purposes will somehow retard the acquisition of English language skills— both oral and reading and writing. Some studies have addressed that issue.

My experience has been with the area of compliance, working in one of the Lau centers. I find school districts very reluctant to change in any way to adapt their systems to serve the needs of the children. The question I am asked is, what is the minimum we have to do to get the feds off our backs? The minimum, unfortunately, becomes the maximum immediately. So we have an educational question that, because of the compliance issue, is resolved legally or by regulation.

> As spokesman for the American Federation of Teachers, James G. Ward, its director of research, was more interested in the idea that bilingualism is seen as a panacea for academic inadequacies and that there is a lack of solid research to sustain that premise. As a union representative, he was concerned too about the goals of any training program that might prepare students to survive in a complex industrial society.

James Ward: I have a friend, a veteran bilingual educator in New York City, who speaks frequently on this topic, and I will share his view with you. He often goes to the chalkboard and writes a number—40, 37, whatever—on the board and says, "Okay, that is the answer, what is the question?" And that is the way we approach bilingual education. Bilingual education has been perceived to be the answer, but what in fact is the question? It might be worthwhile, at least for the context of the question, to look first at the purposes of American public education.

This is, of course, a topic upon which there has not always been a consensus, but if we look at the development of American public education since the first public school in 1635 in Boston, certain things become clear. There are really three broad purposes of American public education. The first is economic. Obviously we educate our children to hold productive jobs and engage in worthwhile work experience. This is no simple task in our increasingly technological society; and our unemployment statistics point out the difficulty, particularly for certain segments of our society, such as young people. A very interesting article by Eli Ginzberg analyzes youth unemployment, pointing out that while the unemployment rate for Hispanic youth in this country is not as high as for Black youth, it is considerably higher than that for white youth. Ginzberg, who has devoted a lifetime to research on unemployment, says very simply that we have not yet done enough research in that area to draw a firm conclusion about the reasons, but certainly they need to be investigated, for they have serious implications for the kinds of educational programs we offer.

A second purpose of American public education is social, that is, preparation for life. The diversity we have had in education for social life in this country has been part of the richness of America and something we should encourage. A third purpose of American public education is political. Freeman Butts, an historian of education, traces this back to Jefferson, among others, and says that American education is not just training for citizenship or civic responsibility, not just preparation of individuals to take part in public life. American public schools have built a political cohesion; and while social diversity has built the richness of America, the political cohesiveness, Butts postulates, has been part of the strength of our democracy, one of the very valuable things the American school has contributed to our society.

I suggest that the context in which to consider the issue of non-English-speaking and limited-English-speaking children in this country is within the three purposes of public education, starting with the economic. Our first goal is to prepare our youth, regardless of their background, to take a full position in our economy. We need to prepare them for life also, to encourage the social diversity that has been so important in this country. And we must consider the political purposes of education—building political cohesion.

The American Federation of Teachers strongly favors bilingual education. We were one of the organizations in the mid-1960s to support the Title VII programs. We were actively involved with congressional staff in the educational amendments of 1978 that led to some changes in the law. We feel that the prime goal (but by no means the only goal) of bilingual education is mastery of English-language skills, not just one or two, but the full range of linguistic skills—reading, writing, listening, speaking. We relate these to the economic goals of education.

One of the difficulties is scarce resources. We must look at the efficiency and effectiveness of present programs, and until we have money to do all the things that the American public schools need to do for all of our children, English-language skills should remain the prime goal of bilingual education. Therefore, we favor transitional programs. (I do not like that term because the use of "transitional" versus "maintenance" only represents the intellectual barrenness in the field. The problem is far more complex than that. No two people define those words in a consistent manner.) We feel that students should be placed in a regular school program as soon as possible. This is a practice that lags because research lags. We need to do a great deal more in the assessment area.

We feel that much more needs to be done too in counseling students of non-English-speaking or limited-English-speaking backgrounds. And we are very concerned about the preparation of personnel, both in the training of new teachers for bilingual programs and in-service training of people already in our schools. Too often because of a lack of in-service training we have two faculties in a school—those in the bilingual program and those not. That should not be.

Again, we need more and better research. This is an area where, because of the newness of concentration on the field, not enough research is readily available. And there has not been work done to translate research into practice. Albert Shanker, the president of AFT, has pointed out that because of certain programs in certain school districts, and more particularly, because of the lack of programs in places where they are needed, we are in danger of creating a new class of handicapped individuals in this country— linguistically handicapped people who are not going to be able to compete in our increasingly technological economy.

We in the AFT are concerned about the best education for all children. Our country simply cannot afford anything less than this.

> Sharon Robinson of the National Education Association reported the policy of her organization as sympathetic to bilingual education as an instructional strategy. Speaking as a Black woman, she advocated multiculturalism but expressed profound concern about the politics associated with bilingual education, which seemed to her to focus less on the needs of children than on other more peripheral issues.

Sharon Robinson: The NEA, philosophically, has always held a strong commitment to equal educational opportunity, based on the fact that its membership comes from a wide range of backgrounds, both in geographical location and subject matter.

But the politics of bilingual-multicultural education suggest that the issue smacks of ethnocentrism on the part of both the advocates and the opponents. Too often discussion of the issue has become an emotional exchange relating to power more than to legality or egality. Some of us, while we resist buying into conspiracy theories, have begun to suspect that the biggest power play around this whole subject relates to the fact that we find ourselves engaged in debate while the educational needs of a large group of children go unattended. If the commitment to equal educational opportunity were real, perhaps we would not have to spend our time in discussion and debate about bilingual education.

Bilingual education recognizes an educational need that a specific group of children brings into an environment. Based on that recognition we should establish the program of instruction best suited to the needs of that particular group, and go on from there to help those children acquire skills needed for full participation within the American society. We have a commitment to realize that objective. But that is not what is happening. We have had some comments relating the tenuous nature of bilingual education to its newness and to the threat that assessment and evaluation might pose. There is also a threat in the suggestion that the program does not work and, therefore, might suffer from a withdrawal of funds.

We cannot ignore the fact that teachers who find themselves meeting a mandate to implement bilingual-educational programs tend to become frustrated. That frustration relates to confusion regarding the objectives of the program. Too often implementation has been based on political factors within the community having to do with providing jobs for members of a bilingual community, or on the exercise of political force by having the numerical power to define the program. The important educational factors are overlooked. We find that programs have been defined universally and very often leave little room for individual difference in terms of what might be best for a particular child. Teachers are in the middle. The in-service programs that have been provided to upgrade the skills of teachers have been inadequate. We find ourselves facing the somewhat untenable situation of defending the efficacy of the program when our training to carry it out has been inadequate. We have not been provided the resources necessary to implement the program properly.

The NEA's position has always been supportive of bilingual education as an instructional mandate, with bilingual education defined as an instructional program that depends on the student's primary language as the medium of instruction until he or she achieves English proficiency necessary to receive instruction in English. I do not know if this is transitional or maintenance. I am not sure that is important.

This definition of bilingual education is based on the following assumptions about teaching and learning. Non-English-speaking children must gain facility with the English language before being required or expected to function at an optimal level in an English-speaking environment. This is equal educational opportunity. This suggests that the child should not have to risk competition in an environment in which he cannot hope to compete successfully. When instruction is conducted in a language that the student comprehends, the curriculum objectives of the instruction are more likely to be achieved, especially if those objectives relate to the learning of English. Language is the most significant instructional medium, although it is only one in a repertoire of instructional media. Language must also accommodate the learning styles of students, and bilingual programs must be implemented in concert with other instructional programs. They should not be isolated. Non-English-speaking children should have an opportunity to interact with English-speaking peers so that all can benefit from social growth and language development that can occur through such interaction.

Bilingual education is often confused with language education or with multicultural education, both of which represent curriculum decisions rather than instructional decisions. Language education represents a decision to afford all students an opportunity to learn other languages; this should be encouraged. Multicultural education is a curriculum issue that involves an objective of recognizing and accepting and enhancing the ethnic and cultural diversity within our national citizenry. Bilingual programs can be implemented with either a positive or negative recognition of both of these curriculum issues. It is preferable that all children experience an instructional program and a curriculum which is designed and implemented in a manner that accepts and fully recognizes language education and multicultural education.

Concerned neither with the effectiveness nor the values related to bilingual education or bilingualism, Abigail Thernstrom, who has written extensively on this subject and lectures at Harvard University, centered her remarks on the origins and changes in the legislation that prompted the current bilingual movement.

Abigail Thernstrom: The issue of the educational value of bilingual education is one about which the most well-meaning people for the most sensible reasons profoundly disagree. What interests me is not so much the educational worth of bilingual education as its political history.

The Bilingual Education Act is interesting legislation, though by no means unique. It is an education act, but it was passed for reasons having only partly to do with education. The more important motivation was political. It was not new educational insights but a different ideological atmosphere that lay behind its passage, and by this I do not mean that it was the fruit of our new ethnically conscious climate. It is very tempting to see the Bilingual Education Act as the product of our recently awakened concern with ethnic identity, but actually to view it as such is to get the chronology wrong. The Bilingual Education Act was passed in 1968 and that antedates by about two years that climactic shift which is described today as the rise in ethnic consciousness.

In 1968 there was little concern about roots, affirmative action programs were still several years off, and ethnic power and ethnocultural maintenance were the slogans of an isolated Black minority, the voice for Black power. I made a check of the *Readers' Guide to Periodical Literature,* and it was fascinating to me that before March 1971 there were almost no articles on minority power, on ethnic studies, or on finding one's roots. The Bilingual Education Act thus antedated our national concern with either encouraging compensatory education for certain ethnic groups or with preserving our multi-ethnic heritage.

What, then, did account for its passage? The act came out of an atmosphere of profound alienation with American values and institutions, an alienation for which, of course, the Vietnam War was in great part responsible. In that atmosphere of alienation and in the midst of widespread doubts about the value of American culture, the movement for Black power and for community control arose. The argument of that movement struck a responsive chord in the minds of congressional and other mainstream liberals who by 1967 had come to believe in ethnic pluralism in society. They were more responsive to ethnic diversity, and the arguments they used were largely adopted from the movement for Black power.

Let me review what the arguments for Black power were and relate them to bilingual education. It was a psychological contention that lay at the foundation of the movement for Black power, and that contention was that American racism had so damaged the self-esteem of Blacks as to make a reawakening of ethnic pride the paramount task. To reestablish a sense of Black self-worth was, thus, what lay behind the demand for institutions run for and by Blacks. Black-run institutions, it was thought, would lay to rest once and for all the myth of Black incompetence. And it was stressed that schools would play a very special part, because in integrated schools Black children were taught the values of white culture, but in Black-run schools they would be taught the worth of their own.

The advocates of Black power never envisioned the principles that they espoused as applying to other groups. In their view no other group had experienced the rejection by white society felt by Blacks. No other group had raised children so outside the culture. As one advocate put it, the identity problem, the problem of self-worth, is not peculiar to Blacks but for Blacks it has a special dimension, "for in the American ethos a Black man is not only different, he is ugly and inferior."

In 1967, however, that point, so crucial to advocates of Black power, fell on deaf congressional ears. Congressional sponsors and witnesses at the hearings on bilingual education extended the arguments for Black power to other ethnic groups. American education, it was said at the hearings, by forcing Hispanic children especially to accept an alien culture encouraged them to reject themselves and, of course, here the self-worth argument was perfectly echoed. The Americans school, congressional witnesses said, "assaulted the cultural identity of the child. A haunting ambivalence of language, of culture, of personal self-affirmation had been created. To ask a child to deny himself and his family and his forebears was to demand a form of masochism which no society should ask. . . ."

One interesting aspect of the Black-power argument and the

contention of those who adopted the Black-power rhetoric for their own ethnic ends was that it precisely reversed the Supreme Court's points in *Brown v. Board of Education*, for what the Supreme Court had said in *Brown* was that children who are racially segregated suffer irreparable psychological damage. That segregation, as Chief Justice Earl Warren put it, "generated a feeling of inferiority unlikely ever to be undone." Black militants and their liberal sympathizers precisely turned this argument around. They said that to *assimilate* children into an alien culture creates a feeling of inferiority. This theme of the danger of assimilation ran through the congressional hearings on the Bilingual Education Act. The psychic cost of the melting pot was never really measured. Not a melting pot but a mosaic was what these advocates wanted, a mosaic built on the principle of diversity. It is not cultural unity but the persistence of cultural difference that makes America so vital, the argument went.

This argument for ethnic separatism, for a more pluralistic society, and for cultural maintenance was a compelling one when made with reference to Blacks, but much less so when made with reference to other ethnic groups because the essential element of massive segregation was missing. It was not the imposition of an alien culture that had been so damaging to Blacks, for other groups had faced assimilation pressure. It was the combination of integration and ostracism that had been so hard. Neither the Hispanics nor any other ethnic group had suffered quite the same denigration of native culture and exclusion from the American culture. The effort to make the history of other ethnic groups fit the pattern of Blacks, and the adoption of Black-power rhetoric for purposes of bilingual education, had important consequences.

There were educational arguments made at the hearings as well, and, if those educational arguments had carried the day, the programmatic implications would have been very different. Arguments about the degree to which the assimilation process assaulted a child's sense of self-worth led in one programmatic direction, while contentions about the Hispanic level of academic achievement and school dropout rate, had they been the most compelling, would have led in quite another. That is, concern solely about the academic record of children of limited-English-speaking ability would have led to unequivocable support for the establishment of transitional programs aimed at giving those children an equal educational start. But concern about the psychological harm of forced assimilation lent legitimacy to the establishment of programs which aimed to promote not scholastic achievement but a greater sense of self-worth by means of linguistic and cultural maintenance. They lent legitimacy to schools within schools, to ethnic educational enclaves run for and by ethnic groups. They led to educational programs much as the Black-power advocate had envisioned, but, of course, not for Blacks.

It is clear that in 1967 Congress envisioned transitional programs—programs that would temporarily bridge the gap between two cultures—to help children of limited-English-speaking proficiency acquire those academic skills that are so essential to economic mobility in our society, but it is clear from the subsequent historical record that what resulted, until 1978, were largely cultural and linguistic maintenance programs. That development can be in part traced back to the genesis of the Bilingual Education Act itself, to the political atmosphere in which it took shape, and to the degree to which profound alienation from American values and commitment to cultural pluralism had moved from the political left to the liberal center.

> Dean Knezevich initiated a general discussion by reflecting on his personal experience and pointing out that responsibility for developing competence in a dominant culture has shifted away from the self.

Stephen Knezevich: As an educator who is very much concerned with linguistic and cultural pluralism, I wonder what language other than English will be taught or will be the vehicle of instruction, or what culture other than American culture will be transmitted by the public school system.

The name Knezevich may not suggest a bilingual/bicultural background, but I did not speak English on a regular basis until I was four years old and went into the Milwaukee public schools. The feelings of those who had a home language other than English, the language of instruction in school, were quite different then from now. I will share with you just a bit of personal experience but

I frame the issues from the educational rather than the political or legal point of view.

One can look upon bilingualism/biculturalism as basically an instructional strategy, namely the use of literacy in one language to facilitate the attainment of literacy in another language. In other words, Spanish, or Korean, or Japanese, or another language may be presented in the public schools as a starting point from which to move to the acquisition of literacy in the primary language of instruction, which is English.

One can also look favorably on the emphasis on culture, the value orientation, the behavior norms that tend to help the individual from a culture different from the dominant one to gain a measure of self-respect. This enhanced self-concept can be a positive force in greater learning acquisition, although we do not have any definite research to suggest that enhancement of self-concept will automatically lead to better learning. One can indeed develop self-pride and end up lacking the requisite skills to succeed in our particular society. So whether it is using a different language in the beginning or talking about a different culture, that is a means of quickly moving into the English language as the basic mode of instruction and the American culture as the culture that is being developed.

One problem we do not have in this country is an alphabet problem. When I go to Yugoslavia I have trouble in Belgrade. I have to decipher the Cyrillic alphabet, and I gain competency in it only to lose it through disuse over a period of four to five years. In Zagreb they use the Latin alphabet, and I have no problem there. In the American culture there is no alphabet problem in dealing with linguistic pluralism. But there may be a different problem because someone may be competent to *speak* in a language and yet not be able to read or write in that language.

Another point of view sees bilingualism/biculturalism as an end in itself. The goal is not to facilitate instruction in English per se but rather to increase fluency in more than one language. Some say that we have a responsibility to transmit not only our cultural heritage but also those of Mexico, Korea, Japan, or whatever, and you can see the problems that would result from that. The suggestion was made that we might in fact run into impediments to assimilation. Some fear we may in this country repeat what is happening in Quebec where there is indeed conflict rather than greater vitality through respect for cultural differences.

Whose responsibility is it that one gains fluency, competency, and literacy in the dominant culture in which he happens to live and must earn a living? Is this the individual's responsibility? It was made very clear to me during the 1920s that it was indeed my responsibility to learn the English language and learn it quickly. It was made clear to all of us in that cultural setting. Otherwise we would be known as foreigners. We were not assimilated even though we were born here, our parents were clearly immigrants, and there was a definite peer pressure for us to pick up the language.

This attitude has changed, and this may invigorate the controversy over responsibility. It has become primarily a government responsibility or society's responsibility rather than an individual or family responsibility to develop language, to understand the mores of the culture. There has been a fundamental shift.

> The first comment and question came from Professor Elliott Barkan of California State College, San Bernardino, who expressed a deep anxiety about the failure of people in other parts of the country to understand and appreciate the extent of isolation experienced by non-English-speaking elements in the Southwest. He was also deeply concerned about some of the implications of past national policy.

Elliott Barkan: One thing that Abigail Thernstrom said left me baffled. Perhaps she would clarify it. She said that in checking the *Readers' Guide* she found no articles dealing with ethnic consciousness or demands in this area prior to March 1971. Later she went back and made reference to the Black-power movement. I got confused as to the timing that she was talking about, because obviously the Black-power movement began in early 1966, before the congressional hearings had taken place, before the 1968 act was passed.

One problem that I sense here is an Eastern perspective—Northeastern perspective—that comes across. I was born and raised in Brooklyn. I came to the West Coast twelve years ago with a Ph.D. from Harvard and did not know that there were living Indians. I did not know there were living Mexicans. Certainly the narrowness, the parochialness, that is bred on the East Coast can be very dangerous.

So one problem is the inadequate understanding of what is taking place in other regions of the United States. How many people really know what the French Canadians in New England went through? How many people really understand what has been happening to the Indians in the Dakotas, or Arizona, or New Mexico? The point is that certainly the Black-power movement ignited a number of power demands. It altered the whole scenario. The rising consciousness in the Chicano movement also began in the summer of 1966, then caught fire with the Indians and others. It changed the whole situation.

There is another point: we are really dealing with a race problem as well as a political problem, and that is not what we were dealing with in the nineteenth century with the Germans, Poles, and Italians. They were white, and the attitude toward them was different. When we say the groups adapted and adjusted, they were adapting as whites in a technologically and socially very different society than exists today.

No-one mentions what happened to the Blacks in the nineteenth century when they wanted to get an education. No-one mentions the price that Indians paid if they wanted to get an education. No-one mentions what happened to the Chinese when they tried to get an education and experienced segregation.

What we are really seeing now in the whole issue of bilingual and bicultural education is the response of society to non-white groups, and that touches on the fact that there have been very deep-seated prejudices within American society that have created an intransigence and an opposition and inflexibility that completely (and I use the word intentionally) colors the whole situation quite differently. The demands in the nineteenth century for unity and conformity were also a reflection of both our fears and isolationist mentality.

The price that was paid was a great deal of ignorance about our minority groups. We have always been multicultural, we have always been multilingual, but society has been unwilling to recognize that reality. The price was ignorance about many groups and that ignorance is what continues, compounded by racial difficulties. When we look at what has happened within the last twelve years and the inadequate implementation, we can understand that inadequacy better if we realize that there was really a failure of will, and that the failure of will was in part due to the very deep-seated prejudices that exist within our society.

> Abigail Thernstrom replied not only to the matter regarding the *Readers' Guide* but to the broader issue as well. She pointed to the tardiness of the popular press to recognize the bilingual issue and went on to say that the perception of Hispanics as a racial group is also relatively recent.

Abigail Thernstrom: You correctly dated the Black-power movement. I was making a distinction between the Black-power movement, which everybody was conscious of, and a much more general rise in ethnic consciousness. We were looking at *Time* and *Newsweek,* and the like, not at professional literature. I was interested in mass culture in the popular magazines, and it was very striking to me that it was not until about March 1971 that interest in the general ethnic consciousness was reflected in the mass culture magazines.

Your point that dealing with a racial problem as well as a political problem makes the current situation very different from that which existed with prior immigrant groups is to some extent true, but it has to be modified. I am not sure that Hispanics in the Southwest do comprise a racial group in the sense that Blacks do. For example, I just came from doing research in Dallas on election rights of Blacks and Hispanics. One clear thing about the experience of Mexican-Americans in Dallas is that they were not considered Black for most purposes, not for restrictive covenants, or in city ordinances making it necessary for Blacks to ride in the back of buses. Mexican-Americans have had a very different experience from that of Blacks, and the result is that they are significantly dispersed throughout the city. They are much more assimilated than the Blacks, and there is tremendous resentment between the two groups as a result. Blacks feel that Mexican-Americans can easily become white, and no matter what a Black does, no matter how middle- or upper-class he becomes, he remains Black.

In the 1930 census, when there was a question of labeling Hispanics a racial group, there was a hue and cry from the Hispanic community because its members wanted to be considered white, thought of themselves as white. Yes, we are to some extent dealing with a racial problem, but I do think that the point has to be clarified.

Abigail Thernstrom's remarks evoked heated rejoinders from both panelists and other conferees.

Josue Gonzalez: The analysis that you came away with after working in Dallas is absolutely incorrect. Absolutely, flatly incorrect. Racial discrimination—racial, ethnic, whichever term you want to use—against Chicanos in the Southwest has been rampant—*de jure* discrimination, restrictive covenants, segregated schools, the whole picture. You are absolutely wrong, and Texas is the best example of the discrimination. I am surprised you did not find it in Dallas. Go to the courthouse and look at the restrictive covenants in deeds of long standing. Children were punished for being what they were. (I was punished for speaking Spanish on the school grounds; it was part of official school board policy.)

I would agree, however, that the *Readers' Guide to Periodical Literature* is not the best source of evidence of ethnic awareness. Awareness in literature of Hispanics in the Southwest dates back at least to the early 1800s and it is in all major libraries in universities of the Southwest. Harvard is not the center of Chicano Studies for the country. I think if we make that assumption, we are better off.

David Maciel: That is one reason why Harvard needs a Chicano president!

Josue Gonzalez: Right. I think it is a question of race, if you define race as a sociological phenomenon, not simply a genetic thing. That puts Hispanics in the same situation as Native Americans, Asians, and other groups of different coloration from European immigrants who have to be dealt with differently. A lot of sociological literature that comes from our friends in the East lumps together ten or twelve million Chicanos with five hundred White Russians in Chicago. This is absolutely incorrect.

How we came into the society is misunderstood. We were not immigrants; the border migrated. The fact of the Mexican-American War in 1846, the land grab by the United States—the history is just so clear to those of us who have spent some time looking at it that a distinction must be made between the Chicanos and other ethnic groups. It is not comparable to the White Russians. You have just to deal with that group differently. The size of the group, the proximity to Mexico, all the factors that speak so clearly to what Elliott Barkan suggested.

As Dean Knezevich mentioned, the schools have a responsibility to carry forth a tradition of the culture of a country. The real question to me is, is this the same culture that Teddy Roosevelt ranted and raved about when he said, if they do not learn English in five years, send them back? Or do we have a different culture in the 1980s from what we had when Teddy Roosevelt was around? I suggest strongly that we have a different culture, that it is diversified. The schools have a responsibility to teach it the way it is, not the way Teddy Roosevelt wanted it to be, and the policies regarding language differences, cultural pluralism, bilingualism, and so forth are in fact conducive to divisiveness when they obstruct the regular process that a society follows in evolution.

People keep pointing to Quebec for some reason, where the dynamic and the history are completely different from what we have here. There is no danger of ethnic separation here. The phrase "ethnic separation" has been used as being almost synonymous with "cultural pluralism," and that is the kind of alarmist language that is very disturbing to me. It is not the presence of bilingualism or the presence of bilingual education that creates a problem. It is the resistance to the fact that people want bilingualism that creates a problem. A divisiveness is created between people when they do not accept a normal evolutionary process of language and culture. All languages evolved out of other languages coming together. All cultures evolved out of other cultures coming together. It is resistance that causes problems, because people resent the imposition of another language over their own.

Ricardo Fernández: Systematic discrimination through segregation of groups in this country usually ends up being described in terms of Black and white, and I think there are historical reasons why that is so. But if we dig a bit into some of the things going on in other groups, specifically among Hispanics and more specifically Chicanos and Mexican-Americans, we find a wealth of legal precedents well before *Brown v. Board of Education* in which Chicanos were fighting for desegregation.

In California, *Mendez v. Westminster* is a clear example of that. A man with a Spanish surname had a son who spoke English, but in spite of that the school system said the boy had to go to a Mexican school. The father protested that the child would not get the kind of help he should have, if he attended the Mexican school, but was told that was the law and there was no choice. So the father filed a law suit and Thurgood Marshall on behalf of the NAACP filed a brief in support of desegregation because Blacks were in that struggle at the same time. In Arizona there was another case— *Gonzalez v. Sheely*—which was basically the same thing.

I found that *Hernandez v. Texas*, which was immediately before *Brown*, is a case that should eliminate any doubts about the existence of discrimination against Mexican-Americans. It is a case about representation on a jury, based on the fact that in the State of Texas, for twenty-five years there had not been a single Mexican-American selected for jury duty in a certain county in which Mexican-Americans constituted 25 percent of the population. Statistically there was no way that that could have happened unless there was a systematic exclusion of Mexican-Americans. It is interesting how Chief Justice Warren of the U.S. Supreme Court said at one point to the attorney general of the State of Texas, who claimed that in Texas Chicanos were white, that it was curious to him that restroom signs in Texas said "Whites only" or "Blacks," and then, "Hombres aquí." So it is clear that Mexican-Americans had to use separate restrooms and those were not the restrooms allocated to white people.

Because the historical analysis that has focused on desegration has centered on Blacks, a number of other groups that have been subjected to segregation policies and have resisted actively in the courts have been overlooked.

Insisting that there was a meaningful distinction between the kind
of discrimination faced by Blacks and that confronted by Mexican-
Americans, Abigail Thernstrom elaborated in her response.

Abigail Thernstrom: My point about discrimination against
Mexican-Americans in Texas was misunderstood. I never wanted
to suggest that Mexican-Americans in the Southwest have not
been discriminated against in a variety of ways. They have. But
there is a distinction between the extent of that discrimination
against Blacks and against Mexican-Americans. The extent to
which Mexican-Americans were discriminated against depended
on exactly how dark their color was, and those who were lighter
experienced less discrimination. I do not want to leave the impression that Mexican-Americans suffered no discrimination.

The nature of the limits and extent of public support of bilingual
education was raised by Dean Donald Dewey of California State
University, Los Angeles.

Donald Dewey: May I ask Ricardo Fernández, where does bilingual education stop? In many California schools it would have to
go beyond *bi*lingualism. If the one-third of the students who speak
Spanish in a Glendale classroom, let us say, should be taught in
Spanish, then should the two students who speak Cantonese, or
those who speak Vietnamese, or Korean in that same classroom be
taught in their native tongues? It can go to the college level as well.
A certain college president had a goal of having engineering classes
taught in Spanish as well as in English. He never reached his goal,
but by now the courses would have to be in Persian, in Japanese, in
Chinese, in Korean, as well as in Spanish and English. How do you
advise that these issues be coped with?

Ricardo Fernández: What you are asking is, how do you implement? What types of services are possible, are required, and are
administratively, financially, and humanly possible? I do not know
what the new guidelines will allow. First, there is one fundamental
point: If a child in a classroom does not understand the language
being used, some steps must be taken; one simply cannot ignore
the fact that the child does not speak English. But it is clear that not
the same types of services can be delivered in all circumstances. In
many districts, such as in Chicago, as many as eighty language

groups are represented in one system. In Washington, D.C., I think this is true also. Any large system would have that diversity, so it is not possible to provide the same type of program (and by that I mean home language or bilingual instruction) to every single child in every single circumstance.

One argument that is used is, if we cannot provide it to every single child then we do not provide it to any child. That is democracy in reverse, except democracy usually means rule of the majority and in the instance mentioned even the majority would not get served. So some districts say, we cannot find any Vietnamese-speaking teachers, therefore we cannot provide home language instruction to Vietnamese. They were probably saying the same thing about the need for Spanish-speaking teachers in Houston, Texas—"we cannot find teachers that are qualified." The issue is, what is practicable? State laws usually set a minimum. For example, if there are twenty or more students who speak a particular language, a class is required. It varies from state to state, the flexibility is there, but *something* has to be done. Those children cannot be allowed to languish; they have the right to participate fully in the educational program of a school.

The second respondent shifted the focus from "how much" to "how good."

Pastora Cafferty: I have three things to say. First, there is an unwarranted assumption being made here that somehow the bilingual individual will be deficient in English. However, there is substantive evidence that being bilingual involves increased skills in both languages. (I am not talking about a transitional program.) Thorough familiarity with the Spanish language does not impair one's knowledge of English. I am bilingual and I am perfectly comfortable in both languages. I do not think it hampered my education. By the way, that is the result of a successful bilingual education, not an unsuccessful one, but so are good math skills and good reading skills the result of a successful education.

I am burdened by being an historian, and it occurs to me that it is not accurate to say that bilingual education dates from 1968 and alienation from America, and that by being bilingual an individual will be relegated to being segregated from society. In fact, bilingual education has been a reality in America since the early nineteenth century, certainly in the parochial school system, as well as in the public school system in a much more limited way.

Second, the end of bilingual education and the change of transitional programs, most in night schools, dates to World War II and xenophobia. Third, and I think most important, if we say that alienation and bilingual education are intricately related, that is, that somehow the Bilingual Education Act of 1968 or today's push to bilingualism from the right is related to alienation and separatism, we would have to say that American assimilation failed completely during the nineteenth and most of the twentieth century. That is a denial of history. We may not be a melting pot, but we do a fairly good job of cohesion as a nation. At least we do not kill each other's language groups.

> Maxwell F. Yalden, Canada's Commissioner of Official Languages, felt that analogies to Quebec were ill-founded. He also questioned the merits and utility of applying civil rights powers—since this would almost dictate answers—and wondered about using political solutions to what are essentially pedagogical problems.

Maxwell Yalden: Quebec has been mentioned here many times—usually very much out of context. Quebec is not a parallel with what you are talking about. French-speaking Canadians have been on the territory now known as Quebec for four hundred years. There are several million French-speaking Quebecers. There are probably three-and-one-half million who do not speak anything but French, and have no need to speak anything but French, any more than a native-born, white American living in Iowa needs to speak anything other than English. They have a full cultural set-up from kindergartens to several universities, theaters, publishers—the whole business. It is not a parallel. If there is a parallel, it is with the French-speaking minority in other provinces like Ontario and New Brunswick.

I want to bring the panel back to the matter of education with questions about some of the assumptions that, looked at from north of the border, seem rather hard to come to grips with. One of them is this: Can you really apply the criteria of the civil rights movement to what is ostensibly a linguistic pedagogical problem? And if you do apply the rules of the civil rights movement—which leads you to equate all languages so that you have, as I am told, eighty-two languages to be taught in a school system in Los Angeles—if you try to do that, is it pedagogically possible? There are, of course, countries with a number of languages—the Soviet Union or, a more successful example, Yugoslavia—but only about four or five languages are involved there. In Switzerland there are three, of which only two are really official; Italian gets second-rate treatment, so that leaves French and German. But when you come to eighty-two, can you make it work?

My second question concerns a transitional system. Can the use of the home language as the medium of instruction ever really work as a tool of humane assimilation? Would you not at least have to try a form of what you call "maintenance," and, if you try that, would you not eventually find that maintenance was not going to work unless it went up through the whole school system? And what kind of an assimilation technique would it be then? Are you not caught in a circle from which you cannot really emerge?

> The first respondent was Sharon Robinson, who denied any special place for English, arguing only that it is a needed skill, and she insisted that there is no threat to bilingual education in using the civil rights movement approach.

Sharon Robinson: The last question assumes a language difference to be a kind of deficiency that impinges on the dignity and worth of the children. I think too often the debate in bilingual education is based on that kind of thought. At the very basis of our acculturation, we assume an arrogance or an elitism about English. If a child has a deficiency in English—and we have to remember that we do function in a dominantly English-speaking society—then the child must acquire English-speaking skills. This does not have to occur at the expense of the dignity and worth of the language that the child brings to the situation.

To draw a parallel between issues of bilingual education and the civil rights movement often encourages an assumption of one group threatening the power base of another. That is unfortunate because for us to be really committed to equal educational opportunity, to full achievement and potential for all people, the basis of one person's success cannot be the denial of an opportunity to someone else. Everybody should have equal chance to compete along more acceptable selection criteria than we have imposed in the past.

Ricardo Fernández: I understand Mr. Yalden's question to mean, what constitutes discrimination on the basis of national origin? That has been defined basically as language or linguistic discrimination. Second, what is required to remedy or to redress that? Fundamentally, that has been answered in terms of limited-English proficiency by the government, by Congress, and by administrative agencies interpreting those mandates.

Because most Hispanic children do speak English, the focus of the Bilingual Education Act, Title VII, addresses only a portion of that population, which has led me to question what happens to the other, even greater, proportion of Hispanic schoolchildren who are not doing very well at all, who are not getting any kind of education. But it seems to me that national origin discrimination or discrimination on the basis of language could take place when a child cannot fully participate in those programs.

> Two non-panelists raised questions about the quality and extent of non-English instruction and the danger of overlooking this critical issue when talking about bilingualism. The first questioner was Donald Hata, professor of history at California State University, Dominguez Hills; the second was Lorum H. Stratton, chairman of the Department of Classical and Romance Languages, and director of bilingual education at Texas Tech University.

Donald Hata: In my position as a university history teacher, all my doubts about the credibility of the public school system in our society have been confirmed, because from the lowest levels in education to the highest I see something very dangerous going on. My question is simple. I would like to know what the panelists' position is on requiring foreign languages for the baccalaureate, because that is where we train the teachers who go out to teach students. In California we do not have any foreign language requirement for college degrees in our publicly funded institutions of higher learning.

Going hand-in-hand with this discussion of bilingualism/ biculturalism should be the question of foreign languages. Otherwise, these kinds of discussions are dangerous. What we ought to be talking about is requiring a foreign language for all of us. I like the comment, "Do not dismiss it because it is not taught well or we would have to get rid of math and science." Noah Webster published something called *The American Dictionary of the English Language*. We do not speak English; we speak American. It is a special language that does, if you look in our standard dictionary, reflect the de facto adoption of a great deal of cultural assimilation from all over the world. Even "samurai" need no longer be treated as a foreign word; it is in *The American Dictionary of the English Language*. So we should start talking about the cultural ambiance of all of us instead of just "them."

Lorum Stratton: I would like to reiterate what Donald Hata has stated so eloquently and add, if we are interested in the long-range goals of bilingual education, we should start foreign-language education early. I know that our most pressing need is to help children who do not speak English, but we want to change attitudes in the next decades so we will not be faced with the situation where an adult says "My kid don't need Spanish. Hell, he can't even speak English." Would a panelist care to address that statement?

> The panelists were not of one mind on the issues raised by Donald Hata and Lorum Stratton. Josue Gonzalez and Ricardo Fernández felt that bilingual education was or would be essential for someone who wanted to be considered educated in our society. Gonzalez, however, did not consider Spanish—nor any language with a domestic constituency—a "foreign" language.

Josue Gonzalez: I do very much support requirements of non-English language for teachers and other professionals. I would advise, however, that we expand from the word "foreign." I would include foreign and domestic languages in that requirement because it still raises that issue of it not being American. It is very American to have a non-English language, and those languages ought to be studied too. I strongly favor the two-way bilingual education that was just touched on. Bilingual education is of benefit to all children who wish to participate as an option. Everyone should have an opportunity from early childhood to develop more than one language.

Ricardo Fernández: I too support the requirement of a language in addition to English for graduation, but I want to qualify that by saying that I support that with a different methodology. I want people who are proficient, not necessarily who got twelve credits or fifteen hours in Spanish or French.

> Pastora Cafferty dissented for many reasons, partly because this is a monolingual society, partly because it raises political questions of a complex nature, and partly for reasons related to the way languages are seen in a pedagogical sense.

Pastora Cafferty: I am treading on very dangerous ground here but I suggest that while, of course, I am in favor of foreign-language instruction, I am also in favor of history, art, music, and a great deal more learning that rounds out an individual. It has always been interesting to me, going back to the 1967 hearings of the 1968 act, that the president of the Modern Language Association testified against bilingual education. There is a difference between being a native speaker of English who acquires a second language, which is seen as a cultural plus in our society, and being a native speaker of another language and acquiring English.

We talk about the lack of English proficiency, but we never speak about having Spanish proficiency and acquiring English. This is a dominantly English-speaking society, and I do not think that any of us should ever suggest—obviously there is a political argument that I will not go into—that an individual should be anything but proficient in English. Yet that does not exclude being proficient in another language. Realistically, in America the acquisition of a foreign language is a cultural asset; it is not a need. That does not mean that a century from now the situation will be the same. But to carry on commerce in this country—to become a part of the economic mainstream of American society—a foreign language is not necessary. That is why foreign languages languish. I am not suggesting that only those things which are necessary or functional should be part of education, but foreign languages must be looked at in the same light in which we look at cultural enrichment programs. I would rather that Americans knew history and understood the place of every group in the society than understood their languages.

> A visiting fellow in political science in Harvard, Tarun C. Bose, who comes from a multicultural/multilingual society, sought to define the problem in terms of his own experience in India. As he saw

it, introducing another language would lead to serious problems and continuing pressures from all language groups.

Tarun Bose: I was interested to hear the comment about the Puerto Ricans being bilingual out of economic necessity. They are bilingual not because they want to be but because they have to be in order to survive.

That brings me to another point, namely, that if you are thinking in terms of introducing another language, would this not place the student concerned at the disadvantage vis-à-vis his counterparts who would be more proficient in English?

I see the problem as basically an economic issue, not so much a political issue, although politicians try to make an economic issue a political issue. But it is basically an economic issue because students—and this reflects what we have in India—have an urge to learn a language because of the prospect that it holds out to them in the pursuit of their careers. This is where English has played a very important role in my country. And my feeling is that the United States, whatever may be the composition of its different ethnic groups, is and will remain primarily an English-speaking society. About that I have no doubt. If this is going to be the case, then if you go on yielding to the pressure of the ethnic groups, and today you yield to the pressures of the Hispanic-speaking group, would it not be impossible for you tomorrow to deny similar pressure from another ethnic group—say the Italians, who are not as numerous as the Spanish-speaking community but sizable? What I am saying is, would not you thereby open a floodgate for other ethnic groups to demand the introduction of their own languages?

> In response to Tarun Bose, Pastora Cafferty emphasized that no-one on the panel was urging a multicultural/multilingual society. They were addressing themselves to an existing need and felt the proposed solutions were both possible and desirable.

Pastora Cafferty: A permanent migrant to this country probably is economically able to function in this society with only one language, if we set aside for the moment the political and psychological and cultural considerations. (I am not suggesting that they are unimportant.) We are constitutionally liable for the education of legal resident aliens, as they pay taxes and have the same access as citizens. I am not going to start arguing for the rights of illegal aliens. But the issue that we do owe an education to a child that will make him able to function economically, socially, and politically was outlined earlier. It is not an issue of one language at the expense of another. Indeed, there is a whole body of literature, not only American but certainly European, that insists that one can learn two languages and doing so enhances the learning of both.

So not for one moment are we arguing about diminishing English skills. A Puerto Rican child should never learn Spanish at the expense of English, nor English at the expense of Spanish. Obviously the Puerto Rican child who is going to live in New York forever probably does not need a bilingual education. If the child never goes back to Puerto Rico, his English skills will be better than his Spanish. If he goes back to the island, his Spanish will probably be better than his English. He will be able to function in both and, by the way, his English will be an economic asset in Puerto Rico. No-one is arguing for a multilingual American society.

Implications of Bilingualism:
The Law

The legal dimension of bilingualism was discussed by a panel chaired by Franklyn S. Haiman of the department of communication studies in Northwestern University, a longtime officer in the American Civil Liberties Union. The panelists were Jaime Fuster, deputy assistant attorney general of the United States and former dean of the University of Puerto Rico School of Law; the Reverend Wayne (Chris) Hartmire, director of the National Farm Worker Ministry; Arnold Leibowitz, special counsel, Select Commission on Immigration and Refugee Policy of the United States Senate Committee on the Judiciary, and president of the Institute of International Law and Economic Development; and Peter Roos, director of educational litigation for the Mexican-American Legal Defense Fund.

Arnold Leibowitz denied the validity of the questions in the conference statement on the grounds that there was no pending legislation that would make the United States a bilingual nation. He reviewed the history of state and federal legislation and litigation regarding the use of foreign languages in this country, noting that most of it was inspired or provoked by the actions of the in-group or "the Establishment," which was afraid of or hostile toward newcomers or peoples who were different.

Arnold Leibowitz: No-one in Washington has any plans to make the United States bilingual. No-one in the 1968, 1974, or 1978 hearings took that position. There is no question now as to whether two or more languages should share official status nor is there any question about the primacy of English. The issue—at least the one that I would address—is the question of what federal and state laws should say about bilingual education. By "bilingual education" I mean the statutory definition—the use in addition to English of another language as a medium of instruction in the school system. That is the only issue when one talks about bilingual education in America.

Let me give some historical perspective. Both federal and state governments have taken positions with respect to language in the school system and elsewhere in American life; most of those positions have occurred at the state, not the federal, level. There are patterns to be seen, so one can, in examining the issue, say what was done when and what the result was and, therefore, what should be done now.

Concern with illiteracy first appeared in American life during the 1850s when nativist forces in Massachusetts and Connecticut, led by the Know-Nothing party and feeling threatened by the flood of Irish immigration—untutored, unlettered, a "criminal element" which clearly would disturb the existing American civilization— pushed through legislation that required a reading and writing knowledge of English before one could vote as a registered alien. (At that time in most states resident aliens could vote! Now in all states one must be a citizen to vote.) This was designed, legislative history makes clear, to keep the Irish from participating in the political process. Such legislation was passed at that time only in those two states.

Elsewhere in the United States there was almost no issue at all with respect to bilingual education or bilingualism. In Cincinnati, by official action, German was permitted in the school system, and in other places German was widely used with little concern. Between 1790 and 1880, about 10 percent of the population of the United States was German. The largest ethnic group that we have ever had at one time was the German immigrants.

In the period between 1880 and 1925 the question of language reappeared when what were called by the Dillingham Commission the "new immigrants"—those from Southern and Eastern Europe—arrived in large numbers. This inflow resulted from the fact that the steamboat replaced the sailboat for transatlantic crossings, making the journey far less hazardous and permitting embarkation farther east. With large immigration from Eastern Europe and Italy, the language issue was openly discussed, both in terms of what the state's legal response should be to immigrants who did not know English, and how immigrants should be "Americanized."

State laws now proliferated. Twenty states by 1923 had English literacy tests as a condition of voting. Thirty-three prescribed English as the language in the school system, and language tests for jobs became standard. Part of this came from the desire for good government and the fear that these new groups could not be trusted. The New York laws requiring barber examinations in the English language and oral examinations for teachers clearly had race prejudice at their base. The in-group worried about the new immigrants and tried to delay their participation in American life.

The voting literacy tests also had a racial bias. For example, in New York the first time reading and writing English became a requirement for voting was 1916, and in 1922 the requirement became a part of the New York state constitution. The law had been passed to prevent a million "unlettered" Jews from voting. It was clearly a political decision. It was very important for Republicans to make sure that these people did not go to the polls; for the Democrats, it was very important that they did. Like the Massachusetts test earlier, the New York test delayed political participation but did not affect it much.

The conference background paper suggests that many earlier ethnic groups chose to handle their educational problems outside the existing structure and that the Establishment accepted this. This is just not true. In California and Hawaii, the Japanese sent their children to the public schools like everybody else from 9:00 A.M. to 3:00 P.M., and then at their own expense set up a private school system where the children learned Japanese history, morals, or whatever. The Japanese suddenly found that the system was controversial. The governor of Hawaii argued that someone should look into what those Japanese were doing. Were they teaching loyalty to the emperor and other un-American values of various kinds? He wanted a full examination of the situation. This is set out in the survey of education conducted by the Territory of Hawaii in 1921. There was fear as to what was going on, and the proposed solution was to legislate the certification of teachers and to spell out the subjects that could be taught, in order to preserve American civilization.

California immediately passed a similar statute, without going through the business of a long survey. The assumption was that if Japanese schools were dangerous in Hawaii they must be dangerous in California. The Japanese parents were shocked and outraged, and litigation ensued. A case went to the United States Supreme Court, then hardly the most liberal we have had, and the Court, in a ruling written by Justice McReynolds, the most conservative of the justices, held the government's actions as unconstitutional. There should be no interference with the Japanese schools. (In 1940 the same issue went up to the Supreme Court again, under very similar circumstances, and for procedural reasons was not heard.) There is no evidence that during World War II Japanese-Americans who had participated in those after-school programs were any more or less patriotic than other Americans.

Why bring this up now? We have all learned. Cannot we say, as has been said here and elsewhere, that if you sit back and relax eventually the system works? After all, the Jews and the Irish are now part of the Establishment.

The fact is, it appears that with respect to the groups who are most seeking bilingual education at this point—Mexican-Americans and Native Americans—the system has not worked. These are not new groups that have suddenly come upon the scene. The Indians, since 1867, have been subjected to the existing school system of English, although they had previously, at least the Cherokee, learned in their own language. The system certainly has not worked for them. So when they appeal for a change in the system, they are basing their appeal on their experience during a time that other groups have "made it" and they have not.

History would show that, rather than say "Relax, it will all work out" to these ethnic groups, it is more appropriate to tell *ourselves*,

"Relax, it will all work out as it did with the immigrants before them." Twenty years from now, or perhaps forty years from now, when someone in California holds a conference concerned about the latest flood of immigrants coming into the American scene, there may well be a Mexican-American professor who will rise and say it is important that these people learn English in the school system if they hope to succeed in the United States.

> The legal status of bilingual education was explored by Jaime Fuster, who examined it from the viewpoint of case law and argued that the conservative nature of the judiciary makes any abandonment of transitional bilingual education in favor of maintenance bilingual systems unlikely. The current basis for what exists is a court-based judgment of statutory, not constitutional, law. He cautioned that a reading by experts is necessary before anyone can claim to understand it.

Jaime Fuster: I do not represent the United States Department of Justice. I was invited here in my capacity as dean of the University of Puerto Rico School of Law. Whatever I say is not the policy of the justice department in this matter. Second, I am not an expert in this issue. I know that lawyers should not begin a statement by disqualifying themselves, but my instincts as a professor rather than as a lawyer insist that I put the cards on the table and say that what I can contribute is a little bit about the Puerto Rican experience, which is very complicated and in many ways different from the Mexican-American experience. Third, I have attempted to respond to the question in the conference paper from the perspective of constitutional law, which I have taught for fifteen years.

The center of concern in this conference, as I understand it, is bilingualism not as a transitional device, but bilingualism that goes beyond the need for solving short-range pragmatic problems. The pertinent question then is, what is the present legal status of bilingualism/biculturalism? To what extent are there new developments? Can they be said to have evolved organically from older constitutional principles? I will give a very brief answer to the questions. Those who are interested in the Puerto Rican experience may wish to ask questions.

What is the present legal status of bilingualism? Bilingualism, in the sense that is the concern of the conference paper and many people here, has no substantial legal recognition, at least in federal law. Whatever exists in federal law, constitutional and statutory, is aimed essentially at transitional goals, and it is largely an extension of older constitutional principles. It is very difficult to say that there are new developments in federal law in the direction of this new bilingualism. The few that exist are subject to debate, and they are essentially statutory developments, rather than constitutional developments. Unless one can make a case for *de jure* discrimination in the case of Hispanic-Americans in the United States, there is nothing in the Constitution as it has been read by the Supreme Court of the United States to guarantee any right to a bilingual education of the type that concerns persons in this audience.

I will be more specific. The classic case in this area, *Meyer v. Nebraska*, has two or three basic principles that are still the law of the land. First, the state can require English instruction in public and even private school systems. There is no constitutional barrier to a state requiring English instruction in schools. What the state cannot do is establish a blanket prohibition against the teaching of another language in the school system, particularly in private schools. The issue in *Meyer v. Nebraska* was a state law making it a crime for any teacher in private or public schools to teach any subject in any language other than English. The Supreme Court struck that down saying that it violated federal due process of law. But the Court did recognize that states have broad powers to regulate education, including the power to establish a requirement that such instruction be given in English. It is not that the states are forced to do that. It is that they have the authority, if they so choose. What they cannot do is to exclude the teaching of other languages in the school system. The reason the Court said that it could not be excluded is because it appeared to be arbitrary to exclude any language from the school curriculum.

Curiously enough, however, *Meyer v. Nebraska* brought a strong dissent from two well-known jurists—Justice Sutherland and, even more important, Justice Holmes—both of whom thought that in any situation there might be an occasion where it is reasonable, to achieve the important goal that all citizens speak a common tongue, to prohibit the teaching of foreign languages.

After *Meyer v. Nebraska* at the Supreme Court level, there is the famous case of *Lau v. Nichols*. In *Lau*, the Supreme Court found that the San Francisco school system failed to rectify the language deficiency of the petitioners, a group of Chinese students who did not speak English and therefore could not benefit from the education offered in the local schools. The failure of the school system to offer a meaningful opportunity to participate in the public educational program was illegal because it violated Section 601 of the Civil Rights Act of 1964, which bans discrimination based on national origin, race, and so on.

In making that ruling the Supreme Court was very careful to point out a number of things that are relevant for this discussion. First, no constitutional issue was decided, and the justices expressly said so. Second, the reason the Supreme Court thought the San Francisco school system was violating federal law was because of the clear guidelines and regulations coming out of the executive branch. The Court doubted whether the language of the statute excluded the type of situation that existed in the San Francisco school system, but it was resolving the doubt in favor of the petitioners because of the clear guidelines that the executive branch, in its right to interpret the statute, had put out. Even more interesting is that the Supreme Court went on to say that the ruling was based on the fact that there were many children involved— 1,800 children—clearly suggesting that in situations in which two or ten children were involved, the justices were not willing to read the statute and regulations as the executive branch has read them.

There was also a final caveat that the Supreme Court placed on the decision. It clearly warned against interpreting the decision too broadly. The justices said it in very express words. They also said that the remedy for the unequal opportunity situation was something for the school authorities largely to decide. They identified two remedies, and as far as the Supreme Court was concerned they were equally good; the Chinese students could be given instruction in their own language, or they could be taught English and, once they were proficient in English, be incorporated into the school system.

There certainly is no way that one can definitively say that *Lau* supports bilingualism. It supports the need to implement a statutorily created right to equal educational opportunities, a right that can be implemented in more than one way, not necessarily through the establishment of bilingual programs, but alternatively by such traditional means as simply teaching English to the people who do not speak the language. If to this case one adds the whole current of contemporary case decisions dealing with intentional discrimination, and observes the way the Supreme Court has been strongly moving in the direction of accepting for adjudication very definite examples of express discrimination, moving away from the original tendency toward resolution of problems of the fact of discrimination, I think that one is on fairly strong ground in saying that there is no constitutional right to any kind of bilingual education, unless one can come up with a clear pattern of intentional discrimination, such as a school system that does not allow Mexican-Americans or Hispanic-Americans to come into the schools simply because they are Mexican-Americans. Arguing discrimination on the basis of people being unable to derive the benefits of education simply because there is something in their condition that keeps them from making use of the right to education is unacceptable; there is nothing in the Supreme Court's decisions that can lead one to believe that people have a claim along those lines. It simply does not exist.

Courts generally are better for preserving an established rule than for changing it. The general idea that courts are centers of social change has been greatly overrated in this country, largely because of the experience with the Black discrimination problem, so one feels very concerned to see people going to courts as if they were a real center of new justice. They are a center for interpreting the law and extending pre-established notions of justice, but not for new versions of that justice, unless something very important has taken place already in either public opinion or in the perception of the national interest by those who are charged with the responsibility for the national interest.

An example of what I am talking about is a decision of the Supreme Court of Puerto Rico. About ten years ago a North American (or as we call them in Puerto Rico, a "continental American," to distinguish from an "island American") was indicted in the local courts of Puerto Rico, and he claimed the right to be tried in English. Of course, proceedings in the local courts in Puerto Rico have been in Spanish since the time of Spain, and this has not changed in the last eighty-two years of Puerto Rico's relations with the United States. But there is a statute that goes back to 1902 that said that "proceedings in the courts of Puerto Rico and in all public offices are to be conducted in the English language and the Spanish language indiscriminately." So the claim by the person who was indicted had a very strong statutory basis. His claim was that Puerto Rican law said he could be tried in English or Spanish. He wanted to be tried in English.

The court in charge ordered a revamp of the whole procedure in order to give attention to the claim. In other words, the trial court respected the claim and gave orders that would have revolutionized the system. The case, of course, was immediately appealed to the Supreme Court of Puerto Rico on an interim basis, and the supreme court ruled that the only right this person had was to have an interpreter, but not a right to have his case pleaded and conducted in English. And this is why the supreme court so ruled (I want to read part of the decision because it is revealing about courts): "It is a fact not subject to historical ratification that the language of the Puerto Rican people is an integral part of our origin and of our Hispanic culture and has been and continues to be Spanish. The determining factor as to the language to be used in the judicial proceedings in commonwealth courts does not arise from the statute which [the defendant] has invoked in support of his petition that the trial be held in English because he did not have a good command of Spanish. It arises from the fact that the means of expression of our people is Spanish, and that is a reality that cannot be changed by any law."

That attitude of the Supreme Court of Puerto Rico is the kind of attitude that largely would be present in the federal courts concerning the "peril of bilingualism." My comment narrows down to two recommendations. To those who are so concerned about the "peril" to the nation posed by bilingualism, my comment would be, "Much ado about nothing." And to those that are interested in pushing for bilingualism beyond what is called a transitional method, you have a lot of explaining to do.

Dissenting vigorously from Jaime Fuster's interpretation of the *Lau* case, Peter Roos presented his own analysis of the case, traced the case law dealing with bilingualism, explained the origin of the "Lau Remedies," and held out the possibility that language maintenance programs could emerge out of the courts.

Peter Roos: I would like to start with the *Lau* decision. There are different ways of looking at that decision that are important for an understanding of the development of the legal right to bilingual education. It is true that the *Lau* decision was not based on the Constitution. It is also worth remembering, although it may turn out to be a footnote in history, that whether there were constitutional rights was not an issue in the case. It was not in the pleadings and, therefore, it is not a matter of the Court saying there was not a constitutional right to either affirmative help or bilingual education; it was just not addressing that issue.

Another very important thing to remember about the *Lau* case: as Jaime Fuster indicated, the Court expressly said it was not ruling that bilingual education or English as a second language or any other approach is per se required. The justices then went on to say they had not been asked, and they were not going to stick their necks out. And they did not. The important point that I would like to leave with you is that they did not say that bilingual education was not required under the Civil Rights Act or that it was required. They did not decide that issue. It may be significant, however, to remember some of the language they used; it may turn out to be instrumental or at least helpful as case law develops.

In my opinion, case law is going to develop a right to bilingual, understandable instruction. Although the Court in *Lau* did not say that any particular form of instruction was required, they did dwell at some length on the fact that one cannot expect equal educational opportunity in a classroom where some of the children do not understand what is going on. If one looks at the pedagogical approaches and the ways of dealing with the problems of limited-English-speaking children, one can certainly say that intensive English-as-a-second-language instruction will at some stage get children to the point where they can understand the subject matter, but in the interim—and there certainly is an interim between the time that they start in the program and the time that they are capable of competing in an English-only classroom—they in fact suffer the same detriments that the Supreme Court pointed to in rendering its decision.

Jaime Fuster also alluded to the numbers issue. Several justices, and they were not the majority, indicated in an often-quoted statement that numbers were at the heart of the game. Some have said that in San Francisco or maybe Los Angeles, where there are large numbers of Asian kids or Hispanic kids who do not understand English, there may be some sort of a right, but, if there is an individual child here or there, the decision in *Lau* expressly or implicitly says a program need not be provided. That is not a fair interpretation of *Lau*. That statement was by a minority of justices.

One cannot really make a principled legal distinction between whether a group of children can understand what is going on in a classroom or whether an individual child understands what goes on in a classroom. Our legal system is not based on group rights. It is based on individual rights. That was driven home in the *Bakke* case, where the Court said very forcefully that individuals have rights and groups generally do not, although group discrimination calls for group remedies. So while the situation concerning small populations may call for different remedies under different circumstances, that is not to say that those children do not have a right to understandable instruction; it is that logistics for those children are somewhat different. It is on the strength of some of the things that Jaime Fuster discussed in *Lau* that it is often concluded, especially by lay people who are not involved in bilingual-education litigation, that since *Lau* did not take up the matter, that pretty well solves the problem, and school districts can do what they want. The fact is to the contrary.

Following the *Lau* decision, the Department of Health, Education, and Welfare called together various experts to determine what their response ought to be to the *Lau* decision. Those experts in the summer of 1975 concluded, in a document known as "Lau Remedies," that the appropriate approach for limited-English-speaking children was understandable instruction—bilingual/bicultural instruction. This document has had a roller-coaster effect on legal interpretation. It has never been published as a formal regulation by HEW and does not have the force of law. HEW also was very ambiguous as to when it would apply, taking the position that it did not describe the basic obligation of the school district. But once a school district was found out of compliance with civil rights laws, this was generally the approach that had to be taken to bring it back into compliance. This is a distinction that the courts and other people have found hard to understand. Nonetheless, it is a document that has been very influential in convincing school districts to implement bilingual programs. Several courts have said that the "Lau Remedies" is a document entitled to great deference and, in concluding that, they have found that there is a right to understandable instruction, bilingual instruction.

While *Lau* is our only Supreme Court case, there are several district court decisions construing Title VI of the 1964 Civil Rights Act and one court of appeals decision, all of which uphold the obligation to provide understandable instruction to children. Those cases, frankly, are the wave of the future.

There are a couple of caveats. As Jaime Fuster indicated, the cases have primarily dealt with the right to transitional bilingual education. In one case from the Ninth Circuit Court of Appeals, the court held that bilingual programs need not be provided for Chicano or Hispanic children merely because of the fact they are from homes in which a language other than English is spoken. Various rationales have been given, one of which is that the grouping of children for purposes of bilingual instruction cannot be justified in the situation where you do not have English-language problems. As Jaime Fuster pointed out, the cases generally have said there is a civil right to understandable instruction in a language other than English for limited-English-proficient children. The courts have generally indicated that there is not a right to a maintenance program. I might make a brief, one not based on a great deal of legal authority at this particular juncture in history, that in a situation in which there is no strong history of providing bilingual instruction to children, but a strong history of discrimination—the *de jure* picture that Jaime Fuster alluded to—under those situations a maintenance program might well be seen as part of a remedy for overcoming that history of discrimination.

As a Presbyterian minister, Wayne C. Hartmire felt out of place among lawyers, but he was not reluctant to point out that language and culture are the mainstays of the farmworkers, that the educational system is structured to assure failure for the poor, that it is ironic that a cause like bilingual education can attract support while social justice for workers in the fields languishes, and that bilingualism/biculturalism have merits because they make a people strong and able to achieve their economic goals—the real issue that transcends matters of race and language.

Wayne C. Hartmire: I am director of a Protestant and Catholic ministry to seasonal and migrant farmworkers that is celebrating its sixtieth anniversary this year, but which in recent years has focused more and more of its life and energy and spirit on supporting farmworkers as they organize into the union led by Cesar Chavez, the United Farmworkers of America.

I had not carefully considered this subject until I read the papers for this conference, because for us in the migrant ministry, two languages and another culture are facts of life. They are there in the fields of California. More than 90 percent of our farmworkers are Hispanic, predominantly Mexican and Mexican-American. They carry their language with them, and they carry their culture with them in their homes, in the churches, in their communities, and in their union. In fact, much of the strength and unity and staying power of the farmworkers' movement have been that shared faith, that shared culture, that shared language. So being with farmworkers in California, in Texas, and recently in Florida, means to accept and respect that other culture and to learn from it, or feel alienated from it.

There are a lot of people in rural California who would accept what I have just said but who have been fighting the Farmworkers' Union tooth and nail for the last fifteen years, and I wonder why it is that bilingual education, particularly as a transition into our society, is so acceptable to people who fight farmworkers as they organize for economic justice. I also wonder if it would have taken Cesar Chavez and the farmworkers so long to win their first victories if they had been struggling for bilingual education rather than for economic justice and political participation in community life.

That leads me to the thought that there is probably in America something that cuts deeper than race and culture and language and that probably cuts deeper in Quebec and in Montreal, and that is economics. People who are poor are going to be taken advantage of. Believe it or not, in the educational system children are not only neglected because they are poor but are programmed in an English-speaking, employer-dominated educational system to fail and to stay poor, and not just because people enjoy having poor people around, but because they need people to work cheaply for them. That may sound harsh coming from a churchman, but it comes out of experience that has hurt a lot of people and educated me.

The economic reality has to be taken into account as we consider any kind of changes in our society. The farmworkers are trying to organize for the sake of equality and human justice, and out of that organizing comes, of course, the group power to participate in community life and political life—a group power that also enables not only poor people, but poor people who carry their culture with them from Mexico, to influence what happens in Sacramento and in Washington, D.C. They have a long way to go before that power will show itself fully as it is going to show itself in the future.

The relationship between bilingualism and biculturalism in Quebec and in California never crossed my mind until I read the conference papers, but I asked myself, can it be bad? How can it be bad for the rest of us, if people grow up strong and accepted and appreciated in the culture and language of their homes and of their community and if they emerge side-by-side with us as mature, strong, independent adults? How can that be bad for us unless we have created such terrible economic inequality that they will in fact then organize to change the whole system.

> The moderator of the panel, Franklyn Haiman, has had a long interest in the criminal justice system. He sought comments on the implications of bilingualism in criminal justice.

Franklyn Haiman: You have talked primarily about what the law is, what you think the Supreme Court thinks it is. But what about what you think it ought to be? For example, ought there to be in the criminal justice system some degree of constitutional protection for a defendant to have trial procedures and the choice of jurors occur in his primary language?

Jaime Fuster did not find the question so easily answered. He recognized the record of oppression that marks the lives of many Hispanics, but he was uncertain how attempting to move toward a bilingual society would overcome the problems—except as "a battle cry." Moreover, he feared that the bilingual effort was draining resources from other movements that might prove more rewarding. He was also troubled by the fact that the advocates of bilingualism were the most cultured English-language speakers in the Mexican-American community.

Jaime Fuster: I am not sure what is fair in this situation. I have no doubts, none whatsoever, that the Hispanic-Americans—Puerto Ricans much less than the Mexican-Americans—have suffered very oppressive discrimination in this country. It is still going on, possibly not as crudely and as intensely as in the past, but certainly going on in ways that are beyond what is acceptable in any society, particularly in a society like the United States that aspires to high ideals of justice. But that is one problem, and it is a very different problem from the bilingual movement.

How does one rectify historical oppression by imposing language goals? I am not talking about transitional bilingualism; if there are people in this country who cannot learn English because they cannot get an educational experience because they do not know English, inevitably there has to be—and there are constitutional authorities for it—a way of helping them become assimilated. But the bilingual premise that seems to worry people—the controversial one—is not the transitional measures; it is something of greater magnitude. I still do not understand the support for it, because there are very serious complications that can come from the proposition that this country can be made bilingual.

To begin with, it is so unrealistic that I do not know how people can even propose it. More than that, I have not heard a very clear explanation of why it is needed. Pastora Cafferty set out one area—the problem of cyclical migration. But the way some of my brothers in the Department of Justice explain their long-range goals transcends cyclical migration in important ways, and as I have said, other than as a battle cry I do not understand it. It is an issue that might be taking the important limited energies of the Mexican-American people away from the area where the real problems are. It is diverting the energies of many valuable people, particularly those that I have seen most emotionally involved in the issue, people who speak English beautifully, who have little vital contact with and do not live as I do in the Spanish culture. I find it puzzling—discrimination has been so profound—that they must come out with this as a battle cry independent of whether it really has any meaning. If my limited understanding of the problem is correct, my brothers might be doing themselves harm because it takes away their great talents from strategies and goals that might be more meaningful.

As a lawyer, I would certainly make all kinds of arguments in favor of somebody who could not be tried in his own language—as a lawyer representing a client's interest in an individual case. As a policy-maker, I would find it difficult to come out and say that the judicial system has to be bilingual. The implications and the complications that would create are mind-boggling.

Arnold Leibowitz: There have been cases where people have asked for some language rights in judicial proceedings. The courts have a standard rule on this. In criminal cases the petitioner is entitled to understand the proceedings regardless of what they are. This does not mean—and the courts have been very clear on this—the proceedings must be conducted in the language of the accused. It means having an interpreter. The Court Interpretation Act of 1979 established that on a federal level for criminal cases. It is acceptable to say that people should understand what is going on. The Supreme Court of Puerto Rico said the same thing.

> A recording technician employed by the technical services in the University of Southern California became so interested in the dialogue that he entered the discussion by claiming that he did not find it hard to see a bilingual society in the future. He set out his scenario and asked for comments.

Joseph Simms: I am a bit troubled, if I understand correctly what is being said by this panel and the one I heard earlier, at the tendency to dismiss the question raised by the conference paper. It seems to me that it is conceivable in this country, say in Southern California, for example in the Los Angeles city schools where Mexican-Americans are already in the majority. It seems entirely possible to me that one state might begin to have a majority in it of people who do not speak the major language of the country, which in this case is English. This is what happened in Quebec. The French were always in the majority there. I am troubled that the panels dismiss out-of-hand the possibility in fifty years or so that something like Quebec might occur in this country. Is that so? Is that impression correct and, if so, why is it so difficult to imagine that kind of outcome in this country?

> There was no direct response from the panel to Joseph Simms's question. Peter Roos commented that the roots of separation were not to be found in language but in the deplorable conditions in the barrio.

Peter Roos: The theme of this conference is broader than bilingual education, which essentially is trying to bring understandable instruction to a group of students who are in the classroom and do not understand what is being taught. It strikes me as disingenuous at best to say that this particular activity is likely to lead to "something like Quebec." There may be other seeds—for example, injustice in barrios, police brutality, the lack of economic development, and so on—that may lead to increased political pressure that someday may lead to some of the problems that Quebec is presently undergoing. I think that to point the finger at bilingual education, or even any sort of bilingual development, is really pinning the blame on the wrong thing.

> Commenting from the floor, Noel Epstein, an educational writer, took sharp exception to the history and interpretation of the *Lau* case as presented earlier by Peter Roos. He thought that Jaime Fuster's interpretation was more to the point.

Noel Epstein: Peter Roos has presented an attorney-advocate's view of how he would like the law to behave so far as the *Lau* decision and the "Lau Remedies" are concerned. He is looking forward in the not-too-distant future to new Department of Education civil rights enforcement of them. I understand his reasons for presenting that view. It is his job as well as his belief; however, I certainly do not think they should go unchallenged.

And, incidentally, one problem in those scattered cases (which, I might say, are thin reeds—educationally and politically—on which to hang the entire justification for the new regulations that are going to be proposed) is that it is very difficult for attorneys to get scholars to come and testify on behalf of school boards as expert witnesses. This is because it is inadvisable, within their scholarly disciplines, even to appear to oppose the maintenance or furtherance of, or to lack sensitivity to, other languages and cultures. Frequently, cases are decided with few if any experts on the school board's side. In fact, that was the situation in a case in Ann Arbor, Michigan, concerning "Black English." There were experts brought in only on the plaintiff's side and not on the school board's side. And in one court case that Peter Roos referred to, even a journalist—myself—was subpoenaed to testify after initially declining, because they could not find experts to testify.

Now to Peter Roos's points. He emphasized that the Supreme Court was not asked to provide a remedy and therefore, he concluded, the Supreme Court did not say that bilingual education was *not* required. The Supreme Court does *not* say a lot of things, and we cannot assume that all those things may therefore be required. We must wait, decision by decision. In fact, it seems to me that since the Supreme Court was not asked to provide a remedy, the fact that it volunteered that there were a number of remedies and that the choice was up to the local school district, suggests that the Court was emphasizing that there was no one way to remedy the perceived violation. Incidentally, the *Lau* decision is not as drastic as many people believe. It is essentially a simple syllogism that comes down to this: If you do not understand what you are being taught, you do not understand what you are being taught. Ergo, schools must do something extra to help you. This left it to the local school district, as Fuster emphasized, to find a way to teach you.

What is really peculiar is that the "Lau Remedies" (which are not law, as Peter Roos pointed out) were drafted by a task force composed chiefly of bilingual/bicultural advocates, a task force made up chiefly of constituents of the civil rights forces. This task force in effect overruled the Supreme Court. The Supreme Court specifically said that giving special instruction in English by itself was one possible way to meet the goals. The task force said special instruction in English must *not* be given by itself. It seems to me a strange thing for a regulatory agency to have done, even though I do not sympathize with just giving students special instruction in English. That kind of authority seems dubious.

Second, the "Lau Remedies" allowed something that is really mind-boggling: the "Lau Remedies" were used to pressure school districts. Their effectiveness has mainly been because the Office for Civil Rights in Washington has threatened or sought to delay federal funds going to school districts that have resisted compliance with the "guidelines." It is not because of any compelling merit in the so-called Remedies that they have had effect in school districts. School districts were pressured into providing, as a minimum, one kind of bilingual education for the affected students—transitional.

Later the Office for Civil Rights sent a memo to its regional enforcement offices telling enforcers that, although these "Lau Remedies" were guidelines only, if a local school district wanted to do something other than what the guidelines say, the district had the burden of proving that what it was proposing would be "as effective" as what the civil rights enforcers were pressuring it to do. The fact is that nobody has any reliable evidence about effectiveness, regardless of what was said by the experts. So the school districts had to prove that something was "as effective" as something else that nobody could prove was effective, which ends up a ridiculous requirement.

Jaime Fuster's statement about transitional programs is interesting. A very important principle is involved here. One of the tragic things about the federal program to date is that it has been spending a great deal of energy and money on the wrong question. We have known for many years that some significant number of children can be helped to some degree by transitional bilingual education. We have also known for many years that some other significant number of children can be helped, particularly those who are from more fortunate socio-economic backgrounds, by immersion bilingual programs (which are not designed to wipe out the native language). The issue at stake here is a very important one: Is Washington going to dictate federal curriculum requirements in schools throughout the nation in sensitive areas like language and history, or is it going to find a way to build in some flexibility for local differences, local needs, to say nothing of individual needs? There are some things that work for one student, some things that work for another. It really does not make much difference what works "on the average." The question is, are we going to have an educational system that still has the flexibility to deal with the many distinct kinds of students, or are we going to set a precedent, which was implicit in creation of the new Department of Education, of increased federal intervention, particularly in politically sensitive curriculum areas? It is not a small question.

> Although he insisted that he and Noel Epstein were in agreement in many areas, Peter Roos marked as areas of disagreement the power of agencies and departments in the government to issue regulations with the force of law and the question of whether the regulations were indeed involving the federal government in matters of curriculum.

Peter Roos: There is a surprising degree of agreement between Noel Epstein and myself, but from some of the things that he has said I feel it is necessary to make certain points. I suppose one area of agreement that we have is that the *Lau* case has been greatly overrated. The reason for discussion of the *Lau* case is because of the next step that Noel Epstein takes, and this is that the *Lau* case does not say that bilingual education is required or ESL [English-as-a-second-language] is required. It leaves that open. Then he is astounded and wonders where the legal authority is for HEW to come out with "Lau Remedies."

I go back to Jaime Fuster's discussion of the basis of the *Lau* decision. What it said was, we have a civil rights law that prohibits discrimination against minority children. HEW has the authority to interpret this, and in the *Lau* case the Court upheld the authority of HEW to issue a very general regulation that said school districts must take affirmative steps to deal with language problems of children. In upholding that, the Court did not say that it was *all* that HEW could do, nor did it say that it had issued its final pronouncement as to whether understandable instruction was or was not required under Title VI. HEW then, with full legal authority, went out and tried to determine what seemed to make the most sense linguistically and pedagogically and came up with the document that we call the "Lau Remedies," with all the problems that we have discussed. HEW most clearly has the authority to issue regulations that require bilingual education, and I think that needs to be remembered. The *Lau* decision clearly did not preclude them from doing that. The *Lau* decision also did not preclude lower courts from hearing testimony that understandable instruction is mandated for children, and a half-dozen courts since then have done so.

Noel Epstein says that the real issue is whether the federal government can prescribe curriculum. I suggest that that really is not the issue at all. The issue is whether the federal government has the right to prescribe understandable instruction. The federal government is not getting into substantive curriculum issues. There are logistical matters that have to be addressed in given localities. Different language groups may have some different nuances that need to be adjusted through federal regulation or otherwise. I suggest that we have never seen, at least in the bilingual area, an effort by the federal government to prescribe curriculum.

Jaime Fuster: I feel constrained to say that, although I do not agree with what Peter Roos said in his original comments on my view of *Lau*, I do agree that there is no question that the executive department has the authority to do all the things that he has specified. There is no question that school authorities are compelled under the law to provide the kind of meaningful education that he has discussed. My point is that this assumption is not constrained by the Constitution, it arises out of a federal statute, but in functional terms one is as important as the other.

In commenting on the Court's actions, Harvard University professor Nathan Glazer pointed out that courts often reverse themselves. He set out many areas of agreement that should be removed from the discussion, but he turned to some of the arguable issues and questioned whether past policies had not brought about the cohesive society that is so important for the nation.

Nathan Glazer: The next time a case comes to the Supreme Court under new guidelines drawn up by this specially assembled group, which are different from the guidelines the Court commented on in 1970, another Supreme Court, or even the same Court, may decide that those guidelines do not say what is in the statute. That is a real possibility too.

There are a number of things I consider not at issue; it is probably good to put down those points of agreement before I get to a question. First, everyone should know a second language, and a second language should be required for a college degree. Second, cyclical migrants in the United States need something in both languages, such as Turkish and Greek workers' children in Germany receive. Third, everyone should have an understandable education, which could also be a year of an intensive program in English as was described in *Newsweek* for immigrants to San Francisco. Fourth, everyone needs services they can understand. Also, Jaime Fuster is absolutely right in saying that it boggles the mind to see bilingualism becoming a constitutional requirement.

Those things are not arguable, but there are still a few things at issue. I want to indicate what is at issue by making an historical reference which probably has influenced me more than it should have and which many of the people here undoubtedly know. Marcus Hansen, in his *History of Immigration,* referred to a time in the 1820s or 1830s when Congress was faced with this question regarding the sale of the public land: Do we sell tracts individually (which is what was being done), or do we make deals with groups of Irish or German immigrants who want huge tracts of land to create a little bit of a new Germany or a new Ireland? They decided to stick with individual sales. Hansen thought that was a very important decision in determining how the country would evolve. There were many other such moments in the history of Wisconsin, Missouri, and Texas. Perhaps I exaggerate the significance of these actions, which are both symbolic and practical as to shaping the future of a nation, and I suspect I do, because in the end, despite all the German schools, German-Americans were very patriotic in the First and the Second World Wars.

Nevertheless, there are actions which shape a future. I want to make another point—a predictive, if not historical point—a reason why how we handle this matter of bilingualism may be important. A couple of years ago a committee of Congress was set up to study immigration policy. It was chaired by Congressman Sawyer. One congressman told me—and he was not a stupid man—that the committee had testimony that by the end of the century there will be 140 million Mexicans, and half of them will be living north of the border. That border itself is an ambiguous thing. As someone pointed out, "We did not migrate, the border migrated." It is an interesting point, if one thinks with that kind of perspective.

I address my question to Arnold Leibowitz. He told an interesting story of the Japanese afternoon schools in Hawaii. I fully agree with him that it was a terrible case of hysteria and prejudice for the Hawaiian state government to look into those schools, and I agree with *Meyer v. Nebraska*. I am a great advocate of private rights, but the question is, would it have been better all around for the Japanese if it had been up to the state schools of Hawaii, under statutory requirements interpreted by some court, to provide Japanese language and cultural instruction in the schools? Consider the alternative and ask, would that have been best for the Japanese and for Hawaii?

Arnold Leibowitz: I do not think from a legal point of view or from the issue of unity or divisiveness that it is significant whether the public school or the private school provided the language and cultural instruction. The issue is whether it could be provided at all.

I differ with others on the significance of the *Lau* case, especially as Noel Epstein has stated it. It is not just that one should be taught things that one should be taught. At the time of the *Lau* case, there were many statutes on the books that said teaching could be done only in English. If anyone wanted something else, these statutes said he did not have the right to it. What the Court was saying in *Lau v. Nichols* is that a person *does* have such a right. The student has a right to understand. The method of making him understand could be compensatory education (something I quite agree with), but there has to be some acknowledgement of the fact that, if the system does not play for you in a language that you understand, then either the language will have to be slowed down a bit or instruction will have to be in a language that you do understand.

I would agree also, from Nathan Glazer's point of view, that what I hope will be evolving, and I think is even evolving under the Bilingual Education Act, is federal support for local accommodation to that basic right—the right of people in various groups, in various stages, at the state level and local level, to demand, if they need it, the kind of education that will be responsive to their circumstances. It could be done as the Japanese wanted to do it after school, or it need not be done at all.

Implications of Bilingualism:
Politics

There is no doubt that the use of languages other than English in the schools and for other purposes as a result of legislation, court orders, and consent decrees has become a hotly debated political issue. It has touched the lives of several of the participants in this panel and, as a result, they hold strong views. The moderator of the panel on politics and bilingualism was the Reverend Max Gaebler of the First Unitarian Society of Madison, Wisconsin. The panelists were Henry Der, director of Chinese Affirmative Action in San Francisco; Father Andrew M. Greeley, director of the Center for Study of American Pluralism at the National Opinion Research Center, University of Chicago, and currently professor of sociology in the University of Arizona; Carmen Diaz-Rubin de Armstrong, coordinator of bilingual education in the public schools of Thousand Oaks, California; and Quentin Kopp of the board of supervisors of the City and County of San Francisco.

Max Gaebler: I grew up in Wisconsin, which was heavily settled by German '48ers. They introduced the kindergarten and free textbooks in the public schools, and although they and their political leaders spoke German they maintained a healthy interest in politics and the republican form of government. Their chief spokesman was Carl Schurz who, as a bilingual politician, bridged the gap between his constituents and the power structure of the Republican party. Ethnic politics are nothing new in America. People who have been able to appeal politically to particular groups on the basis of language and culture have been with us for a long time. I am sure that while the circumstances today are very different from those in the past, some of the phenomena have not changed markedly.

> Henry Der, one of the current exponents of utilizing politics in the interests of a minority, spoke for both the Chinese community and his organization. He denied any interest in living outside the mainstream of American life, pointing out that Chinese for Affirmative Action had pioneered bilingual education on television to teach English to adult immigrants. He denied too that his organization could in any way manipulate Chinese opinion for political purposes. Their struggle is to attain what other groups in the community already possess: adequate police protection, voting rights, and a say in the way the resources of the community are used.

Henry Der: Chinese for Affirmative Action is not a partisan political organization. In order to carry out some of our concerns, and to advocate for the needs of the Chinese-American community in San Francisco, we must deal with political institutions, politicians, and government. In making some brief comments about politics as related to bilingualism/biculturalism I take the broadest definition of politics, including those who are elected and those who are in the executive branch of our government, from the federal level down to the local level.

There are some very basic misunderstandings about why organizations such as ours push for bilingual assistance. First, one prevalent misconception is that there is an inherent dislike within a community such as the Chinese-American community toward learning English. There is very little truth in that. As a civil rights organization, when we were first created in the early 1970s Chinese for Affirmative Action urged one of the local commercial television stations to produce a series to teach English to adult Chinese immigrants. It was the first time that any Chinese community organization had initiated a series of that kind. It won an *Emmy* award. As a result of this effort we received a grant from the

Department of Health, Education, and Welfare to produce accompanying audiocassette tapes so that Chinese immigrants throughout the United States could learn English at home. We have distributed well over 8,000 English tape kits, reaching about 25 percent of the non-English-speaking Chinese population in our country.

Second, there is the general criticism that those who advocate for bilingual programs or ask for bilingual assistance really want to exert political control over language-minority community members. There is very little truth in that criticism. In the San Francisco Chinese-American community, more than a dozen daily or weekly newspapers are printed in the Chinese language. Many Chinese citizens are well-informed. There is no way that our organization or any other could conceivably bamboozle members of the community into voting one way or another in elections or in making decisions that may affect their lives. The basic thrust behind bilingualism—be it in the area of voting rights, education, police services, health services, radio and television programs—is very simple. Bilingualism is only a means whereby members of our community can participate in the broader community on an equal basis.

We do not see bilingualism as an end in itself. We are pragmatic enough to realize that, given the small number of Chinese-Americans, not only in the Bay Area but also in the entire country, it is political suicide and certainly not pragmatic to advocate for the permanent institutionalization of a bilingual/bicultural political system whereby people can participate in American society. Bilingualism is only a means to an essential democratic right of participating and sharing in the making of certain decisions that affect members of our community and the broader public.

Because there has been extensive discussion of bilingual education, I will not comment on how it has affected the Chinese-Americans in San Francisco, but I will, for the purposes of discussion, list the reasons why bilingualism in other areas is extremely important and why politicians and/or bureaucrats sometimes institute or do not institute bilingual programs.

As early as 1975 our organization filed a complaint with the United States Department of Justice Law Enforcement Assistance

Administration about the lack of bilingual police officers and the fact that this lack constituted racial discrimination against Chinese-Americans who could not speak the English language and were, therefore, deprived of essential police services. When this complaint was first filed, justice officials made perfunctory efforts to investigate our complaint, but for a variety of reasons the Ford Administration did not pursue the complaint.

In 1977 we refiled our complaint with the new administration. Justice officials came to San Francisco to investigate and found that the lack of bilingual police officers did, in fact, constitute a denial of equal services to Chinese-Americans. The finding was made right after the mass murders at the Golden Dragon Restaurant in Chinatown, where five persons were killed in a youth gang shoot-out. That incident brought national and local attention to the fact that there was a problem in the Chinese community because of a complete absence of communication between the police department and the citizens of the community. As a result of our complaint and the findings that were made by the justice department, the police department and the justice department signed an agreement whereby the police department would take remedial steps to increase bilingual services to the Chinese-American community.

In addition to this complaint, there was an ongoing Title VII lawsuit against the police department for discriminatory hiring and promotional practices. Incorporated into the Title VII lawsuit consent decree, twenty bilingual police officers were targeted to be hired in response to our complaint filed with the Law Enforcement Assistance Administration. The police department had been unwilling to act promptly in recognizing the need for bilingual police services. It took an outside group, federal intervention, and a couple of other events to precipitate some kind of relief. While we do have relief today, we still feel that we are victims of unequal services. Many crimes go unreported because of an insufficient number of police officers.

Our organization has also been concerned about voting rights. We did not play a major role in the congressional discussion that led to adoption of the 1975 amendments to the Voting Rights Act, but since the enactment by Congress of this important federal law, we have been working vigorously to persuade our local officials to enforce the law in San Francisco. I feel that this federal law is a great service to language-minority citizens. Many Chinese citizens do not speak the English language because of past discrimination, and it is our strong belief that they should not be denied the right to vote. They are intelligent citizens. They are not perverts. They are not criminals who are trying to undo the American system. Their right to vote is as American as apple pie and motherhood, but because of the English-language barrier many of them have been reluctant to exercise this right.

There has been an enormous ballyhoo about the cost of bilingual elections. Problems related to cost are not the fault of language-minority citizens but the product of election officials who have taken very little interest in implementing the law, thereby creating greater problems. In San Francisco, the registrar of voters spends more money on non-voters who are English-speaking than on language-minority citizens. For every election in San Francisco, more than 70,000 English-language ballot pamphlets are returned to the registrar of voters because voters have moved or failed to vote in the previous election. For the registrar of voters to print these ballots in English, send them out, get them back on a guaranteed postage return, hire eight clerks to doublecheck the rolls, then send back a postcard to those homes again to make sure that those voters are no longer there, and then to get a response from the postoffice or from the person, costs well over $100,000 per election. The cost of servicing non-voters, individuals who do not vote but who are presumably English-speaking, is much higher than the cost of conducting bilingual elections, which runs in the neighborhood of $40,000, according to the registrar of voters.

The cost of bilingual elections is a "red herring"; the real complaint about bilingual elections is that a majority of our citizens emotionally and otherwise feel that if you do not speak English you should not have the right to vote. Of course we disagree with that view. In San Francisco (and I mention San Francisco only because what has happened to the Chinese minority there is a microcosm of some of the larger problems faced by other minorities elsewhere) we recently witnessed settlement of a lawsuit initiated by the Department of Justice against the registrar of voters. The settlement asks the registrar to do what he should have been doing all along, as articulated in the federal regulations and federal statutes. After a cost analysis conducted by the Board of Supervisors' budget analyst and by the newly installed registrar of voters, it was found that bilingual elections could be conducted within the economies of Proposition 13 and within the economies of the present city budget. The basic element to the consent decree is cooperation with community groups who are interested in making this law work in San Francisco.

> In strong disagreement with Henry Der, Quentin Kopp, a San Francisco city and county supervisor since 1971, argued that the actions taken by the justice department went far beyond the intent of the law. As for the law itself, Kopp felt that it was the product of both opportunism and weakness, and found proof for his charge in the few language-minorities that were singled out for special treatment. He insisted too that the law placed almost impossible burdens on a community trying to comply, and he argued that its peculiar provisions of finding a community guilty of responsibility for discrimination when there are no specific examples is highly suspect. He predicted that this whole effort would soon be overturned when the people and the courts became aware of what was involved.

Quentin Kopp: The lawsuit to which Henry Der referred has brought absurdity to a new level in contemporary American society. As Abigail Thernstrom pointed out, the original Voting Rights Act in 1965 was predicated upon the principle of giving people access to the ballot. What has happened now is that the right to vote has come to mean the right to an equal result in elections. The most recent amendments in 1975 provided that in any jurisdiction where the Census Bureau said that at least 5 percent of the eligible voters did not know enough English to vote in English, or if the illiteracy rate among that classification exceeded the national average of illiteracy for that particular group, or if the total vote in the jurisdiction in the last presidential election was less than 50 percent of those qualified to vote, then immediately there was triggered a requirement that you fall under provisions of the act. That means, first of all, ballots must be printed in more than one language, that is, more than English.

Of course, the curious thing that commentators have spoken about is that the languages covered by the amendments are limited.

The languages are only those of Asian-Americans, people of Spanish heritage, Native Americans, and Alaskan natives. One absurd provision refers to the fact that some Alaskan natives do not have a written language, so that instructions in all these things must be given entirely orally. I have been through a lot of San Francisco elections, but that provision staggers my imagination with the potential for mischief. Pursuant to that provision, since 1975 San Francisco has had to print ballots in several languages. The San Francisco voter, when he or she opens the mail one day a couple of weeks or so before the election, is shocked to find that it is not printed in type of a size that is easily legible and may wonder what it is all about. [Editor's note: A sample San Francisco ballot appears in the Appendix.]

The lawsuit referred to, however, takes the problem one step further. It is a test case by the Department of Justice in San Francisco, and let me tell you what is at the heart of the case. Henry Der's organization brought suit back in 1975, almost as soon as the Voting Rights Act was extended by Congress. Then in the fall of 1978 the United States attorney brought suit saying that San Francisco was violating the law because it was not enough simply to print ballots in Chinese and Spanish and send them out to people who requested them. (I agree that costs are really not the issue here, although cost does mean something in today's financial climate of government.) What we did was not enough. We were supposed to go out and find people who are citizens but do not speak enough English to be able to cast a ballot in English. We are, of course, limited to finding people who qualify under the four language categories in the federal statute—people who speak one of those languages only or who feel comfortable casting a ballot only in their own language. We have to reach them by setting up tables on street corners, by public service announcements on radio and television, by flyers in the gas company bills, flyers in the phone company bills. The United States attorney says that this could be a lot of fun. We could even do it by putting a trailer behind an airplane flying over the forty-nine square miles of San Francisco, or by balloons that would carry some message in Chinese and Spanish as well as in English about the joys of registering and being able to vote.

Naturally I disagree with the premise of the suit. First, why is it limited to these particular language categories? How about the 120,000 citizens of Italian descent in San Francisco, many of whom do not speak English sufficiently to feel comfortable casting a ballot in English? How about all the other language rights? Second, how about the fact that, formerly under civil rights laws, in order to apply a remedy you had to show there had actually been discrimination with respect to a person or even a group? The Voting Rights Act requires no proof that there has been discrimination against anybody of Chinese extraction or anybody of Spanish heritage in respect to elections in San Francisco. And, finally, how about the English-speaking person who will not be the object of all this government beneficence of trying to recruit him or her to register, and then, after registration, to go to the polls?

I will take Henry Der at face value when he says that the process does not permit manipulation in the actual casting of the ballot. Others, however, who are not as peaceful as Henry Der, know that it might be possible to persuade a person or a group of persons as to where their interests best lie with respect to a particular candidate or particular ballot measure.

To give you an idea, indeed, of how the suit settlement is accepted, the *San Francisco Chronicle* about a month-and-a-half ago ran an unscientific poll; they asked the question, should English be the language in which you are required to cast a ballot? They gave a number to be called to give expression to your view; 22,382 people called in and said yes, and 4,391 called in and said no. Eighty-four percent said yes.

I cannot remember all the details of contemporary political life in the nation's capital in July and August 1975, but I have tried to reconstruct from the *Congressional Quarterly* and other publications just how this ingenious provision came into the law, and I can only conclude that it was a stampede that simply swept politicians of both parties. Former United States Senator John Tunney, a Democract, is given responsibility for the provision about Chinese and Spanish ballots, but how many people here could tell me who the President was who signed this bill? It was Republican Gerald Ford.

My own impression of the matter is that this is part of a seeming reluctance to accept the idea that English is the language of the United States and that English is the language upon which this economy and economic opportunity have been founded. People become shrill and defensive by the very nature of the theory which is contained in these seventy-five amendments of the Voting Rights Act. And interestingly, except when *Harpers* ran Tom Bethell's article and there were some articles in the *Washington Post*, hardly anybody paid much attention to this encroachment on the political process.

I will make a prediction. There *is* a focus of attention on this now. I think the high-water mark has been reached. There are three different bills pending in the Congress, two in the House and one in the Senate, to repeal those provisions of the Voting Rights Act. They have been bottled up in committee by one of the authors of the original 1975 amendments, but they are going to get an airing, maybe not in this election year but I would say within the next year. I think that repeal will take place without denigrating what I know to be the sincere and fervent faith of people who feel this kind of scheme should be part of the American political process.

I think that requiring the printing of ballots in languages other than English is simply too silly for the American people to accept, including the very language-speaking populations who could be beneficiaries of this governmental program if they wanted it. It is too much for them to tolerate very much longer now that the spotlight of publicity has been placed upon them, and I think that probably five years from now this will be as much a thing of the past as that very interesting process of the nineteenth century that is described in the essay by Stephen Wagner. But in the meantime, it certainly is a symbol of a basic part of contemporary American society that has simply gotten away from the original premise upon which the society is founded, and that premise is opportunity.

> One of the nation's leading advocates of linguistic and cultural pluralism, Father Andrew Greeley, favors a society in which all languages and cultures exist with equal status. He feels that he was deprived of his heritage by repressive language practices, and denies that bilingualism impedes an individual's efforts for success. Pointing to the experience of the Catholic parochial school system, he argues that it not only maintained bilingualism but also stimulated

cultural cohesion. The suppression of minority cultures, he insists, stems from ignorance and arrogance on the part of the English-speaking majority.

Andrew Greeley: My premise is that bilingualism is as American as borscht and bagels. My own grandparents were from the west of Ireland. They spoke Irish as their first language. They repressed it utterly—would not speak it with their children—because they feared it would interfere with the children's success in America. Only one word survived. It is the very Irish word "omidon"—the use of which I will illustrate. A husband comes home at 6:30 at night and his wife says to him, "You omidon, what are you late for? Didn't you know we're having guests?" That is an "omidon." It can also be translated freely by the word "igit," which is not quite the same as idiot, but perhaps more descriptive. I feel culturally deprived that a language that could produce such a splendid word as "omidon" has been denied me. They told us that if we gave up our language we could have success in American society and, sure enough, we have. Irish Catholics have recently been made presidents of the Ford Foundation, Harvard, and the University of Chicago. All kinds of nice positions in the society are opening up for the Irish.

I want to talk about politics in the broader sense of whether bilingualism facilitates or impedes the success of a given ethnic immigrant group in obtaining for itself a piece of the American pie. We are all competing with one another in this—if not mosaic, at least stew-pot—society for some kind of affluence and success. Does bilingualism help or hurt? I would point out that as recently as the early 1950s, there were more than one hundred bilingual schools in the city of Chicago. Admittedly, they were all Catholic parochial schools, but a school is a school when somebody wants to study the educational impact. We have in Chicago, and in a large number of other cities, a marvelous natural laboratory to study the effect of bilingual education.

These were not transitional schools. These were schools with people who were probably more English-speaking than Polish-speaking when they went to school. They were people of my own generation, and even after me, and these schools were without a doubt language and cultural maintenance schools. They were designed to be that, and even though it is now clear that one did not have to maintain a Polish culture to maintain his Catholic religion, it was thought to be so earlier in the century. These were schools designed to keep the Polish heritage alive, or the Croatian, or Serbian, or Slovakian, or those of all the other people who were part of the Chicago Catholic school system.

What impact did those schools have on the people who are now adults? One has the impression that they talk a little funny. Michael Bilandic, who was the mayor of Chicago for a while, talked a little funny, but he did not talk any funnier than the folks from New York or Boston. And the reason he was not reelected had nothing to do with his slight Croatian accent; it had to do with his inability to get the snow shoveled. I do not think there is anybody that has argued that going to St. Jerome's Croatian School was the reason he could not get the snow shoveled. Chicago now has a mayor who speaks perfectly good Chicago-Irish English, and nobody's worried about the snow any more. They have more serious worries.

Did the presence of foreign-language and cultural-maintenance programs in the Catholic school system somehow interfere with the cohesiveness of the city of Chicago or the larger society? Were these Poles, Croatians, and others who were students in the bilingual schools of the 1930s, 1940s, and 1950s somehow an affront to national unity? Did their schooling somehow make Chicago Poles, for example, less vigorous and committed participants in the American political experiment? That is a reasonable question. If you ask it that way, you had better smile when you do, because these people have the peculiar notion that not only are they good Americans, they are better Americans than anyone else. The thought that the bilingual education of these folks would propel them into some sort of separatist route just becomes hilarious when you look at the concrete situation. The thought that it was divisive just does not make sense at all. Nonetheless, it would be interesting to see what impact it did have on civic intolerance, and how the people perceive themselves as participating in the larger society because they attended bilingual schools.

There is the pay-off question: What impact did bilingual schooling have on economic achievement? Before that question can be answered, you have to know what people thought about the Poles. For example, the Dillingham Commission thought Polish-Americans were racially inferior because of their inherently unstable personalities. Other groups have been pushed around more than the Poles, but I do not know of any group that is presently accused of being genetically or racially unstable. The Italians were accused by the Dillingham Commission of being genetically criminal. Then came the University of Chicago sociology school (of which I am a late and somewhat illegitimate descendant), presided over by William I. Thomas who said: "I do not want to reject all the important insights of the races, but the problems with the Poles on the Northwest Side of Chicago is not that they are biologically or racially inferior, they are culturally inferior. Their European peasant culture just is not going to be any help to them. It is a terrible problem and they are not assimilating to urban industrial life. That is why they have the high crime rates, delinquency rates, homicide rates, and that sort of thing. Unless we who are responsible for them come in and change their culture, they are never going to make it in American society." The Poles managed to escape the tender ministrations of the University of Chicago sociologists. They kept their language schools. They kept their culture for a considerable time, and many of them still do.

How much of a barrier has this culture been to their economic success? One can say that, nationally, Polish-Americans under forty earn on the average about $1,500 a year more than the average white American, in figures standardized for city size and region and so on. At the least, Polish peasant culture did not impede their assimilation. It is a testable question whether those who went to Catholic schools and were bilingually instructed were impeded at all economically or maybe even facilitated economically by bilingual education.

I have a fantasy that Lem X. Quicksilver, a Martian anthropologist, arrives at my apartment, and we go for a walk in the old Polish neighborhood around St. Stanislaus on the Northwest Side of Chicago. Lem is really very upset because he is a man with deep social concern about the genocide practiced against American Poles. I say, "What do you mean, genocide, Lem?" And he says, "Well, there are none of them here anymore. I can't find them here anymore. I can't find them in this neighborhood, and obviously they haven't gone anyplace else because there are no contributions at all in sociological literature about them since *The Polish Peasant*, the last major study done by W. I. Thomas." No-one would try to explain to Lem that genocide is not the case, but how could one account to him the fact that these bilinguals kept alive a quasi-separate bilingual culture for a long time that has not been studied?

What I would do is take Lem into St. Stanislaus, which, although battered, is still standing in Pulaski Park, where there is the Black Madonna (the patron saint of Poland) on one side of the main altar, and Our Lady of Guadalupe (the patron saint of Mexico) on the other. At the back of the church there are two confessionals. Over one it says, "Confessions heard in Spanish," and something written beneath it that means the same thing; over the other it says, "Confessions heard in Polish," and something written beneath it that means the same thing. On both confessionals it says, "Confessions heard in English." What you have is the mother church of American colonial trilingualism.

Catholic church policy since 1920 in the United States has been assimilationist. The church "bought' assimilation with a vengeance, barely tolerating diversity or bilingualism. The reason for grass roots trilingualism at a place like St. Stanislaus is that the Catholic church is not very efficient. Although it espoused Americanization in the 1920s, it was not very good at imposing its policies at the grass roots. What this salvific inefficiency has done is leave the people at the grass roots free to innovate and come up with what I showed Lem—the Black Madonna on one side of the altar and a brown madonna on the other.

> As director of bilingual education in a California city public school system, Carmen Armstrong explained some of the problems confronted by teachers who are given complicated regulations that are virtually impossible to implement, regulations drafted by individuals of good will but without practical knowledge, regulations that tax the capacity of the systems. Her personal experiences, although unique, shed a special light on the political dimension of bilingual education.

Carmen Armstrong: I would like to start out with a suggestion to all my non-English-speaking friends; they should call themselves

American regardless of what language they speak, so long as they intend to make their homes in this country. My maiden name is Spanish, and I grew so tired of spelling it out to bank clerks and explaining how it should be filed, that I married a man whose name poses no problems to clerks. I have another suggestion—this one to the government and the business community—please provide more space for names on application forms, because Hispanic names do not fit. For Hispanic people entering our communities, it is a mark of our insensitivity. Now to a more serious view of the subject.

Last January I read that State Senator Russell and Assemblyman Mangers were rewriting California's bilingual legislation. I read the bills and decided to make my concerns known to Mr. Mangers and other legislators. The interesting thing to me is that the legislators are so accessible. I often wonder why we educators do not contact them more often. Why is it that educators see a need by their students, see a need in their schools, and do not act? They wait until someone gives them a mandate. Then they must implement something that they do not agree with. A good example of this is the Casey bill in 1964: it was going to make all children bilingual, like it or not. The Casey bill was written by a dentist, and he was mandating how teachers should function.

At the present time I am in charge of a program involving thirty schools, 20,500 students more or less, 650 ESL, NES, LES students [English-as-a-second-language, non-English-speaking, limited-English-speaking] who use thirty-two different languages. I have heard someone say that educators are lying when they say they cannot find a bilingual teacher for a certain language. But I cannot find a teacher who speaks Tagalog, Laotian, or Korean. If I could I would be delighted, but there are none. We had a very large influx of non-English-speaking Parsi students, more than one hundred. How do we teach them and remain in compliance with the law?

Four state bills are presently under review. The current law would be retained under the Chacon-Moscone bill. A bill sponsored by Assemblyman Mangers is a transitional-bilingual measure. A bill sponsored by Senator Johnson would change the number of students required for a bilingual class from ten to thirty. That would really cut down on the number of teachers required per language. Senator Russell also sponsors a transitional bill, but his would change the bilingual class requirement from ten to twenty per grade level. In the case of the 1964 Casey bill, the state provided no special financial support. The only salvation is EIA funds [Economic Impact Aid under Title I and Title VII of the Elementary and Secondary Education Act] and some state funds.

This legislation divides my community. The Board of Education is divided. Some members want bilingual education. Most do not; they do not even want the word used. As director of the program, I am caught in political crossfire between factions. There are several needs which politicians have not addressed, and these are what I tried to explain to the legislators that I talked to. But the answer was always the same: "They are too hot to handle."

Even the so-called easy problems are hard. How do you find trained school personnel? If a teacher is to get a waiver, the teacher must take a test at a university. It costs $50. Who pays the $50? Should the school district pay, the teacher pay? What about in-service programs for these teachers and their aides? How should students be assigned by grade level when they come from foreign schools? Can you imagine an Iranian transcript? Have you ever tried to figure out how old a student is when his culture does not emphasize dates? These are things that bilingual-education laws mandate must be. faced at the local level. What about graduation requirements? What about retention policies and promotion policies? Even more troubling is current legislation that makes it compulsory for a student to pass a language competency test before being awarded a high school diploma in the state of California. These young people have to take the test in English whether they have been here a month or ten years. We have automatically made these individuals high school dropouts or failures.

The State Legislative Audit Committee has prepared a very good brochure on the implementation of bilingual education in California, showing the results of a study completed on March 24, 1980. These are some of their findings: The majority of schools in the state are out of compliance, which means that the current legislation is simply not viable. Staff mandates are not being met; teachers are not on waivers; or they do not have the right bilingual credential. We do not have the correct number of English-speaking students per classroom; the law specifies that one-third of the students in a bilingual class must be English-speakers. We are not assessing the students' English proficiencies in the same manner from one school to another.

The reporting regulation at the school level has become a virtual paper mill. The home-language survey has to be done every year. In my case that means 20,500 per year. The politics of this is interesting because many of the foreign-born people are very much afraid of any kind of reporting, whether they are illegally in the United States or not, whether they are Iranians or Mexicans. They look at reports with a jaundiced eye, wondering why someone wants to know these things about them. They come from a society where citizens fear or distrust their government, or both. We must reassure them that their child's education is based on money generated by this questionnaire and that we do not turn this information over to the Immigration and Naturalization Service. The testing we are required to do for each youngster is an enormous task. This last January we had to do the Indo-Chinese survey. Federal officials told us that in California, since November 1979 about 260,000 Indo-Chinese refugees moved into this state. Forty-four thousand of these are school-age children. The problem is not going to go away. If you think the cost of educating them is high, wait until you start paying the price of welfare that results from ignorance if we fail.

> In discussion that followed the presentation by the panelists, Tarun Bose, a visiting scholar at Harvard University from India, asked if the bilingual issue had attracted the attention of ambitious politicians who could capitalize on it.

Tarun Bose: No-one has mentioned whether the bilingual problem is being taken advantage of by politicians. In my country, whenever there has been so volatile an issue, especially if it happens to concern language, politicians often take a stand on the issue without necessarily taking into account the long-term implications of their position. Here in Los Angeles you have the Hispanic community, a large number of people. Would not it be in the interest of a politician who is looking for votes to take a stand, purely from the short-range point of view, without necessarily looking into the long-term implications?

Quentin Kopp: As a sometime practicing politician, I do not think there is much doubt about the fact that the 1975 amendments to the Voting Rights Act were the product of exactly that. Some amendments that were proposed, even by Republicans in the House, were so modest that I was curious about them. I asked why there was not simply an amendment to delete the provision about bilingual ballots, which has now been read to mean you have to go out and find people who cannot speak English. I was told by a congressional legislative assistant that it simply was not "do-able." And how else do you explain the signing of the bill by a Republican president in a year just before the presidential election? I think for example, that the extension of this legislation to Asian-American groups (with respect to whom no testimony, as far as I know, was given before the House Committee on Constitutional and Civil Rights) was on the basis of seeking political favor, and is an indication of how supinely the majority of both houses accepted the amendments at the last minute in late July and early August.

Henry Der: I respect Supervisor Kopp's views on the Voting Rights Act, and more important, he does represent his constituency very ably. My position on bilingual elections is, while Asian-Americans are beneficiaries of this act, I would like to see Russian-Americans who live in the Richmond district of San Francisco also be beneficiaries, and Italian-Americans who live next to the Chinese also participate. Certainly we do not want, by being beneficiaries, to deny other people similar rights to understand the ballot in their own language and have access to the ballot box.

There is an interesting sidelight to this debate over bilingual elections in San Francisco regarding two supervisors who presently represent the major Chinese neighborhoods. During the last supervisorial election in 1979, both of them in their campaigns took advantage of advertising their candidacy in the Chinese-language newspapers and printed and distributed promotional materials in both Chinese and English, but when it came to the vote on this settlement between the Department of Justice and the Board of Supervisors, they voted against the settlement which would better enfranchise Chinese-American citizens in San Francisco. There are political considerations on both sides; there are many factors in-

volved; but from our narrow perspective as a civil rights organization our one and only concern is that people get out and vote. We
do not care what party or candidate they vote for.

Andrew Greeley: It would be a miracle if I could make some of
the bilingual Poles in Chicago I was talking about actually think
they have a right to elect one of their own people the mayor of
Chicago; everybody knows that is an Irish position. That point is
not altogether facetious or ironic. Ethnic politics are part of the warp
and woof of American life. Yes, of course, people will put these
things to political purposes. The mayor of Chicago, the late Richard
Daley, the *real* mayor, the *only* mayor, was terribly concerned about
getting Hispanics registered to vote because he felt that if they
were registered they would vote right. And he did not mean
"right" in terms of political right and left. So we have to be kidding
if we think that there are not going to be ethnic political in-
volvements. Of course there will be. That is what makes America,
America.

> Taking up Andrew Greeley's comments about bilingualism in
> Chicago, Professor John Allswang of California State University, Los
> Angeles, asked if he did not see a difference between bilingualism in
> a private parochial school setting and in the public schools.

John Allswang: It seems fairly important in the context of this
conference to explain that when Father Greeley was talking about
the parochial school system in Chicago, he was not simply discussing a transitional but a maintenance linguistic and cultural program. It was, nonetheless, a private program, and in that way quite
distinct from what we are dealing with contemporarily in terms of
sought-after government-sponsored, government-maintained,
and publicly recognized programs for a bicultural and bilingual
system, whether it be maintenance or transitional. Whereas the
former was something that existed very much within the mainstream of American political and educational and ethnic life, this is
indeed something different, is it not?

Andrew Greeley: In the years before 1960 the people that wanted
or felt they needed bilingual education for their children probably
had to provide it themselves because the society was so viciously
nativistic that even the suggestion that the public schools in

Chicago, for example, should teach in Polish or Croatian during the 1920s particularly, would have led to horrendous results. Foreign language instruction was done by private organizations because the government would *not* do it. I would be inclined on principle, to which I am committed, to say that it would be preferable for private organizations to do this rather than public ones. But there could be a situation in which the government may very well have to step in—certainly in Carmen Armstrong's district, I cannot imagine there being a network of private organizations that could do it.

I am ambivalent about it, but one could make the case that we simply have a greater conscience now about our obligations to those new Americans that we are permitting into our society than we did when the Irish (and many early Irish immigrants did not speak English) and Italians and Poles and other "wretched refuse of the earth" washed up on our shores.

Quentin Kopp: A little note to that. Foreign language instruction was done privately by other groups, too. In San Francisco, for example, and I am sure in other cities with substantial Chinese population, the Chinese community had schools in the Chinese language and culture that met after regular public school. Then in 1971 a federal judge said children had to be bused from one school to another in order to achieve racial balance, and one of the objections of a segment of the Chinese community, which I represent as a lawyer, was that this would destroy the system of after-school classes in Chinese language, history, and culture. This leads me to believe, as Professor Allswang suggests, that it would be far preferable for this to continue as a private associational activity. What the government does, it can undo.

> It was the observation of Professor Elliott Barkan of California State College, San Bernardino, that changes in law and practice have successfully influenced the way politicians respond to the language issue.

Elliott Barkan: Prior to 1907 the United States government had not centralized the naturalization proceedings; they were left to various state and local courts. Therefore, the standards that had to be met to become an American citizen were quite irregular. It is questionable as to whether immigrants were really asked if they could read English. Certainly, even today in the naturalization proceedings the extent of English that is expected is really quite minimal. So it is clear that to become an American citizen one need not be fluent or even literate in the English language.

Maybe I can illustrate this by a story about a political boss named Sullivan in the Lower East Side of Manhattan, who mentioned that his constituency had been made up of Irishmen, Englishmen, and Germans; he knew a little bit of German and Irish, everything was fine. Then in the late nineteenth century Jews began moving into the Lower East Side. When asked how he dealt with the problem he said, "I learned Yiddish."

The bosses in those days were intermediaries. They translated politics into terms the new citizens could understand. They indicated which candidates would be best to vote for, and the new citizens were more than willing to return the favors that the political bosses had conferred on them. The ballot did not have eighteen propositions, four amendments, and other kinds of complicating provisions requiring a voter to be well-educated to read it. It was a list of names. The voter did not need to be literate, since he was usually being advised on how to vote. Whether in the German community, where people were campaigning in German, or in any other community in rural areas where people were campaigning or giving advice in Swedish or Norwegian, English was not essential.

We are now dealing with a different situation. There are far more complicated ballots and no political bosses or party machines to help translate issues for all these new citizens. Perhaps it is not unreasonable to think that there must be new solutions to deal with people who are not really literate or, in fact, fluent in English. As I understand the naturalization proceedings, asking for bilingual or multilingual ballots is really not a preposterous or unreasonable demand in the light of how our politics have changed.

Quentin Kopp: I have two reactions to that. One is that the immigration law of 1952 requires the naturalized citizen to be able to speak and read and write simple English in words that are in everyday usage. The requirements of the federal law are very easy. They require a knowledge somewhere at the elementary school level. That is the minimal level that is required of all other citizens.

Second, what is suggested by our history is that people in the United States learn to operate in all areas—economic, political, et cetera—in English. And even though the political campaign may be a temporary period for an individual or for a group, it encourages them to learn English. I do not see a great encouragement factor if there is a proliferation of ballots in other languages, which necessarily means for the candidate not only taking out ads in foreign language newspapers but then conducting radio, television, personal meetings, debates, and the like in languages other than English. I have a hard enough time trying to communicate my ideas in English without trying to take on that responsibility.

> Responding to Supervisor Kopp, Henry Der, in a statement that closed discussion on a personal note, defended the decision that forced San Francisco to reach out to voters. He pointed out not only the peculiar circumstances surrounding the admission of Chinese to American citizenship but also the need for understandable literature for the concerned Chinese-American citizen who wants to vote.

Henry Der: A strong case can be made for why Asian-Americans should be and rightfully are protected under the 1975 amendment to the Voting Rights Act. As recently as 1943, Chinese persons were not permitted by federal statute to become naturalized citizens of this country; many of our elderly citizens, who lived with that legacy of discrimination over the years, have been literally discouraged from either taking citizenship or, if they have become citizens, from exercising their right to vote as citizens. There have been many other laws passed by the Congress and by the California State Legislature that have literally deprived Chinese-Americans of occupations and other endeavors in our society. It is this legacy, this pervasive legacy of discrimination, that has kept Chinese-American citizens, as other ethnic minority citizens of this country, from full participation.

The Voting Rights Act in many ways was a signal to language-minority citizens that it is fine if they do not speak English, because English is not necessarily the end-all and be-all of good citizenship. Many persons who, like my mother, do not speak English, want to learn English and try very hard, but because of many incidents in her life and in the lives of other elderly citizens, it is very difficult to learn the English language. New provisions in the immigration statutes permit an individual who has been in this country for thirty years and is more than fifty years old to take the citizenship test in a native language. Come hell or high water my mother, after two years of attending citizenship classes at our community college, tried very hard to take the test. She insisted on taking it in English so that she could show that she at least was making some kind of effort. But when it came to voting it proved virtually impossible for her to understand the complex issues of rent control, Proposition 13, or a veteran bond issue. It does make sense for people who read Chinese or Spanish to have the opportunity to study in their own language the complex election issues so that they can vote intelligently. Because my mother disagrees with my political views, there is no way that I can influence her, and it is just as well that she can read on her own so we do not get into heated discussions at home.

Implications of Bilingualism:
Religion

The relevance of religion to the problems of bilingualism/ biculturalism in American life was addressed by a panel including both clerics and laymen of several denominations. The moderator was Edwin Gaustad, professor of history in the University of California, Riverside. Panelists were Sterling McMurrin, professor of history and philosophy in the University of Utah and former United States Commissioner of Education; the Reverend Frank Ponce, associate director of the Secretariat for Hispanic Affairs, National Conference of Catholic Bishops; the Reverend Carlos Puig, secretary for Hispanic ministries in North America of the Lutheran Church-Missouri Synod; and Moses Rischin, former president of the Immigration History Association and professor of history in the San Francisco State University.

Professor Gaustad began the discussion by emphasizing that religion, ethnicity, language, and culture have always been critically linked in our society.

Edwin Gaustad: Whether or not you accept the thesis that religion is the form of culture and culture the substance of religion, religion and culture, like religion and ethnicity, do interact. Greek

Orthodoxy is probably the best present example of the force of
ethnicity in maintaining enclaves and in keeping to some degree an
ethno-religious group from participating fully in American life.
With respect to language, religion was courageously daring on the
frontier, as, for example, in establishing missions among the American Indians. Moreover, for years the government leaned on missionaries to China and later their sons and daughters for contacts
there. Religion, too, has sometimes been the last refuge of a language that has been abandoned in every other facet of life. Religion
and language have had an interesting and complex relationship in
America.

> Father Frank Ponce, a Chicano Catholic priest, explained why the
> Hispanic-American has special needs, how the Catholic church has
> been tardy in responding to the needs of Spanish-speaking people,
> and how and why the church must change if it hopes to serve the
> emerging masses of Spanish-speaking Catholics in the Western
> hemisphere.

Frank Ponce: I will not bore you with personal facts other than to
say that I was born in Driggs, Idaho, raised in San Bernardino,
California, educated through the doctorate at Stanford University
in English and Renaissance literature, which of course equipped
me superbly to serve Hispanic parishioners. They know all about
the Epithalamion of Spenser! My comments will be more pastorally
oriented than academic, because my work for the Secretariat for
Hispanic Affairs at the Bishops' Conference involves advocacy on
behalf of all Hispanics in the United States—no-one really knows
how many there are—and the problems that most Hispanics face
are really pastoral in nature. They live in a human environment
that is hostile to both their language and their culture.

How can Hispanics who want desperately to become American
(whatever that term may mean), and who want to learn English as
well, function in our society? As I travel in this country I am struck
by the almost unanimous feeling of Hispanics about the importance of learning English. At the same time they tell of the importance of hanging on to their Spanish and passing it on to their
children.

Religion, as Edwin Gaustad said, is an important element and
one that cannot be dismissed, because, along with language and

with other forms of human self-expression, religion is essential in the process by which men and women construct their universe and, by so doing, construct themselves. Whether you think it good or bad, it is an element that we must take into consideration.

As a Chicano priest I am a Catholic who, in the past, was extremely critical of my religion as an opiate, a socializing force that makes people passive rather than active participants in their own history and destiny. I have changed. I changed because, as I became more involved with Hispanics and tried to become a part of their communities, to do what anthropologists call inculturation, I found that Hispanics are extremely religious people.

Gallup did a survey of the socio-religious practices of Hispanics. Some useful statistics were brought out. Of the Hispanics surveyed, religion was very important for 90 percent. When probed as to what they meant by "religion," most of them ignored the traditional practice of attending mass, which was never strong among Hispanic Catholics, but rather emphasized popular religiosity or what anthropologists term "folk religion." Interesting, too, among both men and women the affinity for religious materials—art and especially reading matter—was extremely high. Most interesting to me, but not surprising, was their affinity for religious music, and that was much higher among men than among women. All this points up that if we are going to talk about the Hispanic condition in the United States, about being bilingual/bicultural, religion will be an important element. To assure that Hispanics continue being a bilingual entity, which I believe we are going to be, there will be an insistence on religious music and other materials for Hispanics.

One problem that Hispanics face in this country in order to make bilingualism/biculturalism more of a reality is the cultural arrogance on the part of the population of the United States. I say that not in a vindictive way but simply because it is a fact that I have observed very clearly. The apostolic delegate in a talk to the bishops of the United States in 1976 mentioned two problems that he believed the church would face in this country in coming years. One was the enormous size of churches—their non-human proportions—which is one reason why many Hispanics have left Catholicism, although some do keep a double affiliation. They leave because they find small pentecostal groups offer a family orientation and friendliness that they do not find in huge congregations. The second problem anticipated by the apostolic delegate was cultural arrogance on the part of many Catholics toward ethnic, racial, and cultural minority groups. This has turned out to be a real problem, a major obstacle in making Hispanics accepted in our society in such a way that they feel free to express themselves both in English and in Spanish. The church must somehow avoid attitudes that Emerson saw in the Unitarians. (I hope that I will not offend anybody with this statement.) Emerson accused the Unitarians of believing in the fatherhood of God, the brotherhood of man, and the neighborhood of Boston, which is not the hub of the universe.

Obviously the Catholic church, as Andrew Greeley said, embraced the Americanization process, and I very much agree with that. The church, unfortunately, believed that it was more important to Americanize than to evangelize. One can see this when the Irish and Eastern Europeans came; they brought their priests, their customs, and their traditions with them. The church wanted to keep them intact. It was a defensive posture. The immigrants wanted desperately to be accepted into American society. Who were the first to sign up to go to the wars? They were. They wanted to prove that they were as patriotic as anyone else.

There is now a change in the way the churches—not only the Catholic church but many of the mainline churches, and even the pentecostal churches—view their mission with regard to racial, cultural, and ethnic groups. Ten years ago I would have said that any Hispanic who was converted by a Protestant would be in danger of losing his cultural roots. That is untrue today, because many of these groups realize that the only way they will be able to attract Hispanics and keep them is by demonstrating a genuine appreciation and respect for those cultural traditions that are an essential part of what it is to be Hispanic. There is an evolving consciousness in the church of the importance to minister to people where they are. I told the bishops this when I talked to them on the Hispanic condition. It was the first time in the history of the Bishops' Conference that they had listened to a discussion on the U.S. Hispanic Catholic situation. Taking people where they are is a solid pastoral principle that Thomas Aquinas was fond of stating in

Latin: *Quid quid recipitur, ad modem recipientis recipitur*. Such a practice is much better than imposing on Hispanics *a priori* principles and expecting them to mold themselves into something they cannot be.

Why has the church changed? One reason is a consciousness that the church is genuinely catholic with a small *c*—that it is really universal. Rather than speaking only one language, the church must speak in many languages to many different people, wherever they are. This change was signaled in April 1963 at the second Vatican Council, when the bishops voted on the Constitution on the Liturgy. It was innovative because it decreed that Latin would no longer be the only language for the church—the vernacular could be used. This is an important change. To illustrate, one might say that when a secular empire wishes to consolidate, it imposes language, it imposes taxes. When people accept that, they accept the dominance of whatever empire is attempting to consolidate its power. The church had been very much in the empire-building mode, and at the moment when the bishops decided to opt for the vernacular, they decided it was more important to build the Kingdom than it was to consolidate the empire.

The fact of bilingualism/biculturalism is going to impinge more on our national consciousness, especially as churches realize that we are not talking solely about a regional condition or a national condition, but about an international condition. In a book called *The Coming of the Third Church*, the author makes the interesting observation that by the year 2000 more than 70 percent of the world's Christians will be from Third World countries. By the year 2000, of the 852 million Catholics in the world, 560 million will be from Latin America and the United States. That gives us pause to consider how bilingualism/biculturalism will be colored by those facts.

A Protestant Hispanic, the Reverend Carlos Puig saw no reason why Spanish-speaking people should give up their language or culture because they now live in the United States. He saw no threats to unity because elements in the population might not speak English, or share a non-Spanish culture.

Carlos Puig: The role of religion in the whole matter of bilingualism/biculturalism is extremely significant both to individuals and to the country. I was born in Puerto Rico and educated partly there and partly in New Jersey. I attended Rutgers University law school before turning to the ministry. Perhaps because I too have at times felt discrimination, perhaps because of the sensitivity that one develops when one finds himself in a country that is not supposed to be foreign to him yet is, I have found myself playing the role of advocate very often. There is no way that a person can divorce religion from life. Whether we ascribe to any particular creed really does not matter, because all of us somehow have within ourselves certain guidelines that cause us to behave religiously. We need to be sensitive to one another's needs. We need to be able to respond out of that sensitivity. We need to recognize that even though we may be a little different one from another, that does not make us unequal.

I have been a little disappointed with this conference in that we have failed to address ourselves to the questions that are raised in the conference paper. We have talked around them, and devoted too much time to bilingual education. Let us turn to the issues. First, we need not fear losing the primacy of the English language. It is needed for convenience if nothing else, and that is as it should be. But that does not automatically mean that all other languages should be forgotten. That would isolate us from the rest of the world just as much as from each other. Should the primacy of English be maintained? I say, yes. And I do not know anyone who has ever argued that point.

Second, should the United States become in law and practice a country in which two or more languages share official status—I emphasize *official*—and are widely used in public life and business and education and government? This remains to be seen. I do not worry about it too much because I would rather concern myself with whether we are communicating. If we cannot speak so that we understand each other, we are going to be in tremendous trouble. Relationships are what we are after, and language is essential to good relationships. Without good relationships we are in trouble. If we are to get along with each other, we had better start thinking about that issue.

There is another question: Is it necessary to give up one's heritage in order to succeed? Should I, as an individual, give up what I am? Is it necessary for me to give up my native tongue, my language, in order to "make good?" I do not think so. People who think that are making demands that should not be made. A move to a new country, to a new nation, is traumatic enough without being forced to give up all ties to the past. It is cruel to expect anyone to do so.

Is it possible to have a bilingual/bicultural society? This conference indicates that it is possible; as a matter of fact, not only is it possible, it is desirable. It is possible to function in two cultures without in any way taking away from either the person or the culture. History has proven that bilingualism/biculturalism have no damaging effects upon the nation or the people of a nation. On the contrary, all effects have been beneficial. Is it possible to have a bilingual country without sacrificing unity? Our problem is that we have confused unity with uniformity. They are two different words, two different meanings.

Commissioner McMurrin, although prepared to discuss the unusual circumstances of the Mormon church because it is in transition from being a national church to becoming a universal assemblage, was far more interested in emphasizing the importance of a single language for all Americans.

Sterling McMurrin: I am aware that I was invited to this conference with the specific intention that I make some reference to the Mormon church and the experience of the Mormon people with respect to this subject. Frankly, that experience has very little relevance to the subject because the major issue is not religious at all.

The major issue is that we live in a system of nation-states, and the future of the people of this nation, regardless of what language they speak or prefer, is tied up with the strength of the nation and the culture. Regardless of what our international commitments may be, or of the successes and failures of the attempts at world government of the United Nations, for a long time to come the well-being of the people of this country, as well as those of other countries, will be tied to the fact that all of us live in a nation-state system. Our major concern should not be whether people today can or cannot get along with adequate or inadequate translators. Our problem is with the future. It is not a question of what we face as individuals. It is a question of what we face as a nation over the next decade and, for that matter, coming centuries.

A common language for this nation is absolutely essential to the strength of the nation, and it is basic to the well-being of the people. This is true not only of this nation but of others as well. It would be a disaster—maybe at first a minor disaster but in the long run a major disaster—to legalize and employ in commerce and government more than one primary or standard language. This does not mean that I favor total and complete cultural assimilation, the destruction of the individual and native cultures of the people who have come together in this nation. Far from it. I am very strongly in favor of pluralism in our society, and I deplore as much as anyone the linguistic and cultural illiteracy of the American people. Yet we have to face up to the question of whether we want to have a strong national culture or have it weakened by our over-commitment to pluralism.

America is not simply a federation of cultures from other countries; we have a national culture, and that national culture has been and is tied to the English language. I have no wish to see other languages disappear; on the contrary, we should do far more than we now do to cultivate the capacity to use other languages. But our first priority is not to preserve the other cultures, as important as that is. My point is that there is an American culture, that it is tied to a language, and that it should be preserved. It should be strengthened, and not in some way dissolved by our efforts to preserve other languages and cultures.

This may sound chauvinistic, but frankly it is not. We miss the point if we suppose that the determining factor in this whole matter should simply be the preservation of my Scottish heritage and someone else's German heritage, someone else's Japanese heritage, and someone else's Latin-American heritage. While everything possible should be done to make life more convenient for those of us who do not speak or understand the English language, at the same time our educational operation should be geared to seeing to it that those very people, as rapidly as possible, become competent in the English language. It cannot be done overnight. It can be done over a period of years. The idea is to strengthen the American nation by strengthening its culture, and strengthening the national culture will not be accomplished by having two legal languages.

I am not persuaded by Maxwell Yalden that there are not very serious problems in Canada associated with Canadian bilingualism. I am not convinced that there are not serious problems in Belgium. There are very serious problems in those countries. This is not a religious issue at all, because clergymen seek methods to communicate so they can evangelize or effectively function as pastors. When you come right down to it, this is a political-moral issue on a very large and basic scale. It is political in terms of our living in a world of sovereign nation-states, moral because it concerns the well-being of our people over what we hope will be the long haul ahead. This is not something to be brushed aside in favor of some kind of sectarian sentimentality.

We may just as well face the fact that people who do not learn English in this country are going to be seriously handicapped— very seriously handicapped in more ways than one, but especially economically. That should be obvious to everyone. There is another factor that should not be overlooked. If we are not going to use English as our functional language, then let us give it up and take up Spanish, but let us accept a language that all of us understand or will learn to use and understand, instead of undertaking to utilize two or more languages. I understand that, technically, we do not have a legal language. I do not object to that. What I object to is legalizing more than one language.

Now I will make some comments about the Mormon church and this problem, as I have been requested to do. You should know that I hold no official position and have no official connection with the church. The Mormon church has been intensely American in character, and to become a Mormon in the past meant, in a sense, to gather your family and goods and go to Utah. That began to change a bit after the First World War. It has completely changed since the Second World War. Now, instead of the Mormon church undertaking to gather people into western America and thoroughly Americanize them, the church reaches out to people wherever they are. It is growing very rapidly, and its largest areas of growth are in Mexico and Central and South America, where it is making converts at the rate of something like 100,000 a year.

Because of this, the church faces enormous problems. In the past it has been intensely parochial in character, and now it is under the necessity of some way or another universalizing itself. Obviously, what the outcome will be remains in question.

From the standpoint of languages, it is quite possible that a larger percentage of the population in the state of Utah can speak more than one language than in any similar place in the world, because of the great number of missionaries that the Mormon church has in other countries at any one time—30,000 of them at present. They study the languages of other countries before they leave home. There are those in my expanded neighborhood who collectively can speak as second languages virtually all the languages of Europe and several others. Today in Salt Lake City there are Mormon services in the native languages of Laos, Thailand, Vietnam, and Cambodia, to say nothing of less exotic places. The church has had little experience in treating religion on a genuinely universal basis. What it does have is the experience of being remarkably successful in drawing people from all over the world and turning them into Americans—not Americans who have abandoned all vestiges of their native cultures, but Americans nevertheless. And this has been done largely through the instrumentality of concentrating their efforts on a common language. Of course, as I have indicated, the Mormons have now shifted away from encouraging all their converts to come to this country.

> As a student of immigration to the United States, Moses Rischin is a long-standing advocate of a pluralist society in America. He feels keenly that diversity is what gives America both strength and dynamism.

Moses Rischin: Immigrants to America, most especially those coming from agricultural backgrounds, have undergone a radical reorientation in culture and outlook. Nowhere in the world has there been a country where, for well over two centuries, immigrants of such diverse origins have brought with them such varied and distinctive cultures only to have these cultures—with a few rare exceptions—sooner or later in considerable part lose their perceivable dissimilarities. Upon coming to the United States, immigrants at once become acutely aware of their cultural differences from others. They perceive that they are more bound to their cultures than they could ever have imagined before migrating, and they are driven to construct a new ethnic way of life, different in many aspects from their traditional patterns and gradually assimilating many American habits and traits. They also recognize that to enter the American mainstream they—and certainly their children—will have to make a considerable leap, a leap difficult even for the most gifted and most fortunate, and for most of them unattainable for a generation and more.

For some peoples, the leap has been relatively easy—not a leap at all but in fact just a step or two. This has been particularly the case for those immigrants with a close affinity with Anglo-Protestant America. But others, some illiterate, some isolated by their very numbers from earlier Americans and even from immigrants of other origins, have had great difficulty even in establishing points of contact, whether religious or linguistic, with their neighbors. There has been no more challenging problem in the development of American humanity than this one.

Historians have been drawn to the study of immigration not only because of their conscious or unconscious empathy for humanity, but as much, and more self-interestedly, because of an empathy for the humanity in themselves and in their immigrant forebears. One such scholar was the distinguished Marcus Lee Hansen, who is noted for his grand vision of immigration as a universal process underlying the whole American experience. Hansen insisted that in fact his real interest lay in a totally different dimension of that experience—the role of immigrants as unconscious bearers of culture. "Who Will Inherit America?" was the way he put it in the title of his last lecture just before his untimely death at the age of 45 in 1938. In that lecture, Hansen lamented the fact that a country like the United States, with such a diverse and many-sided cultural heritage, had ordained in its social policy that (in his words) "one set of standards should be the basis of American culture." I do not quite agree with Hansen's doleful interpretation of the American experience, but I do sympathize with his feeling that as a result of civil war, two world wars, and almost boundless social and geographical mobility, generational conflict, and technological change without parallel elsewhere, the United States has experienced a cultural erosion that has had palpable effects on the whole American social fabric.

Perhaps for this reason, among others, many of us empathize so strongly with the dilemmas of the latest immigrants in our midst, especially with the Spanish-speaking, the largest group of newcomers to enter the country in the last four decades. Perhaps we are compensating for the sense of our lost selves or, more precisely, half-selves—for that yearning for the lost world of our forefathers, however romantic—for all of us in entering the modern world have consciously or unconsciously remade ourselves. So many of our political leaders who make policy, and who attempt to do the decent thing, have doubtless been moved by a profound feeling that the Spanish-speaking in America especially are symbolic of our vanished ethnic and regional cultures that only a short time ago were to be found at every hand and that lent not only color and variety but cultural and religious depth to everyday America.

This is meant in all seriousness. I say this as an American Jew representing one of the world's oldest surviving ethno-religious traditions, one that appeared to many to be on the verge of extinction—religion, language, and all—on the eve of World War II. The telescoped story of the rapid modernization of the Jews of Europe, related ironically both to the march of progress and the march of totalitarianism, led either to the cultural dissolution or physical annihilation of a whole people, or both. Yet almost providentially, in the wake of the Holocaust, with the emergence of the State of Israel there also emerged a new American-Jewish consciousness. An awareness of being Jewish, however marginal, was suddenly transformed by the powerful perception of the remarkably vital historical experience that was taking place before the eyes of the world—a literal rebirth out of the ashes of the Holocaust. Within little more than a generation after the virtual extinction of the Jews of Europe and the expulsion of Jews from the new Arab lands of North Africa and the Middle East, Jews of many origins came back to the country of their ancestors, prepared to be remade, not merely to survive, with dignity. In many respects they were like the immigrant pioneers who came to America, but even more so. They confronted the challenge of "Israelization": the transformation of Jews of many languages from many lands into new Israelis, and the creation of a new nation. In this "Ingathering of Exiles," modern Hebrew, a new language known to relatively few Jews, became the primary language of all Israelis. Yet despite the historic religious bond that all Jews shared, the experience has been difficult and strenuous, especially so for Jews of non-European origin. Like America, Israel is an experiment.

Surely in the United States as well, there must be in our time a renewed sense of cultural challenge and a commitment both to the primary American language (as H. L. Mencken once called it) and to our variegated cultures. Those cultures have mutually assimilative capacities. An appreciation of what they have meant to the American people must again be broadly disseminated.

At the same time, enlarged sensitivity both to our own multivalent culture and language and to the dilemmas of immigrants who sense themselves to be at arm's length, ought to inspire confidence in the spirited learning and relearning of our common American language as well as the capacity of the languages and cultures of our latest immigrants to be integrated into our common American heritage and core.

Clearly this nation of immigrants has that capacity.

> Discussion began with a question by Abigail Thernstrom, who found much apathy among Chicanos and questioned Father Ponce about the role of the church in relationship to this feeling among the group.

Abigail Thernstrom: I have been doing research on the politics of the Chicanos in Dallas, and one of the striking things to me is that the provision for bilingual ballots has done so little to improve Chicano registration and voter turnout. Both are abysmally low. Father Ponce, do you see some connection between the political quiescence of Chicanos in a city like Dallas and the role of the church?

Frank Ponce: There is a marked difference in the way the church functioned with European immigrants and the way it functions with those from Latin America, especially those from Mexico. Those who came from Europe brought their clergy with them and established national churches that became social, political, and religious centers—almost theocracies. The churches were able to consolidate and deliver many votes because they were well-organized.

With Hispanics this was not the case. After the Treaty of Guadalupe Hidalgo in 1848, many Mexicans elected to stay in the United States without any clergy of their own, without any people from the church who were Hispanic. We had a Frenchman, Bishop Lamy, and others of his ilk. That situation has continued to this day. In 1910, after the revolution, when a great many more Mexicans came to this country, they also came without their priests. They were uprooted. They came to escape the revolution or to seek a better life, and the church played no role in keeping them together. It did not give them any sense of social identity or political clout. This should be coupled with the fact that in many Latin American countries the people feel alienated from political structures; they see them as corrupt and ineffective. That attitude has been carried to America.

The church now recognizes that it must move into the field of political activity, and it is doing so with great aplomb. For example, our office has worked with Willie Velasquez in the Southwest voter registration project. Yet many Hispanics, particularly Chicanos in the Southwest, feel that even if they register it is meaningless. The problem is eliminating the gerrymandering that makes Hispanics feel that even if they vote it is not going to have any effect. There is the sense of "what use is voting unless we get one of our own people to run for the office?" But the church is addressing the problem by trying to form coalitions with many action groups—UNO in Los Angeles and COPS in San Antonio—that aim to effect political change. The church sees itself more as an agent for political change, and it hopes to be more aggressive.

Abigail Thernstrom: The contrast between the role of the church in the Black community and the role of the church in the Chicano community has been striking. The militants in the Chicano community, at least in my experience in Dallas, continually complain that the message from the church is to keep away from the polls. In a situation like Dallas, gerrymandering is not the issue, because extensive litigation there has had a significant effect in the electoral process. There is not a Chicano district, because the Chicanos are residentially dispersed. That kind of disfranchisement does not hold. So the political activists in the Chicano community complain about the church.

Frank Ponce: In many instances they are right. But I might add that the situation with the Blacks—the way they form their churches—is greatly different from the situation in the Catholic Church, which is a church that was brought here from Europe and, in a sense, imposed on the people.

Ricardo Fernández felt that too much of the conference had centered on "either/or" situations.

Ricardo Fernández: The bilingual problem has been discussed here generally in terms of either/or: we are either one or we are many; we are either united or we are divided. For example, one question raised was, where does responsibility for learning the language lie? Is it in the family or with the government? I think that can be viewed not in terms of "either/or" but rather as "in addition to"—with responsibility first on the individual and then on the family, and I suppose eventually on the group, the society—and ultimately the government has to play a role. It does not really pay to look at it as either/or, and yet consistently these discussions and comments are of an either/or nature. Is that part of our philosophy and historical development as a people? Do we tend to look at things in terms of either/or? Should we not perhaps look for other approaches?

Sterling McMurrin: That is an important point. I am in favor of preserving cultural heritage and preserving language, and I cannot see why it cannot be done, at least to some degree, within the framework of what I simply refer to as a national American culture. I agree it is difficult to define that culture.

But I do hold strongly to having only one legal language. I am adamant on that point. It has nothing to do with the immediate future when, obviously, many people are put at grave disadvantages and difficulties. I am thinking in terms of the long-range future of the nation, the culture, and the well-being of the people.

I am Scottish by descent. There is a Scottish organization in my city, and it holds meetings. I could not care less what it does. To those of us who have no great interest in preserving the culture of some distant ancestor of whom we have never heard and could not trace back to even if we tried, I say let that culture disappear in this country. On the other hand, for those people who want to keep their cultural traditions alive, I am all for that.

> Frank Ponce saw cause for concern because some groups in our society have been ignored by American historians and feel that they are not a part of the society. They are therefore distrustful of the future.

Frank Ponce: I strongly believe that it cannot be permitted to become an either/or situation. Go back to what Sterling McMurrin said about a national American culture. There has to be some type of American culture, and he admits that it is difficult to define. I submit that whenever we begin talking about what different racial, cultural, and ethnic groups here have contributed to the American scene, one of our problems has been a profound historical dislocation.

I think that the crisis of culture we have in this country is really a crisis of history. We have lost contact with what we have been so we are unable to say what we are now and where we are going. Involved with that, therefore, is a crisis of trust; we do not trust each other. Therefore, we tend to say, I am better than you are, and my culture is much more important than yours.

Part of this historical dislocation is related to who it is that has written the history, those books that try to define what American culture is. I am not a cultural historian but when I was at Stanford I attended some of the courses of David Potter. His book *People of Plenty* seemed to me a brilliant analysis of the American character. But nowhere in his treatment, and almost nowhere in the work of Sydney Ahlstrom, nor in the work of Perry Miller, or of Henry Steele Commager—all eminent scholars—nor in the work of the nineteenth-century romantic historians like Parkman and Bancroft, do I find real sensitivity toward cultures other than Anglo-American.

Each of us, whether or not we know it, has an ideological stance toward the way we see the world, and I think it is often colored (and I use the word advisedly) by how we have been formed with history. I submit that many of these cultural historians have not really taken into account anything other than the "Anglo" experience. (I use the phrase for lack of a better one; I know terms are slippery.) Our thinking has been formed by these people. I have read Potter and I look in vain for any reference to the Latin-American experience, which is part of American culture as well. I think we are still ethnocentric, we are afraid of people who are different from ourselves, and this is all part of that historical dislocation that creates a crisis of culture, which is basically a crisis of trust.

> The moderator, Edwin Gaustad, who is an historian of religion, remarked that he would be inclined to talk about American cultures as plural rather than about a singular American culture, because of the difficulty in finding a homogeneous pattern from one coast to the other. Carlos Puig saw the issue very differently, attributing American behavior to chauvinism and insisting that Americans should be not only sensitive but active in learning other languages.

Carlos Puig: We as a nation expect the whole world to know English, but we cannot be bothered to take the time to learn somebody else's language. I think relationships would be much better if we would get away from monolingualism. It really does not unite the country. The country is divided anyhow. We should think in terms of being part of a universe that is shrinking constantly and that badly needs to be understood through communication.

Sterling McMurrin: The world *is* shrinking, and anyone who has been around it knows that it is shrinking with one language, and that is the English language. We may as well face that. Since Frank Ponce mentioned the writing of American history, I should mention that I am the first author to publish in the United States a history of philosophy that gives serious attention to Latin-American philosophy.

Noel Epstein: Frank Ponce asks about including the perspectives of other groups and other cultures as part of American history. This is part of a long-standing trend in this country—starting in the 1920s—called the "intercultural education movement." It was revived in the 1960s. There was the *Roots* phenomenon, as well as demands by Blacks, American Indians, and women to revise American history books. Of course, what happened was that the more everybody demanded, the more we got away from the central themes of America, its political and economic history.

There is another reflection of this in our civil rights movement today. One group after another has come in and claimed injustices. Everybody says, you think that *you* had it bad? We had it worse. The staff director of the Civil Rights Commission told me not too long ago that the constituency of the United States Civil Rights Commission today is made up of roughly 80 percent of the population, if you include women, the aged, and all religious groups; only 20 percent are left to be the oppressors.

Government agencies cannot cope with the overwhelming demands of all these groups, because almost every group to some degree or another has been subjected to some kind of injustice in the past. In the same way, quite frankly, how can all these groups be accommodated in a way that fits into a single American history text? Here is one example of what is happening. In some of these cases where American history texts have been revised to get in more information about ethnic and cultural groups, it has been necessary to eliminate almost entirely the Age of Exploration for lack of space in the book or time to teach this subject. The explorers have been reduced to a paragraph in some instances.

Frank Ponce: Let me give the question a different focus. I dare not speak for other groups, such as the Asians or the Blacks, but as an Hispanic what offends me when I read school textbooks is simply the fact that there is a distortion of exactly how this country was formed. Some Catholic authors talk about Catholic schools as beginning in the East, unaware that in Florida and in the Southwest there were such schools. In the whole question of the discovery of this country, the emphasis is on the landing of the Pilgrims on Plymouth Rock and the settlement in Jamestown, overlooking that in 1564 in St. Augustine the first mass was offered in America by a Spanish priest. These are the things you never read about. This is distortion of history.

The other extreme could be the writing of history in such a way that there is no cohesion to it, that we lose the large focus. I am not an historian, but I would hate to see history written in that manner.

I do not have an answer, but I want to avoid the cynical attitude that says that if you cannot do everything you do nothing. There has to be a process by which, with good consultation, the people of each group are able to get their own priorities in order to say what is most important for them to be included in America's cultural history.

Stephen Wagner: I am a history teacher in Wayland High School in Massachusetts. I have taught courses in Black history and courses in immigration and Americanization as well as general American history. For the last several years, in practically every class at one time or another I have asked my students to estimate the percentage of the population of the United States that is Black. I teach in a wealthy suburban town where nearly all the Black students are bused out from Boston and our only Hispanic students are a few Cuban refugees. I almost never get any estimate of the Black population of the country below 30 percent. If I ask for estimates of the Black population of Massachusetts, again it is way too high. The reason for this is that there has been so much attention to minority problems, perhaps not in the textbooks but in the materials that the students read, in what the media show, that students even in a white community like mine are more conscious of minorities in this country than we may appreciate.

I have a question tied to religion. At the risk of appearing thoroughly reactionary I would like to ask Father Frank Ponce if he is absolutely sure that abandonment of the Latin liturgy, which after all was everywhere essentially the same, has tended to make the church more universal? Has it no tendency to increase differences among Catholics of different backgrounds?

> Frank Ponce did not answer the question whether shifting from Latin to the vernacular had made it more difficult for Catholics to communicate among themselves or share a common language experience in the mass. He saw the issue in terms of the insensitivity of the church's hierarchy.

Frank Ponce: The shift from Latin to the vernacular in the mass was received ambiguously by Catholics throughout the world, but that ambiguous reception was due not so much to questions about the wisdom of the course of action, but rather to the manner in which it was done. That is to say, many of the bishops, as they went back to their home countries, still considered themselves the "head honchos," the feudal lords of their dioceses, and they simply dictated that this was to happen, starting next Sunday. Now, *there* is an example of insensitivity and historical dislocation! How can something that has been going on since the 1500s be eliminated, legislated right out of existence between one day and another? People naturally resented it.

A professor of history from El Camino College expressed her feeling that the panel had side-stepped the key issue of the conference.

Nadine Hata: I have been disturbed that with the exception of Sterling McMurrin the panelists have not directly hit the issue of religion and bilingualism/biculturalism. My question is this: "Should the church mainstream its congregation or should the church preserve and perpetuate the language and culture of the group it serves, whether they are Jewish, Japanese, Greek, or whatever?

Carlos Puig: There is no way in which a denomination or church could possibly divorce itself from the people's language and the people's culture. It serves each of its constituent groups in its own language and culture as best it can. This we see as absolutely necessary. As individuals become "Americanized," they will tend to drift or shift into those congregations where they feel more comfortable. They might be English-speaking.

The fact that I have a position as secretary for Hispanic ministries within the Lutheran church is indicative of the fact that the Lutherans take this seriously. My job is exclusively to deal with Hispanic matters, whether they be congregational life or literature or whatever. We have to reach people with the Gospel. We have to do it in a way they understand. There is no way a person who has no facility in the English language can get anything out of an English service. We are "where the rubber hits the road."

Frank Ponce: My answer is unambiguous. The role of the Catholic church today, at least in the United States, should be that of serving the people in their own language rather than mainstreaming them into society. That is really what I meant when I said that the church's job is not to Americanize but to evangelize, to preach the Gospel. And it should be done with respect for the language and customs and traditions of the people, taking them and their relationships as starting points, not romanticizing the past in an ethnocentric way, but always purifying the cultural tradition so that people can develop and become members of society in full standing. What we do not want to do is to create yet another barrio or ghetto in a religious sense.

Sterling McMurrin: We have heard enough to convince me that the task of conveying the English language and American culture is not one for churches. There are people out to learn English as rapidly as possible and to use English in every way in everyday life. And *that* is a task for the schools.

Implications of Bilingualism:
The Media

The critical role of the media in American society, not only as the
vehicle by which issues are brought before the public but also as an
employer, a major area of investment, and a role model for community behavior and values, was noted by moderator Thomas Plate,
associate editor and editor of the editorial pages of the *Los Angeles
Herald Examiner,* as he introduced the panelists considering media in
relation to bilingualism/biculturalism.

Participants in this last panel of the conference were Phil Kerby,
prize-winning editorialist of the *Los Angeles Times;* Félix Gutiérrez,
associate professor of journalism in the University of Southern California and executive director of the California Chicano News Media
Association; Eugene Fuson, editorial director, KNXT-CBS, Los Angeles; and Aida Ferrarone, staff writer for *Imagen,* a Spanish-
language weekly paper published in Culver City, California.

Phil Kerby, a longtime advocate of personal and group freedom of
action in society, began the discussion by expressing his concern for
the divided nature of American society and his hope that the issue of
language would not divide it further.

Phil Kerby: Bilingualism is a very controversial subject in the
editorial conferences of the *Los Angeles Times,* and I do not speak

here for the newspaper. I have brought it up rather frequently, and people seem to hedge around it. There is a certain amount of tension when it is discussed.

This country is divided on many issues. There are some things that divide a country, some things that unite it; a single language is possibly the most cohesive force in a nation. The United States is the most fascinating country in the world because it has numerous ethnic groups, each with feelings for its past, for its culture, for its customs. That is great. That is one of the splendid things about the United States. But if we in this country attempt to make two or more languages officially recognized, it would in my opinion be a prelude to disaster. Many of my liberal colleagues disagree with that position, but it seems to me that the United States is already divided along many lines. There is already much controversy. To add the divisive element of language to all the other problems we now encounter would be a tremendous historical mistake. Yet I have a hunch that this is the way the country is going.

> Félix Gutiérrez did not share Kerby's apprehension about an American society with mixed language usage. He traced briefly the development of the bilingual press in the United States, pointed to the government's support of non-English-language radio and television stations, indicated that business was the primary economic factor in the non-English media, and predicted that in the future many people may be able to live their lives bilingually.

Félix Gutiérrez: Most of my research has been in the area of the Spanish-language media in the United States, its history, and its contemporary growth. In doing this research I found that the proliferation of bilingual media is in the tradition of the press in the United States. The first bilingual publication in this country dates from 1784 in Philadelphia, less than ten years after the signing of the Declaration of Independence. Newspapers were published in both French and English. The first bilingual Spanish-language newspaper in this country, *El Mississippi*, dates back to 1808 in Louisiana. As a matter of fact, in 1810 there was a trilingual newspaper—French, Spanish, and English—published in New Orleans. A bilingual press is nothing new in the United States, and the threat that people may see in this growth is invalid. In the past almost 200 years bilingual journalism has done nothing to divide the country.

Moreover, the bilingual media traditionally have been encouraged by both the public and private sectors. The first newspapers in the Southwest, after it was conquered from Mexico and made a part of the United States, were bilingual. They were subsidized by state and local governments because of the provision in the Treaty of Guadalupe Hidalgo, which insured bilingual rights to the residents in this area. Publications in the bilingual format were subsidized by tax dollars in those days. In fact, the first daily newspaper in Los Angeles was supported by state funds to print the laws in Spanish.

The federal government has licensed foreign-language broadcasting since the 1920s and shows no inclination to do otherwise. The growth of Spanish-languge broadcasting in the 1970s was spectacular. In 1973, when I started keeping track, there were 250 radio stations that broadcast some or all of their programs in Spanish. By 1978, only five years later, the number had increased to more than 600. These are not all full-time non-English-language stations, but part of their programming is in Spanish.

We will see a growth in the 1980s of media in a bilingual format in the sense that they actually use two languages. Traditionally in the recent past of this country, newspapers have been entirely in English or in Spanish or in Chinese or in another language. What we see now is mixed media: for example, Spanish-language radio stations that play English-language songs. We will see more magazines, hear more songs, and see more forms of media in two languages that people can relate to.

This growth is directly related to the proportion of people living in this country who prefer to use languages other than English. But the more direct relationship is to the investment of advertising dollars in these media by advertisers who want to reach this audience. People who are concerned about the rapid growth of the Spanish-language press or Asian-language broadcasting in this country should talk to Sears, J.C. Penney, McDonald's, Montgomery Ward, and other major corporations that now invest more than $100 million a year in advertising in Spanish-language media.

This is where support for bilingualism in the media comes from.

The implications are clear. The growth of media in languages other than English increases the utility of these languages in other sectors of society. One can do more things in our society, particularly in commercial transactions, without having to learn English. One can also become informed, entertained, and acculturated as a consumer without learning English.

Census data indicate that, in the case of the Hispanics at least, retention of Spanish does not mean that people do not learn English. It simply means that Latinos feel they do not have to forget one language in order to learn another. Long-range projections indicate that the proportion of our population that prefers English over Spanish will experience its greatest growth over the next generation. This is one reason that media that use both languages will be the ones that grow the fastest. Bilingual media exemplify the bringing together of people of different language traditions. Developing plays, articles, and short stories in two languages so more people can identify with them, so that everyone can understand them, is in the highest tradition of the United States.

> Broadcaster Eugene Fuson had a contrasting view. He attributed opposition to bilingualism to fear of personal displacement, and reported his observation of strong forces in the public determined to maintain the status quo because substantial economic interests are involved.

Eugene Fuson: I am not as optimistic as my colleagues. I am a ninth generation Hispanic Californian. I have been working in the media in California for thirty years, and I wrote pro-bilingual editorials ten years ago when bilingual education was just beginning, when it was a seedling. My argument was that if we can use English to teach children Spanish, why cannot we use Spanish to teach them English? I got a tremendous adverse reaction then and the subject still gets a tremendous unfavorable reaction, not so much in the big cities, but in Middle America. It is away from the big cities that one encounters the fear of displacement, a kind of reaction that says, "Why the hell don't they speak American?" The evidence is that there is a growing antipathy probably based on this fear of displacement.

Television is the biggest of the media and probably has more effect on people than any other. A technological revolution in television will come about in the next few years. The whole system is going to turn upside-down. Some people say that we will still have networks; others say that we will have fifty channels of cable television. *Time/Life* owns 63 percent of the cable market. Getty Oil and Warner Brothers and other large companies put together a $2.5 billion combine to go into cable. Moreover, there are advances in video discs and home tapes, and no-one knows what other changes may come.

My guess is that we will not have a bilingual society. There are strong forces in this country that require uniformity and want to maintain the status quo. Moreover, we already know that our economy is in a recession and maybe a depression. With this comes great unemployment. With great unemployment will come civil unrest and scapegoating, aimed at minorities such as the Latinos who are here illegally. We have seen much of this already in Florida in reactions toward the Cubans who are pouring in, and the Haitians. People there are really bitter. When unemployment becomes widespread, there may be more riots and burnings of the kind seen in Miami. Discontent, friction, and civil unrest bring as a reaction a rising antipathy toward any kind of foreign languages or foreign people. While it may seem a grim forecast, that is the future I see.

Aida Ferrarone found unusual problems and opportunities in the non-English-speaking community. The lack of ability to communicate is the most serious problem.

Aida Ferrarone: As my experience in broadcasting has varied, so have my thoughts about bilingualism/biculturalism. My experience as a Peruvian reporter in Washington, D.C., was far different from my experience as a sociological researcher in the Los Angeles barrio trying to do so-called bilingual/bicultural programs. But the attitudes of people are changing. When I do interviews or reports for *Imagen* now, I find that the large company or the major university always has someone who speaks Spanish.

Bilingualism/biculturalism tend to be a two-way street. In a way technology is changing everything. But the Hispanic population is growing very fast, and I see a merging of the languages. Some futurists are talking about unilang—a combination of a very technical English language, such as is used in computers, and Spanish. What I see in the future is a merging of the two cultures in which Spanish will persist and be used as a vehicle to communicate what America is to people of other cultures. Spanish, rich as it is, lacks the technical terminology to explain and express the developments of American society.

There is a language problem within the Spanish-speaking community. When I talk in my "educated" Spanish to people who are directors of bilingual programs, often I cannot communicate with them. Therefore we speak English. When I was producing a public affairs program for radio station KNX, I had great difficulty getting people who could speak Spanish to take part. Perhaps this is a transitional period; international broadcasting in the Spanish language is coming.

We Spanish-speaking people will have to compromise. I hope that we do not lose our culture and that Hispanics can continue to have radio stations that broadcast in good Spanish, television in good Spanish, and newspapers that are well-written in Spanish. But I also believe that it is essential for all Hispanics to learn how to express themselves in English.

> When moderator Thomas Plate asked, "What role should the media play in pressing for assimilation or alternately what role should it play in pressing for bilingualism?" he drew a response from Phil Kerby, who argued that the media has a task of their own and should not assume moral superiority in dealing with the issues of society.

Phil Kerby: If the media aggressively report events in this country and where the country is going, they will be doing quite well. The media are not professionally or morally superior to the people of the United States. They have enough to do just to report vigorously and objectively what is going on so the people can have the facts. Then the media can express their own views in their editorial columns.

The speakers in this discussion are very interested in the background of all of this, but the question was, "Should the United States have two or more official languages?" That is an important question, and I did not hear anybody address that particular question directly. Should we or should we not?

Thomas Plate: But should our view of the desirability of having two languages, whether official or semi-official, affect our functioning as journalists, and if so, how?

Félix Gutiérrez: There are two levels of decisions that the media must make—one is editorial and the other is economic. An example of the editorial decision is, how should a newspaper cover changing demographic patterns? In the case of California, a state that borders on Asian nations and Latin America, obviously there will be some language overlap, as there are along international borders anyplace in this world.

An example of the economic is, how does a newspaper function as a business? Media enjoy some degree of freedom because of the First Amendment, but they have to survive as economic institutions. There are business decisions that have to be made. Should the paper address this growing population in the language in which they are most comfortable? If so, how does it do it? We see in the case of the established predominantly English-language newspapers in this part of the country a willingness to pass off the non-English-speaking audience to other media. That is why there are new papers starting up. That is why there are full- and part-time Spanish-language television stations. That is why the number of Spanish radio stations has grown from three to eight in the 1970s. Advertisers go to the media that can deliver the audience that will spend money, and if the traditional media cannot do it, advertisers go elsewhere.

The *Los Angeles Times* has done extensive marketing studies of the Latino community and has not come up with an editorial strategy beyond adding to its staff some employees to address that community. What we have here is a medium deciding that it will deliver its message in a particular language to a particular segment of the population. If other segments of the population that do not speak English are seen to grow, those will be someone else's market, somebody else's audience to cultivate. Then, of course, that business decision has an effect on their news coverage as the marketing studies tell them. The basic decision is, are these people, as viewers or readers, worth going after editorially in terms of how they are covered?

Thomas Plate: The *Miami Herald* has been publishing a single-page Spanish-language edition on a daily basis.

Eugene Fuson: The *San Diego Union* was doing that about twenty years ago. They had a two-page section on Sundays that was a digest of everything that was in the rest of the paper so they could open up the Mexico City market, which they did quite well.

> Employing Hispanics is not a solution unless the individuals are sensitive and knowledgeable, argued Thomas Plate, giving as an example an unfortunate experience of his own newspaper, the *Los Angeles Herald Examiner*.

Thomas Plate: We hired as a columnist a Nieman Fellow from Harvard named Tony Castro, who had written a book called *Chicano Politics*. This may demonstrate the simple-minded thinking of editors. They think that if they hire a Chicano columnist it might help them in the eyes of the Hispanic community. The key fallacy here is "Hispanic community." It is not one community. If the newspaper columnist pleases one segment of the community, he might alienate other elements of the community. The man hired to speak to the entire community may speak to only a part of it. This can prove an educational experience for an editor. It is difficult really to reach the "Hispanic community" in any significant way.

> Communicating within the Spanish-speaking community is not easy even for Spanish-speaking reporters, Aida Ferrarone agreed. Not all people of Hispanic background have an adequate working knowledge of the Spanish language.

Aida Ferrarone: When a native-born Latin American encounters the Spanish language as it is spoken in California, he resorts to English. In fact, the reason that I joined *Imagen* instead of other papers is because the editors and owners, who live in Mexico City, made a point that they wanted it to be written in Spanish that could be understood by everybody who speaks Spanish. For Chicanos this is not possible. Perhaps it is possible on the East Coast, where the Spanish-language press has been in existence for thirty years and uses excellent Spanish. The international media that address Latin America from London or Washington on shortwave use one kind of Spanish, and the people understand it because it is a common denominator. But here in California the situation is somehow different.

Times have changed, argued Eugene Fuson, who pointed out that it has now become economically advantageous to have a Spanish surname if one is in the media.

Eugene Fuson: Between sessions of the First Amendment Congress in Philadelphia, a group of reporters—members of the National Broadcasting Editorial Association—was watching television and saw Geraldo Rivera report a major scandal, a big exposé. One reporter looked at it and said, "Jesus, you know how long I have been in this business? I knew him when his name was Jerry Rivers." When there is money in being an Hispanic, it will happen and not before.

Félix Gutiérrez pointed to the fact that the new non-English media are often funded from the mother country and that this could have an important social impact.

Félix Gutiérrez: In the growth of the Spanish-language and Asian-language media in California there is heavy involvement from the mother country. In other words, *Imagen* is financed from Mexico. Spanish International Network (SIN), the major Spanish-language television network in this country, is owned by the Mexican television network, Televisa. Asian programming in this country is heavily dependent on both investment and programming from Korea, Japan, and Taiwan. The records one hears on the Spanish-language radio stations are largely imported from Latin America. If you turn on the evening news on Channel 34, you will be watching a direct satellite broadcast from Mexico City. Is that a concern to anyone on the panel?

Phil Kerby: It adds to the variety, the marvelous variety of this country. I have no objection to all the groups in this country developing newspapers, broadcasting, all the media to their fullest extent, but I think the question still remains, are we going to have a unified country in which everybody shares, everybody is equal? I think that is the question. But it is the variety in this country that makes the United States the most fascinating place in the world.

Thomas Plate: I wonder, as a representative of a metropolitan newspaper, if I am not too easy on myself. If the desirable goal is to have diversity within stability, should the metropolitan Los Angeles newspapers be more involved in the process of integration?

Phil Kerby: As President Kennedy once responded to a woman at a press conference who asked him, "What are you going to do about women?" he agreed that he had never done enough for women. And so far as social issues are concerned I think that is true of newspapers and all the other media and other parts of the economy. Of course, newspapers do not do enough. Of course, newspapers are not sensitive enough. Of course, newspapers should always do a better job. But the point is that a newspaper should try to reflect the reality in this country as best it can. Metropolitan newspapers today, like the *Herald* or *Times*, are far different publications than they were twenty-five years ago. If you compare the publications of that time with today's press, you will be absolutely astonished. Newspapers, and the media in general, are trying to reflect in a sensitive way what is going on in this country.

> David Maciel, who had participated in the panel on culture and bilingualism, raised the question of tokenism. He feared that newspapers are more interested in looking good than in achieving a genuine balance within their staffs.

David Maciel: When you hired Tony Castro, it seems to me that this was a kind of tokenism, a very slight gesture. It is only one reporter; how about seven reporters? In Albuquerque where, supposedly, the population is 42 percent Chicano, there is not one editorial writer who is an Hispanic. The same is true in Phoenix. The question of whether the language employed by reporters is standard Spanish or barrio Spanish is glossing over a much more serious problem. Why only one Chicano at a major newspaper?

Thomas Plate: There are problems. Chicano reporters have to speak and write excellent English because they are writing for an English-speaking readership. The individual must be as fluent in English as in Spanish.

Phil Kerby: The newspapers are slowly beginning to recognize some of these things, and as David Maciel said, why not seven reporters, why not eight, why not eighteen? That is always true.

I wish we would reach a point in this country where we would not be concerned at all—we would hardly know who was who on the staff. I agree that in this interim period we are going to have numbers, and we will look at proportions and increase opportunities for everyone. I will not live to see the day, yet I would like to have this country reach a point where nobody is really aware that someone's a Chicano or a different kind of Chicano or speaks a certain kind of language and does not speak English. All of this makes me ill-at-ease. In the interim period, of course, we must try to make sure that all the minorities in this country are fully, not partially but fully, and fairly represented.

> Thomas Plate pointed out that Hispanics suffer in news reporting very often because the press tends to emphasize the exceptional and the negative. This frequently works to the disadvantage of minority groups.

Thomas Plate: It is totally incontestable that the media will present a somewhat distorted image of almost anything that they cover. They will tend to emphasize the negative for two reasons. One is because the negative is more immediately apparent and visible. It is difficult for journalists, by reason of training, by reason of educational orientation, and a number of other reasons, to do otherwise.

But there is a more cynical reason that is involved. One of the true geniuses of contemporary magazine design, Milton Glazer, said, "Let us put out two papers every day; one is called 'Good News' and the other is called 'Bad News.' Three months later 'Bad News' will be doing great. 'Good News' will fold." There is much truth in this. It also bodes ill for minorities.

> Continuing this line of discussion, Frank Ponce, who had been a member of the panel on religion, queried why the press had so crudely, if not dishonestly, reported on the number of Mexicans crossing the border without proper immigration certification.

Frank Ponce: If the function of the news is to report inequality, that can be manufactured as well as encountered. The question I have concerns the reporting of newspapers like the *Los Angeles Times*, the *Washington Post*, and the *New York Times* on the undocumented workers, so-called illegal aliens (which is a term that is fairly repugnant to most Hispanics). I kept a file of many clippings from newspapers like the *Los Angeles Times* and the *Washington Post*; their treatment was universally unsympathetic, using inflammatory language such as "brown hordes invade" and that sort of thing. Has this editorial policy been modified?

Félix Gutiérrez: I have done research on this. I studied fourteen months of coverage in California newspapers and found that the reporters were guilty of one-sided reporting in that they relied very heavily on law enforcement and public officials as their sources. Out of 114 articles that I selected at random throughout California newspapers over a fourteen-month period, about 80 percent of the stories had law enforcement as their primary sources. In only four of the stories did the reporters actually use undocumented people as sources, talk to them, quote them. So while they were talking about this great number of people, in only four cases did the reporters actually talk to someone from that group. Similarly, church groups and legal aid groups were largely unrepresented. They did not have a balance in reporting.

Interestingly enough, I separated out data on Spanish-surname reporters and found that their coverage tended to be more balanced. They went to the law enforcement sources as did the non-Spanish-surname reporters, but they also went to sources on the other side. The *New York Times* was particularly guilty. The *Herald Examiner*, prior to the changeover, ran "Alien Horde Threatens State" as a front-page banner headline off the *New York Times* story. When the networks sent crews to Tijuana to find the Mexicans in track shoes lined up at the border ready to come across, they found that there was no story there. It had been fabricated by the *New York Times*.

The *Washington Post* invented the term "Mexamerica," a term I have never heard. In a series they ran in 1978 they said there were a lot of people out in the Southwest who called it "Mexamerica." Well, I have lived in "Mexamerica" all my life and I have never heard a Chicano use that term. I had an occasion to meet Benjamin Bradlee, editor of the *Post* a few weeks later, and asked him where he got that term. He said one of his headline writers probably thought it up. That kind of coverage may sell papers to Anglos but it does not accurately reflect Latinos.

Phil Kerby: I can tell you about the *Los Angeles Times* because I have been involved in their editorial conferences on this subject for ten years. The *Los Angeles Times* has been profoundly sympathetic to the cause of the undocumented workers, entirely sympathetic to the reasons why they are coming into this country, and has been pushing the federal government constantly to take a flexible and understanding attitude toward this whole problem. It is very easy to make a remark about newspapers in general, but the *Los Angeles Times* is not one of those you describe.

> Max Gaebler, who had moderated the panel on politics and bilingualism, believed the issue to be more than merely one of language but certainly one of social justice. He asked the panelists whether a more sympathetic response from the press to the needs of the Hispanic community might not slow the pace of growth of non-English-language media.

Max Gaebler: One message that seems to come through loud and clear in this conference is that what is centrally at issue is not just language but rather the aspirations of Hispanic people for proper recognition and for social justice. What do you think would happen if, in support of those very legitimate aspirations, the media became responsive to the interests and concerns of the various Hispanic communities in the kinds of effective ways that have been suggested here, but do so in the English language? Do you think that the future then of Spanish-language media would be somewhat more limited than in the event that that kind of response were not forthcoming?

Félix Gutiérrez: Yes.

> A member of the Spanish Department at the University of Southern California, Esther Nelson, referred to Félix Gutiérrez's discussion about the role of foreign capital investments in American media. She disagreed with Phil Kerby's assessment that this was not objectionable.

Esther Nelson: I am concerned about foreign control of the media that reach Hispanic minorities. Unless the mainstream media in this country, the large media, reach out to these people, we are going to have a polarization politically, not just social segregation. We are going to have a tendency for minorities to identify with the foreign country that is feeding them the news, and to produce a rather monolithic group among Hispanic minorities instead of a whole spectrum from conservatives to liberals, because they are getting news and views on television and in the newspapers which are being paid for from Mexico. Obviously, the foreign-language media are not going to foster any kind of pro-United States position on anything where Mexico, despite being a friendly nation, may have its political differences with the United States.

Félix Gutiérrez: Well, I raised the issue, and it is a fact. The investment is here, and the programming too. What is happening is that Hispanic people are commercially integrated through the Spanish-language media. American advertisers ask that money be spent here, but the television stars are from Mexico. The news is from Mexico, except the limited amount the stations have to put on to fill their Federal Communications Commission requirements. The actors, actresses, entertainers are all from someplace else. It limits our ability to perceive ourselves as full actors in the United States. What this says is that it is fine to earn money and spend money here in the United States, but if you are Spanish-speaking and want to be a television star, you must go someplace else. It cuts across to films, records, and newspapers—across media lines—and although it enriches the variety, it has to be of some concern to me because the Hispanic element is a reality in this country, and this is not well-reflected in the English-language media, and it is not well-reflected in the Spanish-language either.

> Acknowledging that *Imagen* is funded from Mexico, Aida Ferrarone denied Mexican control of editorial content.

Aida Ferrarone: The money is from Mexico, but in *Imagen* we are not, except for two pages, presenting news from Mexico or ideas from Mexico. Reporters like myself, most of them free-lancing, are putting together new material. Our aim is to make the Hispanic reader understand what is going on in all fields of American society.

> Gilbert H. Scott, who attended the conference as part of a Canadian group invited by the Center for Study of the American Experience, questioned Eugene Fuson about the implications of the new technology for language usage in our society.

Gilbert H. Scott: Mr. Fuson, do you conclude that the technical advances in media and further advances that are on the way will inevitably lead to monolingualism, monoculturalism, or a certain homogeneity of culture? And will they displace producers, writers, directors, researchers?

Eugene Fuson: No. What I meant to say, if I did not make myself clear, is that there is so much new technology that we are just now confronting. All the large newspapers are investing very heavily in the cable networks, and so are the publishing houses and the oil companies. Nobody really knows what the outcome will be. I certainly do not know what is going to happen.

Noel Epstein was curious and amused by the reaction of the Hispanic community to being discovered by the major media. He asked why it had taken the media so long to begin reporting about the Latin community.

Félix Gutiérrez: I could sound like Spiro Agnew and say it is because the media are all based on Manhattan Island and everything west of the Hudson River is Indian country to them. That may be one factor.

Blacks have been a more visible minority on the East Coast where corporate decisions tend to be made, although the city with the largest Latino population in the United States is New York City. But I am not sure that is the reason. Perhaps it is that, because of voting and other patterns of discrimination, Hispanics have not participated in the political processes much, so we do not have nationally recognized leaders to the extent that other communities have. The fact that many of our group speak Spanish makes it harder for reporters to cover our community and easier to pay attention to other communities. Also, we have a tradition that is reinforced with interchange with Latin America. This has limited our participation in the institutions of the United States.

There is no single cause, but all these factors have militated against a very fast recognition of us. Even today, in areas where we are numerically more numerous than other minority groups, our participation in the media, particularly as television anchors, is limited. There may be a blind spot in American life that we represent, but we are coming into better focus, better view, and will continue to do so.

Phil Kerby ended the discussion by pointing to the fact that the media comprise a human institution with human frailities, and like other American institutions, this one is struggling to respond with acquired sensitivity to a society with large numbers of individuals who speak a language other than English.

Phil Kerby: Events occur and force things to the attention of the media. We have to admit that the media have their share of errors, stupidities, and blindness, just as do education, medicine, and other professions. This is an imperfect world. But the big newspapers are beginning to become sensitive to a lot of problems, whereas twenty-five years ago they were not, and incidentally, no-one else was. We sometimes act as though each of us understood all these things a generation ago. We are not all born sensitive and caring, with the knowledge to do absolutely the right thing and do it with genius. We are just human beings. Now this country seems to me to be struggling in many areas to do the right thing, and the newspapers are doing a little struggling right along with everyone else.

IV. The New Bilingualism: An American Dilemma

The New Bilingualism: An American Dilemma

Martin Ridge

The dominant English-speaking American society faces a genuine dilemma when it is confronted by bilingual/bicultural peoples who ask for public policies that will allow them to retain their identities. On the one hand, English-speaking Americans have traditionally paid at least lip service to the words of Emma Lazarus on the base of the Statue of Liberty, prided themselves on a willingness to accept the principle of diversity within unity, and, in recent time, hailed a new spirit of pluralism that encourages Americans to reclaim a sense of self by preserving or seeking their ancestral heritage. On the other hand, changes in technologies, laws, business practices, and national goals (defined or implicit) raise serious doubts about whether the bilingualism/biculturalism now advocated is really a repetition of past experience. Or is it a new phenomenon that should be seen in a new light.

Advocates for a more bilingual/bicultural society have clouded discussion of the issue by insisting on talking about it in terms of older questions dating from before the First World War, when nativists were more interested in segregating bilingual/bicultural groups and in denying non-English-speaking peoples access to advantages of mainstream society. More serious advocates argue that it is unfair, if not cruel, to ask peoples who have migrated within the United States from centers of limited-English usage such as Indian reservations or have come from foreign nations—both traumatic experiences—to abandon their mother tongues and cultures for the English language and the values of our society. Some Indians and Spanish-speaking peoples insist that merely because their ancestors succumbed to English-speaking conquerors does not mean that their children must be denied their native language and traditional culture. It is worse than cruel, it is devastating to a child's self-respect, the advocates contend, when a child is forced to give up a family language when attending school. This denigrates not only the mother tongue but also the value system of the home culture. Little wonder such children do poorly in school. Educating children in part in the language of their homes—at least until they have mastered it—is as important as learning English. This, it is argued, will create a spirit of self-respect and self-confidence in students. The advocates of bilingualism/biculturalism who demand language and cultural preservation, for whatever reason, insist that the majority society encourage a wide range of options for minority groups.

Today's critics of extending the bilingual/bicultural option to public policy believe that these contentions are specious. They want to accelerate the assimilation of non- and limited-English-speakers into the mainstream of society as quickly as possible. They are appalled by the nurturing of bilingual/bicultural maintenance through federal, state, or local laws. They see such programs as a threat to the economic and political power of individuals as well as to the functional unity of the society—reinforcement of the segregationist tendencies that have compelled people in the past to live virtually outside the English-speaking economic and political structure. They deny they are nativists and insist they are not concerned about what bilingual/bicultural groups do in their private lives, in what languages they carry on their business, or what voluntary organizations they establish or maintain; it is only in the area of public policy that they ask for a careful reassessment of what the courts and government agencies have mandated.

CIVIL RIGHTS, "ROOTS," AND PLURALISM

The discussion of bilingualism/biculturalism was inconceivable prior to growth of the civil rights movement and the age of entitlements created by federal statutes to protect laboring and dependent groups in our society. It would also have been inconceivable prior to the awakening among American Blacks of a desire to recapture their "roots" as an essential to grasping their full sense of citizenship and person.

As recently as twenty-five years ago a discussion of public policy regarding bilingualism/biculturalism would have been strangely out of place. Although the federal courts had denied states the power to exclude subjects from the school curriculum—especially languages other than English—the states retained the power to determine the language of instruction. Therefore, in the public schools English was used to teach even non-English-speaking immigrant children and limited-English-speaking children born in this country. Moreover, the public schools almost universally taught the doctrine of the uniqueness of American culture and stressed values implicit in American democracy in distinction to other systems in the world.

To the extent that there was a pluralist perception of America and an attempt to maintain other languages and cultures, they existed in church-supported school systems. But because parochial schools were sometimes viewed as suspect by the dominant segment of society, they so taught the themes of Americanization and the uniqueness of this nation's past that within a few generations they had almost lost their ethnic character and constituencies, and they were less associated with bilingualism/biculturalism than with religious and sectarian values. In addition, the rising costs of private education, the need to prepare children to function in mainstream society rather than in a confined ethnocultural community, the increasingly secular nature of the public schools, and the generally ecumenical character of American churches seriously threatened the persistence of parochial bilingual/bicultural education.

A DOUBLE STANDARD FOR MINORITY CULTURES

If American society was not pluralist in its goals, in some ways it was pluralist in its means; public policy by tradition was broadly tolerant if not sympathetic and supportive of bilingual/bicultural groups. So long as the minorities' purposes were meritorious and eleemosynary the state did not intervene in their activities. Ethnocultural hospitals, schools, youth and adult clubs, camps, and church groups were exempted from taxation, even though they were often rigidly sectarian.

In the wholly private business sector the government's policy was strictly laissez-faire. If employers imposed bilingual/bicultural conditions or quotas for employment, their practices were not in conflict with governmental regulations or court mandates. The same detached attitude also prevailed in the media, where non-English and bilingual radio stations proliferated as readily as had foreign-language newspapers in the nineteenth century. For some bilingual/bicultural groups this laissez-faire attitude meant they had an option: they could accept or reject as much of the dominant society's values and practices as they saw fit.

Other bilingual/bicultural elements did not enjoy this opportunity. For example the federal government for years fought efforts by American Indians to preserve their languages and cultures. And even in the 1930s when this attitude began to change, Indians were far from free to pursue a style of life compatible with their traditional values. To the extent that their languages persisted it was because of past failures on the part of government to eradicate them. For some Spanish-speaking groups in the Southwest, public policy was equally repressive, although the law—as it does in New Mexico—mandated acceptance or parity for the bilingual/bicultural group.

There, then, were two bilingual/bicultural elements: those who through voluntary efforts sustained programs that nurtured their cultures through the media, schools, and charitable institutions—all in the traditional American sense of accepting diversity within unity—and another element that persisted because it was denied the opportunity to enter the mainstream. The former, steadily shrinking in number, in large measure shared the values of the majority English-speaking community; in fact it would have resented deeply any implication that it was not *the* mainstream. The latter, however, were often physically and economically segregated as well as politically and socially isolated.

RISING AWARENESS OF A MULTI-CULTURED SOCIETY

All of this began to change after the Second World War as Americans entered an era of critical self-evaluation. The ideals espoused during the war and in the following decade led to a searching reassessment of the contradictions between national values and public policy. A vital part of this process focused on the disadvantaged status of minorities—especially Black Americans—but it gradually broadened to encompass a concern for the developmentally disabled and the handicapped, women, and bilingual/ bicultural groups. The initial changes came with Supreme Court decisions that extended the umbrella of civil rights protection to housing and education, interstate commerce, and voting rights. The Court's extension of protection led first to implementing legislation and finally to federal regulations established within executive agencies with legal divisions that could compel enforcement.

The purpose behind the initial thrust for civil rights was to break the barriers that had kept minority groups from complete participation in the majority society. The results of these early efforts, however, were far from effective. Removing the restriction placed the burden of action on individuals or groups who could ill afford to claim the opportunities available to them by law. Increasingly the courts, the Congress, and the executive branch of the government became involved in compelling local, state, and private agencies to provide services for previously disadvantaged groups or to make it economically costly to be out of compliance with federal rulings.

Although compliance often involved dramatic changes in policies, when it dealt with problems of language it became complex. Multilingual ballots, multilingual voter registration and voting drives, and methods of teaching non-English-speaking and limited-English-speaking children all became part of mechanisms for implementing governmental regulations rooted in civil rights legislation.

In many instances states and cities, acting on the same humane premises and without federal prompting, made genuine efforts by enacting laws and writing regulations that permitted individuals to function in their own languages when dealing with the government. Miami, Florida, for example, with its large Cuban immigrant population became a bilingual community transacting all official business in both English and Spanish. (This ordinance was later repealed by a general referendum.) In many states election ballots, state tax forms, and driver license examinations were printed in bilingual or multilingual fashion. Multilingual signs were placed in public buildings and in state and municipal agencies.

RISING EXPECTATIONS BY MINORITY-LANGUAGE GROUPS

This shift in public policy no doubt strengthened the rising level of expectation among many bilingual/bicultural groups. Supported by friendly legislation and governmental action and sustained by a generally sympathetic public, they sought logically the boundaries of opportunity that had been opened to them. For example, could an employer require that a bilingual employee speak only English while at work? To what extent and under what conditions could a school district be compelled to provide instruction in languages other than English while children learned English? Was there a basis in law to ask, as compensatory education, that school districts be bilingual/bicultural, if a group had suffered sufficient discrimination because of language in the past? Was there some entitlement on the part of children who do not know English to secure from public schools the kind of cultural maintenance, albeit without the religious structure, that had in the past been provided by parochial schools? Could local governments and school districts be mandated to employ bilingual/bicultural workers to guarantee services to individuals unfamiliar with English-speaking regulations and practices? If the boundaries were vague, they were to be tested whenever possible. That is, after all, the American system for securing answers to social questions. Bilingual/bicultural groups found in this changed environment that the law—or the Constitution—which in the past had been a shield against the threat of majority repression was now a sword for achievement of greater opportunity to exercise the right of option.

THE CHOICE NOT TO ACCULTURATE

Perhaps the most significant result of altered public policy was the option for many bilingual/bicultural people to "stand the purpose of civil rights legislation on its head" and live outside of the English-speaking community. This is more easily possible today than it was in the past not only because many functions of citizenship no longer require the use of English but also because modern technology has made possible continuing close contact among peoples of common culture. Satellite transmission of television broadcasts from abroad, more effective shortwave radio systems, the speed and low cost of international travel, multinational corporations that maintain communication systems and move people, along with the ease of printing newspapers and distributing movies have made it simple for bilingual/bicultural people to have a full creative life without important contact with the majority community. Even the churches, both Catholic and Protestant, have willingly embraced a bilingual/ bicultural position in the United States and abandoned their former "Americanizing" practices in the competition for converts.

Critics hold that the linchpin of sustaining bilingualism/biculturalism is not how many governmental services exist for bilingual/ bicultural groups or how vital the private sector is in capitalizing on the market they represent, or even continuing immigration: the critical factor is how much and at what stage languages other than English will be taught in the schools. If the children of the present generation of bilingual/bicultural individuals are not taught their home language effectively and for prolonged periods, that group will undoubtedly lose its capability to maintain its cultural and economic unity to an extent necessary to retain its exclusivity. If it were possible for ethnocultural minorities to perpetuate their exclusivity through voluntary action, there would be fewer impassioned arguments on the centrality of bilingual education. For this reason the debate about teaching bilingually or through some other method has become an issue in public policy discussions; its significance for the persistence of a bilingual/bicultural society is really what is at stake.

The bilingual/bicultural dilemma is no stranger to other nations in the world. Few countries count on the benefits of having a homogeneous population; fewer still have enjoyed internal calm. Most have faced domestic rivalries, separatist movements, covert discrimination, or militant repression. A few have suffered because their minorities became pawns in international affairs when politicians sought to capitalize on latent ethnic hostilities. None of this is likely to happen in the United States, although in the past there has been discrimination and hyphenated Americans have tried to influence foreign policy.

The American situation is unique. This nation during the present generation has moved steadily toward integrating all its people into a society of equal access to opportunities in the public and private sectors. Education, housing, civil rights have been major issues that the nation has debated and resolved. If there is a disagreement on the means of satisfying our national goals there is no disagreement on end. We have accepted a new pluralism based on profound mutual respect and a belief in equality of opportunity.

OPTIONS FOR MINORITIES—AND FOR AMERICA

Yet the mechanisms for implementing these goals have led to a contradiction: the hopes for a more open society have created options for an officially sanctioned bilingual/bicultural America. This does not mean that Congress will consider passing an act placing another language on a par with English (which itself does not possess official status except in the courts), but it does mean that a plethora of regulations, court actions, and state and local laws may extend the options that will make it possible for people to function fully as citizens without the use of English.

Whether this American dilemma is resolvable is, of course, a subject worthy of discussion. It is always an error when a society pursues public policies that have not been fully explored and adequately discussed beyond governmental agencies or even the Congress. Historically, ours is not a society where policies can persist in defiance of the public's wishes. This has been proved from the days when politicians tried to manage the slavery issue by a patchwork of compromises to the recent past when the public reached a consensus about the war in Vietnam that forced an end to that conflict.

What we do about the options for minorities to live within or without the mainstream of the English-speaking community is something only an informed public can decide. It should be apparent that the nation now is at something of a crossroads, because the extent to which the federal government will sustain bilingual education is now and will be before Congress in many forms ranging from education bills to reenactment of civil rights laws. This is a suitable time to decide, and only after candid discussion, whether we want to be as pluralistic as the Canadians or as demanding as the Mexicans in our search to maintain diversity within unity. The decisions should not come by default at the hands of a bureaucracy or through any mechanism other than action by an informed electorate, for in the United States we still hold to the revolutionary idea: *salus populi supreme lex*—the will of the people is the highest law.

City and County of SAN FRANCISCO

Muestra de Papeleta de Votar
選 票 樣 本 **Sample Ballot**

RUN - OFF ELECTION	*ELECCIÓN FINAL*	市 長 複 選
DECEMBER 11, 1979	*11 DE DICIEMBRE DE 1979*	一九七九年十二月十一日

PUNCH OUT BALLOT CARD ONLY WITH PUNCHING DEVICE ATTACHED TO VOTOMATIC; NEVER WITH PEN OR PENCIL. INSTRUCTIONS TO VOTERS: To vote for the candidate of your choice, punch the ballot card in the hole to the RIGHT of the name of the person for whom you desire to vote. To vote for a person whose name is not printed on the ballot, first write the title of the office in the blank space provided for that purpose on the write-in ballot envelope and then after the title of the office write his name in the blank space provided for that purpose. All distinguishing marks are forbidden and make the ballot void. If you wrongly punch, tear or deface the ballot card or tear or deface the write-in envelope, return it to the inspector and obtain another.

PERFORE LA TARJETA DE BALOTAJE UNICAMENTE CON EL PERFORADOR PROVISTO EN LA "VOTOMATIC"; NUNCA USE PLUMA O LAPIZ
INSTRUCCIONES: Para votar por cualquier candidato de su preferencia, perfore la tarjeta de votar por el aguijero proximo a la DERECHA de nombre de ese candidato. Para votar por una persona que no está en la tarjeta, escriba primeramente el titulo del cargo en el espacio en blanco provisto para este fin en el sobre para votar por otros candidatos, y después del titulo del cargo escriba su nombre en el espacio en blanco provisto para este fin Si usted equivocadamente perfora, rompe o estropea la tarjeta de votar o el sobre para votar por otros candidatos, devuelvalos al inspector de la eleccion y obtenga otros.

只可用選票機上之打孔器來打孔，切勿用其他筆或鉛筆代替。
選民注意：用你自己的抉擇去選舉。在你要選的人的姓名右方打孔．如你要選的人的姓名未列在選票上，則將該人姓名、官職清楚地寫在選舉信封的空白位置。切勿塗改、損毀、劃記號或打錯了孔在選票上，如有以上情形，請即向監察員索取新票重寫。

**Workers are needed at the polls in many
San Francisco neighborhoods.
Apply now in room 155, City Hall**

**Se necesitan trabajadores en las urnas electorales
de muchos barrios en San Francisco. Preséntese
ahora en el cuarto 155 del City Hall.**

徵聘雙重語言人員
在選舉站協助選舉
薪酬三十二元五毛或以上
請即向市政廳一五五號室申請

City and County of SAN FRANCISCO

RUN-OFF ELECTION DECEMBER 11, 1979

市長複選
一九七九年十二月十一日

ELECCIÓN FINAL 11 DE DICIEMBRE DE 1979

Alcalde 市長候選人

MAYOR

Vote for One
Vote por Uno

請選一名

DIANNE FEINSTEIN
Mayor of San Francisco
三藩市市長
Alcaldesa de San Francisco

2 ➡

QUENTIN KOPP
Member, Board of Supervisors
市參議員
Miembro, Mesa de Supervisores

4 ➡

Fiscal de Distrito 地方檢察官候選人

DISTRICT ATTORNEY

Vote for One
Vote por Uno

請選一名

JOSEPH FREITAS
District Attorney of San Francisco
三藩市地方檢察官
Fiscal de Distrito

9 ➡

ARLO SMITH
Senior Assistant Attorney General
資深助理檢察長
Asistente Jefe del Abogado General

11 ➡

Alguacil (Sheriff) 承法吏候選人

SHERIFF

Vote for One
Vote por Uno

請選一名

GENE BROWN
Sheriff
承法吏
Alguacil (Sheriff)

16 ➡

MIKE HENNESSEY
Corrections Administrator, Attorney
感化院行政員、律師
Administrador de Correciones, Abogado

18 ➡

EVEN # DISTRICT

APPLICATION FOR ABSENT VOTER'S BALLOT
APLICACION PARA PAPELETA DE VOTANTE AUSENTE
缺席選票申請表

NAME: _____

PRINTED NAME *CON LETRAS DE IMPRENTA*

I hereby apply for an Absent Voter's Ballot for the election noted on the reverse side of this form. I expect to be absent from my election precinct on the day of election or unable to vote therein by reason of physical disability or other reason provided by law.

Por la presente solicito una Papeleta de Votante Ausente para la elección señalada en el lado reverso de esta forma.

Espero estar ausente de mi precinto electoral en el día de la elección o no poder votar allí por incapacidad física u otra razón prevista por la ley.

本人因故缺席或因病缺席，不能依法於選舉日在指定之選舉區內親自參加投票，特此申請發給缺席選票一份，以便依照本表格背面所証明之辦法作缺席選舉投票。

BALLOT TO BE MAILED TO ME AT: *ENVIEME LA PAPELETA A:* 請將選票寄給本人下列住址：

_____

_____

_____ Zip Code
Area postal
郵區號碼

X _____

SIGNATURE OF APPLICANT IN FULL
FIRMA COMPLETA DEL SOLICITANTE
申請人簽名

Application must be received in the office of the Registrar of Voters no later than the seventh day preceding the day of election.

La solicitud debe recibirse en la oficina del Registrar de Voters no después del séptimo día antes de la elección.

申請表必須在選舉月七天之前寄到選民註冊官辦事處。

(DO NOT WRITE BELOW THIS LINE) *(NO ESCRIBA DEBAJO DE ESTA LINEA)* （請勿在此綫下填寫）

Signature and registration verified as correct.

Date _____ _____
Deputy Registrar of Voters

Registered San Francisco Address of Applicant
Dirección del solicitante registrada en San Francisco
申請人在舊金山登記選票之住址：

MAIL TO: **ABSENT VOTING SECTION**
ENVIARA: **REGISTRAR OF VOTERS OFFICE**
郵寄至： **ROOM 158, CITY HALL**
SAN FRANCISCO, CA 94102

From
REGISTRAR OF VOTERS
City Hall
San Francisco, Calif. 94102
*POSTMASTER: IF ADDRESSEE
HAS MOVED, DO NOT FORWARD*
★ ★ ★ ★ ★ ★ ★ ★ ★ ★ ★ ★ ★ ★ ★ ★ ★

BULK RATE
U.S. POSTAGE
PAID
PERMIT No. 4
San Francisco, Calif.

EVEN # DISTRICT

POLLS OPEN AT 7 A.M. AND CLOSE AT 8 P.M.
LAS ELECCIONES EMPIEZAN A LAS 7 A.M. Y TERMINAN A LAS 8 P.M.
選舉站開放時間由上午七時至下午八時

── **VOTE HERE** ──── *VOTE AQUI* ──── 請在此投票 ──

Precinct

── **NOTICE** ──

If you find that for any reason you will be unable to vote in person on election day, promptly complete and sign the application for an absent voter's ballot printed on the reverse side of this page and return it to the **Registrar of Voters, 158 City Hall, San Francisco, 558-6161.** Your application may be submitted not more than 29 days before the day of election but must reach the office of the **Registrar of Voters** not less than 7 days before the day of election.

── *AVISO* ──

Si usted, por cualquier razon, no puede votar personalmente el dia de la eleccion, llene y firme enseguida la solicitud para votante ausente que esta impresa en el reverso de esta pagina y devuelvala al **Registrar of Voters, 158 City Hall, San Francisco, 558-6161.** *Su solicitud puede presentarla no antes de 29 dias antes del dia de la eleccion pero debe de estar en la oficina del* **Registrar of Voters** *antes de los 7 dias anteriores a la eleccion.*

── 注　意 ──

若你因故不能在選舉之日親自前來投票，請在此表後面之缺席選票填安簽字，寄回Registrar of Voters, 158 City Hall, San Francisco, 558-6161。申請缺席選票可在選舉日之前二十九天提交，但必須在選舉日之前七天交到Registrar of Voters（選民註冊官辦事處）。